Cover Name: Dr. Rantzau

FOREIGN MILITARY STUDIES

History is replete with examples of notable military campaigns and exceptional military leaders and theorists. Military professionals and students of the art and science of war cannot afford to ignore these sources of knowledge or limit their studies to the history of the US armed forces. This series features original works, translations, and reprints of classics outside the American canon that promote a deeper understanding of international military theory and practice.

SERIES EDITOR: Joseph Craig

ZMS Bw

An AUSA Book

Cover Name:
Dr. Rantzau

Nikolaus Ritter

Edited and translated by Katharine R. Wallace
Foreword by Mary Kathryn Barbier

K UNIVERSITY PRESS OF KENTUCKY

The original German edition of this book was published as "Deckname Dr. Rantzau: The Records of Nikolaus Ritter, Officer under Canaris in the Secret Intelligence Service" (Hamburg: Hoffman und Campe, 1972). First English language edition published by the University Press of Kentucky.

The University Press of Kentucky,
scholarly publisher for the Commonwealth,
serving Bellarmine University, Berea College, Centre
College of Kentucky, Eastern Kentucky University,
The Filson Historical Society, Georgetown College,
Kentucky Historical Society, Kentucky State University,
Morehead State University, Murray State University,
Northern Kentucky University, Transylvania University,
University of Kentucky, University of Louisville,
and Western Kentucky University.
All rights reserved.

Editorial and Sales Offices: The University Press of Kentucky
663 South Limestone Street, Lexington, Kentucky 40508-4008
www.kentuckypress.com

Cataloging-in-Publication Data is available from the Library of Congress.

ISBN 978-0-8131-7734-2 (hardcover : alk. paper)
ISBN 978-0-8131-7735-9 (pdf)
ISBN 978-0-8131-7736-6 (epub)

This book is printed on acid-free paper meeting
the requirements of the American National Standard
for Permanence in Paper for Printed Library Materials.

∞

Manufactured in the United States of America.

Member of the Association
of University Presses

For Ian, Thomas, and Kate
A glimpse of your history

Spying as such is not a crime; it is not even immoral, provided it is not pursued out of greed, but rather for the sake of patriotism.

—Friedrich von Martens, *Das Internationale Recht der zivilisierten Nationen* [International Law of Civilized Nations]

Contents

Foreword

During World War II, as has been the case in most conflicts, particularly modern ones, the major nations involved engaged in the intelligence-gathering game by employing spies and double agents. It was imperative to learn the enemy's plans and to counter them. Understanding the extent of the enemy's military might was crucial to defeating them. Neutral countries like Switzerland and Portugal became playgrounds for spies and their contacts as they engaged in their craft; however, intelligence-gathering operations occurred in other locations. For example, in 1943 the British ambassador based in Ankara, Turkey, was compromised when Elyesa Bazna (aka Cicero), his Albanian-born valet, systematically photographed "highly classified documents," which he then sold to the Germans.[1] Richard Sorge, an undercover German journalist, set up a—briefly lucrative—spy ring in Japan, where he gathered information for his real bosses, the Soviets.

Some spies, known as double agents, worked for both sides. Some of these double agents volunteered for their new roles. Others chose the lesser of two evils. Working for the enemy beat the alternative—death. While some double agents provided information about damage caused by bombs, the location of airfields, the training and movement of troops, and factory output, others served a more targeted purpose. They participated in deception operations designed to mislead their original employers or to increase the possibility of their new bosses' success in battle. For instance, scholars have shed light on Operation Fortitude—the Allied cover plan for the Normandy invasion—that has revealed the use of double agents in what was initially a secret, undercover operation. In the aftermath of the Second World War, spies, double agents, and handlers remained, for the most part, reticent to speak or write about their wartime activities.

With the advent of the Cold War and the ratcheting up of the espionage and counterespionage game, the climate wasn't right for transparency. In the last few decades, however, shifting winds have cleared the way for firsthand accounts, historical narratives, and movies about the espionage game. The spy novels written by John le Carré and Ian Fleming, among others, helped pave the way. Along with the James Bond movies, they romanticized and glorified the work of spies. Secret agents with access to incredible gadgets represented good and successfully defeated evil time and again. While James Bond, George Smiley, and others like them operated during the Cold War, the roots of these fictional characters can be found in the real-life Second World War spies, double agents, and spymasters, like Nikolaus Ritter, some of whom experienced lives fraught with excitement, intrigue, and danger.

Numerous men and women did their part for the war effort by working for the intelligence services. Not all of them gained notoriety after the war, but as time has passed, more and more of them have had their stories told. British agent William Stephenson established a spy network that successfully operated against the Germans throughout the war. Virginia Hall, or the Limping Lady, first a member of the Special Operations Executive (SOE) and then of the Office of Strategic Services (OSS), worked with the French Resistance during the war. Her work was so damaging that the Gestapo put a price on her head.

Several spies worked both sides, and their stories have added a new layer to an understanding of the espionage game. Eddie Chapman, aka Zigzag, a longtime criminal, chose to circumvent the pitfalls of living under occupation by becoming a spy for the Germans and then selling them out to the British. Seeming to flit back and forth between the two intelligence services, Chapman's loyalties were hard to determine. Three who willingly became German spies and acted as double agents to help bring down Germany were Dusko Popov (Tricycle), Juan Pujol Garcia (Garbo), and Lily Sergueiew (Treasure). Each in his or her own way contributed to Operation Fortitude. Each had a personal agenda in agreeing to spy for Germany, and each understood the dangers of their chosen path.[2]

What has become increasingly apparent, as more firsthand accounts and other narratives about these spies and double agents are published, is that the story is generally not told from the perspective of the handler—the spymaster. In addition, the majority of the recent English-language publications provide the inside story of American, British, or French, but not German, spies and double agents. *Cover Name: Dr. Rantzau,* the memoir of Nikolaus Ritter, will fill a gap in our understanding of World War II German intelligence operations by providing the unique perspective of a handler in the German Intelligence Service (*Abwehr*). His engaging narrative of the war years illustrates the complexity and danger inherent in his job as he endeavored to recruit legitimate spies and to turn enemy operatives into double agents who would advantage the Abwehr. In order to fully appreciate Ritter's story, however, it is important to understand who Nikolaus Ritter was.

Born in Rheydt, Germany, to Nikolaus Josef Ritter and Käthe Hellhoff on January 8, 1899, Nikolaus Adolph Fritz Ritter lived for a time in a suburb of Mönchengladbach in the Rhineland. His family did not remain in one place for long when he was young. From 1905 to 1910, he attended an elementary school—the Volksschule—in Bad Bederkesa. For the next four years, he received an education at the Klostergymnasium in Flensburg, which was close to the Danish border. He received his high school education at the Domgymnasium in Verden an de Aller, which was southwest of Bremen. After receiving his diploma (*Abitur*) Ritter enlisted in the German Imperial Army and was assigned to the 162nd Infantry Regiment. Serving on the Western Front, he was wounded twice and was promoted to lieutenant in June 1918.

Following the war, Ritter relocated to the former Lauban, Silesia (postwar Luban, Poland). There he apprenticed with a textiles company from 1920 to 1921. After his apprenticeship, Ritter enrolled at the Prussian Technical School for Textiles in Sorau, Poland. Once he passed his final exam and qualified as a textile engineer, he returned to Lauban, where he gained employment as a superintendent of a different textiles company. Declining economic conditions in Germany convinced him to make a life-changing move. He set sail for the United States, where he hoped opportunities for advancement and success would be better. Arriving in January 1924, Ritter landed a job as an office clerk with the Mallinson Silk Company in New York. This job did not last and was followed by menial, low-status, blue-collar jobs—parquet floor layer, dishwasher, metalworker, house painter—over the next few years.

In 1926 Ritter married a schoolteacher, Mary Aurora Evans; he subsequently found a job with the Melliand, Inc. textiles firm, settled down with his wife, and had two children by 1934. By 1935, however, he had switched jobs again. Although he was gainfully employed as a representative of Consumer's Credit Corporation, the position was less than satisfying. His lack of job progress was discouraging. His economic status and future prospects were again poor, primarily as a result of the Great Depression. Disillusioned by reality in "the land of opportunity" and wanting his father, who was ill, to have the chance to see his only grandchildren before he died, he made the decision to uproot his family and return to Germany. It proved a fortuitous choice.

In 1936, Ritter found a home in the Abwehr because he was an experienced army officer and he had lived in the United States for over a decade. The Abwehr, as a new organization, desperately needed staff, anyone with a firsthand knowledge of the United Stated—even a down on his luck salesman. More important, however, was his ability to speak "near perfect American English."[3] Ritter very quickly became one of Admiral Canaris's rising stars, largely because of his great success in recruiting and running agents in the United States and Britain. Although he did not embrace the Nazi Party, Ritter was loyal to Germany. Motivated by a sense of honor and patriotism, not money, pressure, or duty to the party, he strove to do his new job well. When he returned to Germany in 1936, he had a new appreciation of and devotion to his homeland. The outbreak of war in 1939 drove him to do his best for his country.

While Ritter found a new purpose with his career, the resulting situation was less than ideal for the family as a whole. The stress of his new career caused a rift in the family and resulted in permanent separation. Not only did Ritter neglect his family, but having an American wife also did not bode well for his intelligence career. As Ritter went home less and less, his wife, who was actually very happy in Germany initially, slowly realized that she had no husband. After a strained divorce, she endeavored to return home with the couple's children; however, the Gestapo abducted the children and wanted their mother to leave for America without them. Although she gained their release, she did not obtain permission to take her children out of Germany. The outbreak of war further complicated the situation. Mrs. Ritter and the children were unable to leave Germany until the end of the war, and it was only then that Mrs. Ritter learned the truth about her former husband's career and his relationship with his second wife. Ritter, on the other hand, with barely a backward glance, moved on and married Irmgard von Klitzing, whom he met through an intelligence colleague. Before and after they were married, Klitzing occasionally worked for Ritter and his colleagues.

Responsible for aviation intelligence at the Abwehr branch in Hamburg, Ritter traveled far and wide to meet with his agents. He sent spies to Britain, where success was fleeting. Initially, however, his efforts in the United States bore fruit. Relying on contacts that he had made when he lived there, he recruited several agents, including Herman Lang. A German-born American citizen, Lang was an inspector for the Norden Corporation, the developer of the Norden bombsight. Acquiring the plans for the Norden bombsight, which, at the time, was the most sophisticated and accurate device for bomb targeting, was a real coup for Ritter. Although a carefully guarded secret, the bombsight plans that Lang provided brought Ritter great honor. He was awarded a medal, which he received personally from Canaris. In addition to the Norden bombsight, Ritter acquired plans for an autopilot device that was developed by the Sperry Gyroscope Company in Brooklyn from an agent employed there.

Despite early successes in the United States, a poor decision (in hindsight) on Ritter's part destroyed his spy ring. One of his recruits, William Sebold, was an FBI double agent. Breaking a rule to keep his agents separate, which he had established early on, Ritter allowed Sebold to send communications for other spies. Although this proved to be a costly move, it seemed to be the only option at the time. Once he learned the identities of these spies, Sebold turned the information over to the FBI; the agency arrested thirty-three German agents in June 1941. Not only did the FBI bust Ritter's spy ring, but they also compromised his cover as Dr. Rantzau. After the very public destruction of his American spy ring, Ritter's career in the Abwehr became tenuous. For a time, he ran intelligence operations in North Africa for Field Marshal Erwin Rommel before being transferred to Hanover as antiaircraft auxiliary combat commander until the Allied bombing of the city. He ended his career in the Harz Mountains as brigade commander on April 20, 1945.

After the war, Ritter was incarcerated by the British for two years and then faded into obscurity, which was perhaps not a surprise. After all, most intelligence operatives position themselves in the background, where they can observe rather than be observed. In 1972, after years of encouragement, particularly from his family, Ritter decided to write his memoir about his life during the war.[4] *Cover Name: Dr. Rantzau* is an interesting memoir that offers useful insight into Nikolaus Ritter's wartime work with the Abwehr and its operatives. What is evident from the beginning is that Ritter was a confident, intelligent man, who took to intelligence work easily and who very quickly determined how to take advantage of connections that he had established during the interwar period. That he was able to operate so successfully for a time demonstrates his intuitive grasp of what sorts of factors might increase the possibility of discovery and disaster. At the end of the day, Ritter's efforts as an intelligence officer mirror, to some extent, an Abwehr writ large that failed to achieve long-term success during the war. Furthermore, in a wider and more regrettable context, Ritter, like so many of the Third Reich's functionaries, emerges from these pages as a "good German," a man who strove to do his best for his country without inquiring into the wider ramifications of his service.

Mary Kathryn Barbier

Notes

1. Keith Jeffery, *The Secret History of MI6, 1909–1949* (New York: Penguin Press, 2010), 503.

2. For more on these spies and double agents, see David Stafford, "'Intrepid': Myth and Reality," *Journal of Contemporary History* 22, no. 2 (1987): 303–17, http://www.jstor.org/stable/260934; Elizabeth P. McIntosh, *Sisterhood of Spies: The Women of the OSS* (Annapolis: Naval Institute Press, 2009); Judith Pearson, *Wolves at the Door: The True Story of America's Greatest Female Spy* (Lanham, MD: Lyons Press, 2008); Ben Macintyre, *Agent Zigzag: A True Story of Nazi Espionage, Love, and Betrayal* (New York: Broadway Books, 2008); Russell Miller, *Codename Tricycle: The True Story of the Second World War's Most Extraordinary Double Agent* (London: Pimlico, 2005); Juan Pujol Garcia and Nigel West, *Operation Garbo: The Personal Story of the Most Successful Spy of World War II* (London: Biteback Publishing,

2011); Mary Kathryn Barbier, ed., *I Worked Alone: Diary of a Double Agent in World War II Europe: Lily Sergueiew* (Jefferson, NC: McFarland, 2014).

3. "Josef Jakobs—1898–1941: The Story behind the Last Person Executed in the Tower of London," http://www.josefjakobs.info/2015/11/the-german-spymaster-and-alabama.html, accessed February 21, 2018.

4. "Josef Jakobs—1898–1941: The Story behind the Last Person Executed in the Tower of London," http://www.josefjakobs.info/2015/11/the-german-spymaster-and-alabama.html, accessed February 21, 2018; "Nikolaus Ritter," https://en.wikipedia.org/wiki/Nikolaus_Ritter, accessed February 21, 2018; Sherryl Connelly, "New Yorker Risks Life as Double Agent in Nazi Underground, Brings Down Duquesne Spy Ring: New Book," *New York Daily News,* July 12, 2014, http://www.nydailynews.com/news/world/new-yorker-risks-life-double-agent-nazi-underground-brings-duquesne-spy-ring-new-book-article-1.1864628, accessed February 21, 2018; Benjamin Fischer, "A.k.a. 'Dr. Rantzau': The Enigma of Major Nikolaus Ritter," *Center for the Study of Intelligence Bulletin* 11 (Summer 2000): 7–9, https://permanent.access.gpo.gov/lps19742/www.cia.gov/csi/bulletin/cs/11.html#toc7, accessed February 21, 2018.

Preface

After much urging and encouragement from other like-minded World War II authors and researchers, in the United States and abroad, who wanted me to produce an English translation of Nikolaus Ritter's war memoir, *Deckname Dr. Rantzau*, I began exploring options.

The memoir was published in German by Hoffmann und Campe Verlag, Hamburg, in 1972. The work documents my father's achievements and mishaps as Chief of Air Intelligence in the Abwehr under Admiral Wilhelm Canaris, Chief of the Abwehr. The content covers his entry into the service, the 1937 theft of the Norden bombsight, details of securing, indoctrinating, and training various agents, his interfaces with Admiral Canaris, the stationing of secret transmitters in England, his African mission with Count Almásy and the resulting plane crash into the Mediterranean Sea, and his imprisonment at Neuengamme and Bad Nenndorf.

It is one of very few historic memoirs written by an ex-Abwehr officer.

The Abwehr was the intelligence unit of the Wehrmacht, Nazi Germany's military until the end of WWII. I think it is appropriate to mention here that the Abwehr was not a murderous organization and that Admiral Canaris avoided hiring members of the Nazi Party. When Admiral Canaris offered the Austrian General Erwin von Lahousen a position in the Abwehr, he said it was with the understanding he should bring his "best men with you but none of your damned Austrian Nazis. I don't want any of those swine—or at least as few of them as possible in the Abwehr."[1]

CIA History Staff member Benjamin Fisher wrote

> The Abwehr, Nazi Germany's military intelligence service, is better known for its failures than its successes, especially with regard to agent operations. Perhaps its heart wasn't in winning Hitler's war. It was a hotbed of anti-Nazi conspiracy even before the war. Admiral Wilhelm Canaris, chief of the service from 1935–1944 was one of the first senior officials to conclude that Germany would lose the war. (Once, after the admiral had delivered a pessimistic assessment of operations on the eastern front while briefing the High Command, Hitler grabbed him by the lapels and demanded to know whether he was a defeatist.) Never a Nazi, Canaris permitted some of his officers to use the Abwehr as

cover for political and religious dissidents such as German Pastor Dietrich Bonhoeffer.[2]

Bonhoeffer was an anti-Nazi spy who tried to help Jews flee to Switzerland. He and Admiral Canaris, with his chief of staff, participated in the various assassination plots against Adolf Hitler and were hung on April 9, 1945, in the last days of the war.

The Abwehr was also the rare organization under Adolf Hitler to tolerate employment of Jews in its service. Both Admiral Canaris and General von Lahousen worked silently against Adolf Hitler and his select generals. General von Lahousen was sent to the Soviet front in 1943 and thus escaped arrest. He later volunteered to testify at the Nürnberg trials against many of Adolf Hitler's inner-circle officers.

As I immersed myself in the memories of my father, I was mindful of the damage he caused our family, but I also remembered him, on the rare occasions we visited, as a playful and fun parent. Although my focus was on detail and technical content, I also wanted to bring out his dry wit and often self-depreciating sense of humor. It was not unusual for him to sheathe himself in a mantle of great importance in business and social affairs. He loved high society and glowed in the presence of domestic and military high-ranking achievers. However, his proclivity for elitism was never lost on him, nor did his occasional hyperbolizing make him blush. He bloomed where he was planted and adapted exceptionally well to unaccustomed environments, without displaying defeat or depression.

His military career gave him an identity, but he never considered himself a spy and never joined the Nazi Party. He took pride in working for his fatherland as a gentleman as well as an officer. In this translation, I strive to preserve my father's distinctive character and emotions in a first-person narrative and to reconstruct a document that describes his wartime occupation in his own voice. I did not undertake this project to glorify his career, but rather to share a glimpse of the day-to-day operations within the Abwehr and to leave his American family with a sense of who Nikolaus Ritter was and his place in chronicles past.

My father's wish to write his war memoir came to fulfillment in the late 1960s after he became aware, through personal interviews with the American writer Ladislas Farago, author of *The Game of the Foxes,* that operational intelligence data, including names he thought were still classified, were already cataloged in the National Archives and Records Service, Washington, DC.

In the introduction to his memoir, he discloses a collaborative agreement for drafting his manuscript with an American author, Beth Day (later Romulo), whom he met while visiting Mr. Farago in his New York home in the spring of 1970. Since my father's book had already been commissioned by a German publisher, Mrs. Romulo agreed to take the assignment. According to my email exchanges with Mrs. Romulo, she received some royalties. Unfortunately, she does not have a copy of the original English manuscript; therefore, I approached the translation as a new document. Other attempts to locate the English manuscript have failed. However, my father was generous in providing information to authors and journalists, who have widely quoted and critiqued his experiences. Many years have gone by since 1972, and new documents and research abound regarding my father's activities. Speculations about whether he knew that agents sent to England became turncoats also abound. Few captured agents chose execution over working with the enemy against their own country. My father was sociable, charming, and maybe a little bit too trusting, but he served his country loyally.

Rantzau is written in a conversational style. To help the reader engage with the story, the English version needed contractions, exclamations, questions, and a more active voice. I deleted many of the repetitive words, strings of articles, and superfluous verbs that caused confusion. Events, dates, and places are recorded as in the original memoir. The appendix allows the reader to take a look at the age-old necessity of espionage. Aliases were modified through research. It provides a brief history of espionage and an insightful justification of the author's view of his career. Most importantly, however, my focus remained on maximum comprehensibility and flow while deviating as little as possible from the original text.

My father died at age seventy-five in March of 1974.

Katharine R. Wallace

Notes

1. Charles Wighton and Gunter Peis, *Hitler's Spies and Saboteurs* (New York: Award Books, 1958), 10.

2. Fisher, "A.k.a. 'Dr. Rantzau,'" 8–11, https://web.archive.org/web/20010417015403/http:/www.cia.gov/csi/bulletin/csi11.html#toc7.

Notes from the Author

All events herein correspond to documented evidence. The names of my associates and almost all the agents mentioned in this book are bona fide, and those who are still living have given their express consent. Cover names were used in only a few cases, because the persons connected with them either could not be found, or they are undercover for business or personal reasons. I want to emphasize that I, of course, revealed nothing about any agent and informant whose name had not already been exposed in the most recent British and US intelligence publications—and that adds up to quite a number. (Cover names are italicized.)

Introduction

My name was *Dr. Rantzau* in the autumn of 1939 when I crossed the border into Belgium, a few months before the Blitzkrieg rolled over Holland, Belgium, and Luxembourg. In Hungary, my name was *Dr. Jansen*; in Holland, it was *Dr. Reinhardt*; in Germany, I called myself *Dr. Renken*.

When I went to the United States in 1937 to recruit secret agents, who were later referred to en masse by historians of World War II under the catchphrase "The Ritter Ring," I sailed under my own name. I stopped using it immediately after arriving in New York. During my stay in the United States, I used, among others, the name *Alfred Landing*.

Nikolaus Ritter, cadet in First World War, age 18. From the editor's private collection.

Today, sitting in my cozy little study in Gross Flottbek among the many books I have accumulated over the years, rejoicing at the sight of the fresh, green grass and the blooming roses in the gardens, it almost seems unreal as I think back to the tension and excitement of those days more than thirty years ago. At that time, I was a member of the Abwehr. I was assigned to the Hamburg Intelligence Station, where it was my job to procure secret information on enemy air forces—above all, those of the United States and Great Britain.

It was my agents who were able to procure the Norden bombsight and the Sperry gyroscope. Both of these devices contributed significantly to the rapid buildup of an effective German Luftwaffe. Until now, it never occurred to me to disclose any of my classified operations. After the war, I was interned for two years as a former intelligence officer, and thereafter, with considerable difficulty, I laboriously rebuilt a new life. At first, I did just odd jobs; then I traveled all over the world in the import/export business. From 1954 until my seventieth birthday, three years ago, I was the managing director of the German Aid Society in Hamburg.

During the early fifties, the market was overflowing with books and articles on espionage, spies, and agents of World War II. I received continuous encouragement from all sides, urging me to write about my involvement in this great world event. I repeatedly declined. In only two instances did I correct misrepresentations of my own work.

Many aspects of my activities have remained classified. The American Intelligence Service, for instance, never learned about my trip to the United States or about my recruitment of agents.

There were various reasons why I decided not to write a memoir. Anyone who at one time or another belonged to the Intelligence Service, or so I thought, has a natural disinclination to talk about things that were previously confidential and secrets they were expected to keep.

Additionally, any reports on espionage might easily expose a former coworker who had not yet been revealed. I also had a third reason, albeit a purely personal reason. It went against my principles to reveal my feelings, and those of my comrades, about the mistreatment of German intelligence officers by the British after the war. The time had not yet come to talk about that without bitterness; therefore, I was determined not to say a single word in that regard. But then, in the summer of 1968, I received a call from the former director of the Hamburg Intelligence Station, Navy Captain Herbert Wichmann (Ret.), who asked me if I would receive the American writer Ladislas Farago. Farago happened to be in Hamburg at the time to interview former intelligence officers as part of his preparations for *The Game of the Foxes*, a book on the German, English, and American intelligence services. Wichmann advised me, however, to be cautious.

When I received Farago in my office, I was astonished about everything he told me and even more so by the documentation he showed me: countless photocopies of classified and even secret documents of the German Intelligence Service. Among these was a series of documents that detailed my activities. Until now, we had always been certain all of these documents had been destroyed at the end of the war, but Farago had the papers with him and explained that the originals are well preserved in the archives in Washington's National Archives and Records Service.

So, now there were no reasons to keep secrets. I realized that from an historical viewpoint, it would be foolish not to cooperate with known writers and espionage specialists such as Farago. Preventing them from publishing was impossible, but we could try to prevent our own work from being misrepresented.

While I was in the United States in April 1970 to visit my older daughter in St. Louis, Missouri, I also took this opportunity to visit Ladislas Farago in New York. During dinner in his apartment on Park Avenue, I met his book agent, Maximilian Becker, and the charming American author Beth Day. In the course of the evening, both persuaded me to at last tell my story about my activities in the Abwehr. Miss Day agreed to work with me.

My wife had always encouraged me to commit my personal notes to paper. And since she had been employed by German Intelligence as well, she had preserved many notes and all letters, and thus, so to speak, had assembled an unofficial journal of my intelligence work.

When I spoke with my wife in Hamburg about the plan of writing about my experiences, she embraced the idea enthusiastically. "Just do it!" she said, using the figure of speech that had been a stock phrase in our family when my father wanted us to accomplish a task.

In September of the same year, Miss Day came to Hamburg, where we assembled all the materials with documentation to create our first rough draft of a coherent work. So began the history of my experiences, which also chronicles the experiences of my colleagues in the Abwehr. My assignment during the last years of peace, and during the first two years after the outbreak of the Second World War, was organization and direction of the Luftwaffe branch of the Hamburg Intelligence Station. I was to build up and manage an agent network in Europe and in the United States.

Regarding domestic and foreign policy at that time, I refuse to make any hindsight judgments, because that would yield a completely false image of the situation and of our actions at that time. I was a soldier, and I served my country under Kaiser Wilhelm II in World War I and under Adolf Hitler in World War II. If, God forbid, there were to be a third war, I would serve any other leader who happened to be at the head of my country.

Many books have been written about individual agents or espionage cases, but they do not produce a true picture of the sober and nerve-wracking mosaic work that spread over entire continents, and without which no intelligence work could be successful. That will be shown by the history of those men and women who worked for me. They were not Hollywood heroes, but rather human beings of flesh and blood, with much courage, selfless commitment, and great idealism. But there were also issues of greed, foolishness, and treason.

May the story of these events and their actors provide an insight into the work of the Abwehr such as it really was, and is, and always will be, and may the reader be aware of how easy it is to become unsuspectingly entangled in the snares of the Abwehr.

Hamburg, summer 1972, Nikolaus Ritter

1

Arthur Owens
(aka *Snow* and *Johnny*)

I began my work for the Abwehr on January 1, 1937. I sat at a desk in Hamburg, looking over a pile of questionnaires and other papers in front of me; my assignment was to recruit as many agents as possible to assist the Luftwaffe Operations Staff concerning the British Royal Air Force and aviation industry, and I was close to losing courage. The fact is, I had no prior knowledge of anything of that nature. All my knowledge about aviation was based on two reconnaissance flights as an infantry observer in an old open-cockpit Bücker double-decker. All I knew about espionage came from reading spy novels.

I had never received any special intelligence training. My short period of service in the army in 1935 and at various headquarter units in the autumn of 1936 merely helped to refresh my military knowledge. Now, I was sitting in Hamburg without the slightest understanding of the unfamiliar paraphernalia surrounding me. Previously I had reported to my immediate superior at general headquarters, Lieutenant Commander Joachim Burghardt, chief of the Intelligence I Subgroup. He was a roundish little man with thinning dark hair and a rather long nose. He greeted me jovially and briefly explained the organizational setup of the subgroup, but then he passed me along to another salt and pepper, extremely reticent gentleman by the name of Major Hilmar G. Johannes (Hans) Dierks.

Dierks was a section chief in the Navy Intelligence Service. He showed me a narrow, almost empty office, said I was to call him if I needed him, took his leave with a slight smile, and closed the door behind him.

A table, two chairs, and an empty safe stood in my barren office. I sorted through the papers on the desk. Baffled, I looked at one sheet of paper, put it down again, and picked up another one. Letters, numbers, and incomprehensible words danced before my eyes. They did not make sense. Burghardt and Dierks, of course, had explained to me beforehand the organization of Subgroup I, Secret Intelligence Collection for Navy, Army, industry, and Luftwaffe; but no one in Berlin had given any details as to how and where this procurement was to come from. I was simply told it was now my task to recruit agents and to answer the pressing questions put to us by the Luftwaffe operations staff.

But what were those questions? Looking at the questionnaires on my table, I read the following: ABW, L I/6, Ast-W-haven, Nest-Bremen, Gkdos, urgent, airport and factory Speke, details about Stapleford . . . and so on—just a bunch of mysterious abbreviations, numbers, and figures.

So, there I sat without a clue about where to begin. I had no predecessor's files relevant to my assignment. I did not want to go to Lt. Commander Burghardt. It was hardly his task to teach me the meanings of abbreviations and the like. I needed someone who had time and patience. I thought of the man with the somewhat faded blue eyes who had taken me to my office. Fortunately, I remembered his name among the many introductions to other employees. Somehow, I felt he was knowledgeable. I had just gathered up my courage to look for Dierks when the door slowly opened.

I turned around, and Dierks stood before me. "Well," he said in his usual calm style, "are you making any progress?"

"What do you mean 'are you making progress?'" I murmured. "I was just coming to find you."

"I knew that," he said quite casually. "Come on! Let's go have a cup of coffee." He pointed at the papers covering my desk. "Put that stuff in the safe and secure it."

Vaguely relieved, I stood up and did as I was told. Then we went through the iron fence that separated our wing from the other military duty stations of General Headquarters; we passed the gatekeeper and the guard and walked into the street.

On the way to the little café around the corner, Dierks said in a rather comradely tone of voice, "In the first place they shouldn't have had you come here at all. It would've been better if they'd run you first through the wringer for a couple of weeks in Berlin."

"One fellow," I replied, "a very distinguished looking older lieutenant colonel with a monocle, I forget his name, made a veiled reference to that also when they were shopping me around in Berlin. But the others thought I should first start in Hamburg, so they could report to Admiral Canaris that the slot had been filled." At that point, I gave Dierks a sharp look. "They said, there are enough experienced people in Hamburg who could show me the works."

"Well," he smiled, "I'll be one of them. By the way, the gentleman with the monocle you described, his name is Seber. He's a very keen and unusual man. It's a pity he's assigned to work on matters concerning the East and not in your territory."

So, we sat in the café, drinking a coffee spiked with some cognac. I used the occasion to take a closer look at my new colleague. He was the kind of fellow I would hardly have noticed under ordinary circumstances. Dierks was about ten years older than I and already had completely gray hair. He had a high, intelligent forehead, but his mouth was too narrow for his face, which, upon closer observation, actually seemed ugly but still rather sympathetic. Listening to him for some time and observing him, you would automatically have been captivated by his entire personality. Later on, I found out, to my genuine astonishment, that he had something that was extremely attractive to women, women of any age, any type, and any nationality. He told me that he was divorced and his young son spent one day with him each week.

Coming from a Friesian farm family, Dierks displayed the slow, contemplative style that characterizes the Friesians. Friesians think first and talk later. They do not speak any more than necessary. They rarely display any excitement.

Dierks had a brother who was a kind of clairvoyant, and he himself, as I learned later on, was the type who would run around with a divining rod. He had been a reserve officer in World War I and was in Intelligence even then. Although he had been in the insurance business before he joined the Abwehr, I always had the feeling he already worked for Intelligence in the Black Reichswehr. He was ever so knowledgeable, and like an old fox in this field. I could not wish for a better mentor.

Dierks gave me a detailed overview of our organization, its mission, its operating procedures, and its contacts. Sitting back at my desk, I was able to put some order to my stacks of papers with the hitherto incomprehensible hieroglyphs.

"And don't think that somebody expects you to answer all questions right away," Dierks counseled me. "Before you can actually get down to work, you have to find someone who will go to England for you and make inquiries there about places, factories, and other things. Since you're an Intelligence officer, you yourself must never visit the country you're working on. On the other hand, you can travel all over the world to find suitable people."

"So, where am I supposed to start?" I asked, somewhat subdued.

"I've got one for you," Dierks said. "He's a Welshman who offered his services to our embassy in Brussels when I was stationed there."

"Why don't you keep him for yourself?" I asked.

"No," Dierks said, shaking his head. "I can't use him because he has more contacts with the Luftwaffe than with the Navy. I have his address and a few notes concerning him. You can start with that. As you'll see, the notes will give you an idea of how best to contact him." I was much delighted. This was a good beginning.

"And then," Dierks continued, "go to the Chamber of Commerce, and talk to Mr. Lerner. He's our contact man there, and you'll certainly get valuable contacts through him. He knows all the importers and exporters who work with Scandinavia and England." "And," he added with his characteristic, barely noticeable smile, "do not exaggerate things, do not get nervous, and do not expect any immediate success in this type of business. And if you write letters, you might never get an answer. That calls for patience on your part."

I thanked him. He had given me far more than I had ever dared hope for. Before Dierks left his office that same evening, he gave me the notes concerning the Welshman. His name was Arthur Owens. I gave him the cover name *Johnny* [*Snow* to MI5].

Johnny was an electrical engineer and ran his own little company with a workshop in England. Additionally, he was a representative of foreign companies, including the Dutch Philips-Werke. He was thus able to move all over the continent in an official capacity. During a business trip to Brussels, he had made himself available to the German embassy. He gave as his reason for wanting to help that he was a Welshman who hated the English and therefore offered to provide information on the British aircraft industry.

I pored over the notes concerning *Johnny,* and I kept wondering with growing excitement whether this Welshman might not become my first "spy."

2

Dr. Rantzau

The next morning, I wrote my first letter to *Johnny*; I described a new type of dry battery and offered him a chance to import it into England. This was a battery built in Hamburg by a company that specialized in dry batteries and was owned by one of our trusted contacts. I indicated that, if he was interested, I would be happy if he would visit me in Hamburg. I signed the letter, which was written on company stationery, using the name *Dr. Rantzau*. That was a routine business contact for *Johnny's* alibi.

After the First World War, I had studied business administration; I had been a mercantile managing director in both Germany and America and was familiar with international commercial practices. In civilian clothing, I was primarily considered to be a businessman, so my camouflage was genuine in every respect. We rarely wore our uniforms.

Our cars displayed ordinary license plates without any military symbols, and our drivers were civilians. Dierks was the only one who had his own car at that time. Whenever appropriate, I posed as a textile merchant. That was the field in which I was technically and commercially competent. But, because I spoke fluent English, it was also quite natural for me to act as an interpreter for *Johnny* and the technicians making the batteries. This was later also the case with other contacts.

There were four telephones on my desk; three were used exclusively for my various business contacts. When one of the managers picked up the receiver, he always used the company name, but everyone else had strict orders to only answer with the relevant number. In this manner, *Dr. Reinhardt*, *Dr. Jansen*, or whoever was requested, would be called to the phone. In any country where I happened to be traveling, I had other names, each with a corresponding passport. In Hamburg, I was *Dr. Renken*, an emissary of various German companies.

Over time, with the help of Mr. Lerner of the Chamber of Commerce, I established a series of solid connections with Hamburg companies, for whom I often acted as representative, and as assistant to the managing director, who happened to be traveling abroad. In that way, it was quite natural that on some occasions I would need to correspond with my agents on the respective company stationery displaying their unique business logo.

Gradually, I became familiar with the practical side of the Abwehr, with all of its nuances, subtleties, and wiles. In many cases, my education and my past civilian experiences constituted a foundation that was not to be underestimated, and without which quite a few connections and successes would not have been possible.

I had been brought up according to the strict Prussian principles of my father—obedience, justice, decency, and good manners. I was raised to be God-fearing and patriotic. Our motto was "One who is free, does what is right and strikes what is wrong." I had been taught to believe every person was good. That rule, in my later life, constituted a heavy burden and was often sorely tried by my knowledge of human nature.

My father would have liked for me to study theology, but I always was inclined toward the military. I was an inspired soldier during World War I, before I had any concept of the dedication required by a military career and of my life in general. In the army, I quickly discovered that not all men were honorable and that I had to remain vigilant lest I be driven into the wall.

What had begun during my hardened soldiering days was now behind me in New York. My beginning in New York was a difficult learning experience. I found it most demanding to defend myself against the rudeness of the reportedly "nice" people. But I soon learned the key phrases, and my English vocabulary expanded with the addition of expressions that, to this day, I have not found in any dictionary.

In 1935, the German Consulate General in New York contacted me and asked whether I might want to become an officer again; so, I went to Germany, took an exam, and returned to the United States somewhat frustrated. The following year, General Friedrich von Bötticher, the military attaché in Washington, asked me to contact him. He shared with me that the Wehrmacht High Command, the Foreign Bureau, was interested in me. Well, that was more like it. In the meantime, the president of my textile company in New York had died, and the firm was now in other hands. That made it easier for me to make my decision. I accepted the offer and returned to Germany.

My new military career started in Bremen on September 1, 1936; from there, after a short time, I was transferred to the Wehrmacht High Command, Foreign Bureau–Intelligence I, under Admiral Canaris.

Nikolaus Ritter. From the editor's private collection.

3

The Abwehr

I had never seen Admiral Canaris before I reported to him. I simply knew him from hearsay as the legendary chief of the Military Intelligence Service, the Abwehr; and I knew nothing at all about the Abwehr.

Secret intelligence is as old as history. The former German Intelligence was disbanded by the Allies after the First World War and was secretly resurrected a few years before Hitler took power. It was a powerful organization that developed gradually out of a small group that was originally affiliated only with Army General Headquarters. In the beginning, it engaged not simply in military affairs, but also in political intelligence; furthermore, it procured domestic political intelligence for the High Command of the Reichswehr.

After 1935, the political intelligence service was gradually removed and transferred to the SD [*Sicherheitsdienst*]. In 1938, after Admiral Canaris became Chief of Military Intelligence, he reorganized the Abwehr into three sections. Its activity was confined purely to military counterespionage and intelligence collecting.

The OKW [*Oberkommando der Wehrmacht*] Abwehr consisted of three departments:

- Intelligence I (Abw I)—foreign intelligence collection, espionage
- Intelligence II (Abw II)—sabotage
- Intelligence III (Abw III)—counterespionage

Departments were subdivided into four or five branches of the Wehrmacht: e.g., Heer (army, I H), Marine (navy, I M), Luftwaffe (air force, I L), and Wirtschaft (economy, industry, I Wi). In other words, I H, I M, I L, and I Wi and each branch of the service had further subdivisions, such as technical, communications, and Central intelligence (Z, the department for secret records), administration, and so forth. All were combined under the Foreign Bureau and were affiliated with the Armed Forces High Command in Berlin (OKW). The co-headquarters under the command's defense positions were organized similarly under the Bureau.

When Canaris came into office, he was a naval captain. He had been a follower of National Socialism even before 1933, but he did not belong to the "inner" circle. Canaris was an active-duty officer and was, above all, governed

Admiral Canaris, Chief of the Abwehr. Organizational chart. Originally published in *Der Stern*, March 15, 1953, page 14.

by the Old Prussian rule that an officer does not engage in politics. Until 1919, active-duty personnel were even forbidden to select a party.

Canaris's office in Berlin sat in the old buildings of the Wehrmacht High Command on Tirpitzufer 72 in the so-called Bendler Block between the canal and the zoo.

When I reported to Canaris, I was astonished to discover he was rather short and squatty, entirely different from the way I had imagined him. He was actually quite colorless, but he radiated a striking air of calm. His movements were measured; he spoke in soft, reflective tones; his eyes were an undefinable blue; his facial features were regular, but in no way outstanding.

Basically, he was difficult to describe. Although he was not yet fifty, he appeared old at first glance. His hair and eyebrows were white. He looked tired. In the agency, he was not called "the Old Man" like any other chief; instead, he was frequently referred to as "the Greek."

At our first meeting, we merely exchanged a couple of words. I just had to answer a few questions. Canaris was obliging, but rather impersonal. He asked about my military past and refrained from any extraneous statements. There was nothing particularly impressive about him, and yet, I was impressed. Though some of his subordinates were afraid of him, he struck me as someone I would never have any reason to fear, but also as someone I would never really get to know well. He confirmed I would be assigned to Intelligence I Air, specifically to the Intelligence Duty Station attached to the headquarters of X Army Corps in Hamburg. He then escorted me to the door and asked his secretary to take me to Colonel Hans Piekenbrock, Chief of Joint Group I.

Piekenbrock was the exact opposite of the pale, inscrutable Canaris. He was tall, friendly, open, and frank. He was an active-duty officer who knew what he wanted. I felt I could trust him, and I felt drawn to him from the first moment we met. He explained to me, briefly and clearly, that my job was to build up a new desk in Hamburg for the Abwehr of the Luftwaffe, and that this would not be an easy task.

The Luftwaffe, which was being built up under Hermann Göring, needed everything that could be procured in terms of technical and military information from other countries; in my case, England was the priority. We needed to make up for lost time and to set aside maximum funding for related research and development. Piekenbrock personally escorted me to my department head, who introduced me to a number of staff members and then discharged me to go to Hamburg with all his best wishes.

My territory, thus, was England. I had been told that various desks of the other Wehrmacht components already had a series of agents. My first agent was to be the Welshman, whom Dierks had lined up for me, and now I impatiently waited for his response to my invitation.

Two weeks later, I received a short letter from *Johnny*, informing me he was interested in the batteries, and that he would be in Hamburg on a certain day in March. I showed Dierks the letter and asked him whether I should meet with *Johnny* directly at the battery manufacturer's plant or someplace else. It was obvious that we could not receive any agents at our duty station lest we expose our identity and risk endangering our operatives. Military duty stations were always under observation. Dierks said, "The first time you must meet him alone before you go with him to the plant. For that occasion, I'll let you use my office in the city on Spaldingstrasse, but then you have to find your own office as soon as possible."

He gave me the address of an imposing office building in a rather out-of-the-way but heavily traveled street behind the railroad terminal that would be difficult to find for the uninitiated. This way I was able to make a start with *Johnny* and to concentrate on the recruitment of other agents.

"Try to meet as many people as possible who have some dealings with foreign countries, but be rather choosy in your selections," Dierks advised.

Mr. Lerner from the Chamber of Commerce called me from time to time when he was visited by foreign or German businessmen who might be of interest to me. Sometimes, I would meet them in the Chamber of Commerce, but frequently we would first go someplace and have a glass of wine, just to establish a business relationship without discussing my real "business."

One day, I received a call from my Hamburg optician. I met him through Mr. Lerner, a man I had used as a researcher. He told me that over the next several days he would be visited by a Mrs. Erikson, a naturalized Swede of German extraction. Her Swedish husband had passed away some years ago, and she had accepted a position as housekeeper with a British Royal Navy Air Arm in Grimsby. Her children were attending school in Stockholm, where she visited them twice a year. On one of those visits, she also stopped over to see her friends in Hamburg. I asked the optician to invite me to meet Mrs. Erikson. Shortly after her arrival in Hamburg, we met at the home of my researcher for a cup of tea.

Mrs. May Erikson—or *Lady May*, as we later called her—was about forty-five years old, tall and stately, with chestnut-brown hair and strikingly beautiful, melancholy doe eyes. She exuded an atmosphere of confidence and reliability. On occasion, she could be rather jolly. I chatted with her for quite some time. She told me of her life in Scandinavia and her current job in England. I detected in her a possible employee. I told her that I frequently had business in Stockholm, although I had never been there before; I just might be able to visit her the next time I was in Stockholm. She expressed that that would give her pleasure. Through our own informant, I had the local police trace her history and reported the new contact to Central in Berlin. I was to arrange a trip to Stockholm, provided nothing negative was reported on *Lady May*.

Mr. Moll was to help me. He was a deputy section chief, and in the past had had the job of bureau chief for I Army [I H] and I Luftwaffe [I L]; later, as my work kept growing, he was assigned to my section. We generally called him *The Skipper.* He had indeed been a "skipper." In other words, he had been the captain of a small merchant vessel. He was in his early fifties, medium tall, sturdy, lots of fun, sly, intelligent, and painstakingly correct in terms of attitude and work. He never lost his typical seaman's gait. He spoke fluent English and had an extraordinary knowledge of human nature. New recruits, who were referred to me for briefing, constituted a welcome prey for him.

Once, I observed him lecture one of these officers who had rather timidly asked if he should not use blue eyeglasses and a moustache for a particular mission.

"That's just the sort of thing we've been waiting for," he retorted rather dryly, and smiled mischievously. "No, Captain. No Sherlock Holmes stuff—just plain and simple, just like the good Lord put the nose on your face. At most, now and then, a different hat or just ordinary eyeglasses—plus a good memory so you won't suddenly use a different name in the same hotel to the same doorman who, as we all know, always has good recall for people's names."

The Skipper did everything. He took care of passports, monitored records, made all important trip preparations, plus much more. He was an old fox in this field and rarely lost his cool. But when he became really excited, you could always tell, because he kept buttoning and unbuttoning his jacket without being aware of his action.

Mr. Moll, *The Skipper,* had several female secretaries working for him; all had been screened thoroughly. Whenever I wanted to know anything specific, they would always say, "You have to ask Miss von Klitzing."

I had run into Miss von Klitzing frequently in the past, as she hustled past me along the long corridor, acting quite reserved, courteous, and friendly. At that time, I did not know that, deep inside, she was always laughing at me.

"I always had to restrain myself," she said about me. "He looked so American. He shook hands with everyone. He always raced through the hallway in his light-colored raincoat and a frightfully bright-gray Stetson hat. And when I happened to be passing his office, he was always sitting at his desk and pensively rolling a thick cigar between thumb and middle finger."

Miss von Klitzing, at that time, was on friendly terms with Dierks, although it seemed he took the friendship more seriously than she did. She was impressed by his extraordinary intelligence and realistic attitude toward life, which distinguished him from most of her other, younger acquaintances. But he was almost twenty-five years her senior, and in him she hardly saw a man she might marry someday.

Miss von Klitzing's father had been killed in action in 1914 during World War I shortly after she had been born. She was living at home with her mother and grandmother in Rothenbaumchaussee, an elegant residential district in Hamburg.

Besides the secretarial staff, our floor also housed other units in the department, including sections I H and I Wi.

Major Lips was head of I H. He had lived in England for several years and had the same assignment for the army as I did for the Luftwaffe.

Dr. Karl Prätorius was the head of I Wi. He was privately called "the rat catcher" because of his special skill in recruiting agents.

Just a couple of rooms down the hall sat the capable chief of our photography laboratory, who was particularly skilled in working with covert photographic techniques, such as invisible inks, in his darkroom.

Everyone had their own cover names, which were made known to others in the event they happened to work together as agents. Secretaries were also given cover names to use when they made contact with agents. Miss von Klitzing, for example, took the very bourgeois name of *Busch* and, of course, was subject to the same strict secrecy rules as the rest of us.

Every evening, we had to empty the wastebaskets into the "wolf" [shredder] in the basement to avoid all legible paper trails. The officer on duty had the job of double-checking all rooms to make sure that there were no papers lying around and that all desks and safes were properly secured.

The Skipper told me that, sometime earlier, an officer had left a letter stamped "Secret" on his desk. As required, the officer on duty reported the offense, and the careless fellow was transferred to field duty.

Something far more serious involving one of the female secretaries occurred not long after I reported for duty.

One day the officer on duty was looking for a rubber eraser. He opened a desk drawer and found a sealed, addressed envelope. At first, he almost pushed it aside without any further thought, until he suddenly realized the recipient had a foreign name. Upon closer examination, he established that the recipient of the letter had to be a Swede. The Swede for whom the letter was intended happened to be a lumber exporter. The entire scenario looked suspicious to him and he took it to his superior, who decided to open the letter. It was a love note. They were going to put it back and just reprimand the female secretary, but then they read the following in the second sentence:

"I fall in love again and again with your accent, and when you hold me in your arms at night . . .." Whoa, they thought. A foreigner with whom she goes to bed? And then they could not believe what they saw next. Here is what it said verbatim, "Please be careful concerning the issue which I told you about last Sunday. It is a Top Secret matter. I felt terrible about that. But I know that you love me and will make no use of it."

With whom the girl went to bed was her own business, but the fact that she was so enamored with this foreigner that she would divulge secret topics . . . that was treason. Indeed, it was "negligent" treason, but in any case, it was still treason. She was immediately taken into custody, and therefore was of no further use to our Intelligence or to any other military or civilian duty stations.

That was quite a shock to us all. At the time it concerned me only somewhat marginally.

For now, my travel claims were giving me a headache. My records had to match exactly with the original documents, such as hotel bills, receipts, and so forth; all of these documents had to be submitted. Our first paymaster was a petty-minded peasant who had not the slightest idea about the Abwehr. That's why we had various difficulties with our accounting. With current regulations, it was impossible to maintain secrecy about meetings with all the bells and whistles, since everything had to go through the administrative offices. After a great deal of bureaucratic back-and-forth, Berlin ordered new accounting procedures that prevented the exposure of secrets to the paymaster's department.

I had become entrenched in my work, and I was most enthusiastic. My family had moved to Hamburg, where we found a cozy apartment not too far from General Headquarters. The children had adjusted quickly, but the more I was consumed by my work, the unhappier my wife seemed to be. As an American, she understood neither my kind of work, nor the extraordinary stress to which I was exposed as a result of my duties. Naturally, I could not discuss any details about my work with her, and the more I became embedded in it, the more anxious she became. I suffered a great deal over the situation, but I assumed everything would improve once she had suitably settled in.

One morning in late summer, without any prior warning, right next to my plate at breakfast, I found a letter from an attorney whom my wife had contacted without my knowledge. It stated that she wanted to get a divorce and go back to America with our children. I offered her an opportunity to first visit the United States for a quarter or half a year, just as a trial to make some comparisons and to think through all of this calmly before she made her final decision. But she insisted on leaving.

Per regulation, I requested my chain of command to approve the divorce, which was granted after a careful check. I refused to let the children go to America with her, so my ex-wife remained in Germany until finally, after the war, without my knowledge, she returned to America with the children while I was imprisoned.

After my divorce in November of 1937, I moved into a small bachelor apartment and delved even more deeply into my work. I was embittered and missed my children. In later years, I was able to establish close contact with them, but many years passed before that time.

4

Launching a Network

One of the first discoveries I made during my intelligence activity was that practically everybody is a potential spy. Not because the work might appear romantic—although it is said that "there is an adventurer hidden in each of us"—but rather simply because an individual may not have a choice. One fellow finds a discarded blueprint, the other happens to be listening in on a conversation not intended for just anyone, or the chambermaid finds thoughtlessly scribbled notes on the notepad next to the phone or in the wastebasket.

That is why the chambermaids and cleaning personnel play an important role as agents.

An American ambassador assigned to a Central European power had the habit of throwing his notes and other papers in the wastebasket by simply crumpling them up instead of destroying them. One day, the cleaning woman picked up a crumpled scrap of paper that had fallen next to the wastebasket, and to her astonishment, she discovered it contained notes about Washington that certainly were not intended for the general public. She let us have the scrap of paper, in return for pay, and was recruited as a steady informant. As long as that particular diplomat was in his office, and as long as she worked as a cleaning woman for him, this wastebasket was a great source of classified information regarding the government of the United States.

But it was not just chambermaids and cleaning personnel who were of great interest to the intelligence services of all countries; all indigenous employees of foreign missions and agencies were of equally great interest to the Abwehr.

Only the Russians had drawn the proper conclusion from this reality and always, exclusively, employed Russians abroad. But many people, especially tourists, are also agents or spies without knowing it. They talk a lot without ever being asked any questions, and they photograph everything they can focus their cameras on. The latter category also includes seamen. They photograph every harbor and every coastal strip and allow the so-called harbor photographers to make copies. And since we were very much interested in these pictures, we recruited local harbor photographers. They made duplicate copies for us, which were then evaluated accordingly. In foreign ports we naturally tried to encourage our agents to adopt these same procedures.

We had already assembled a myriad of images of harbors such as Gibraltar, Malta, Singapore, and countless other small and large ships and airports. Although most of the time we did not gain much new information, every now and then we were able to spot a warship or a flying boat. We were also able to obtain images of the new naval air station at Grimsby.

In his usual dry manner, *The Skipper* used to say, "It's a good thing there are so many seafarers who always happen to take photographs where that sort of thing is not permitted." My assistant Lieutenant Commander Tornow loved to show a photo of Singapore and comment, "I never saw Singapore from that angle. That shows you once again how much better a little picture is than a long letter."

This is all part of a collection of countless little mosaic pieces that are indispensable to complete the Big Picture. Actual success or failure, however, depends on the people who, in international lingo, are referred to simply as "spies." In the old days, this word meant nothing more than a scout or a snoop. Here is what it says in the 1813 Prussian National Guard Regulations, paragraph 54: "This kind of snooping, far from being contemptible, is a duty to be pursued against the enemy; it is of utmost value and must therefore be encouraged everywhere. No undertaking can succeed without it."

Over the years, the term "spy" acquired a rather repulsive connotation, particularly due to the espionage laws. The general public almost always associates a spy with a traitor or criminal. But for the most part, spies are absolutely honorable informants, and many are the closest collaborators and associates. So, if we speak of undercover agents today, we simply talk about "V" people [*Vertrauensleute*]; in other words, trustworthy people.

In broad terms, four main groups of spies can be identified.

First, we have those who do this type of work as a matter of principle, in other words, those who are totally committed to their assignment on the basis of their very innermost morality—for example, our friend the Welshman, whose motive sprang from his personal hatred of everything English. These people are idealists who often blindly pursue their path without considering themselves or their family.

Then we have the professional adventurers, who are enticed not simply by adventure but mostly by money. They will take American dollars just as well as British pounds, Russian rubles, or German marks. You never know where their real sympathies lie. They are often referred to as "double agents," who work for both sides at the same time.

Another category consists of people who have been blackmailed. Generally, we do not go for blackmail. This form of agent recruiting is primarily a privilege of the Communists. Such agents are frequently unreliable.

And finally, at least in peacetime, the best and most dependable informants are the businessmen, who travel all over the world and who do not merely report what they routinely hear and see, but also keep their eyes and ears wide open to see and hear beyond the ordinary.

One such ideal example of the businessman informant was Mr. Everett M. Röder, the owner of an old Hamburg import-export firm. I met him through Mr. Lerner. He impressed me, not just because of his business activity and his frequent travels—above all, to England—but also by his personality. He was approximately 5'10", slim, and bent slightly forward; he had blond hair, a little blond moustache, and could at all times be considered a typical Englishman of good society. He smoked a pipe, and he wore tweed suits and, frequently, also the well-known checkered Sherlock Holmes–type deerstalker cap. As a child, Röder had attended school in England for quite some time and spoke perfect Oxford English without the slightest German accent.

I had taken a close look at Mr. Röder, and he agreed without hesitation when I approached him about possible collaboration. He was a good German, and he considered it quite natural that he should work with us. His company had regular business dealings with Great Britain long before World War I; all those on the other side of the English Channel were always open to him.

The most important aspect of Mr. Röder's usefulness was that he was an amateur aviator and was familiar with aviation and the aircraft industry, not just in Germany, but also in England. I could not find a more suitable associate, and I never found anyone better. It is not the number of agents you engage, but rather their ability and aptitude that count.

No matter how willing a person may be, you cannot assign just anyone to reconnoiter an airfield nor can you expect a mechanic to penetrate into the secrets of a chemical laboratory. By the same token, you cannot expect a small-town hero to establish contacts on the parquet of high society. All of this had to be taken into consideration as we were recruiting our investigators, informants, or spies in the countries where we were working.

Naturally, first Germans by birth and those of German descent came under consideration, although here again we had to be cautious because they were not simply suitable candidates for us; they were equally in the crosshairs of the counterintelligence service of the country where they resided. Particularly in the event of political tensions, they would be subjected to selective monitoring. Such is also the case for diplomats.

The safest recruits, but also the most difficult to find, were usually locals. They included mostly the anti-Communists, the fascists, and the dissatisfied minorities.

In poetry and drama, the success of a particular intelligence service is based almost exclusively on the skill, the security consciousness, and boldness of the individual. In reality, however, besides conscientious planning, mutual trust, and close cooperation, the most important requirement for success is the support of a group of qualified associates.

In the event an agent or spy decides to work as a loner, his success is limited. Success within the management organization cannot be guaranteed except through genuine teamwork. That was something I did not find in most Germans, after I had learned all about teamwork in America. The German language has no translation for the word *teamwork,* and the fact that I had to use the English term proved how unaccustomed the Germans were to working as a team. That was probably rooted in the character of the German who would, so to speak, encapsulate himself in his problems and jealously guard his achievements in order to receive credit for his success. I believe that greater success could have been achieved if we had encouraged more teamwork.

At that time, Dierks was just about the only individual outside of my circle of associates with whom I was able to work openly and without compromise.

Mr. Lerner of the Chamber of Commerce was another man not reluctant to part with his experiences and contacts. One day, he alerted me to a Hamburg manufacturer whose products were shipped mostly to Sweden. Of course, Lerner did not know whether I could persuade this gentleman to work with us. Nevertheless, I asked him to arrange a meeting.

As I entered Mr. Lerner's office, I saw an older, very distinguished-looking gentleman rising from his guest chair next to the desk. At first sight we realized that he was not accustomed to taking orders. It was immediately obvious from his overall demeanor that he was a widely traveled businessman, and because I also had lived abroad for a long time, I immediately recognized his personality type. After the usual formalities, I went directly for my target.

"Now that Mr. Lerner has introduced us, I'd like to ask you first of all not to worry about my identity. You can easily tell where I come from on the basis of our conversation."

I noted that he became a little more reserved, so I added, "Perhaps to calm you, I might point out to you that I have nothing to do with the "Party" [Nazi Party]. I'm speaking to you about things which are of interest to Germany, and also to your own interest as an exporter." Now he listened attentively.

I continued, "As Mr. Lerner informed me, most of your business is in Sweden. We're not interested in your business. On that score, you undoubtedly and unfortunately have enough trouble with foreign currency and other problems. What we'd really like to know, and you could certainly help us with, is the following: Some of your instruments are used in Sweden's aircraft industry. The same special instruments are made by your competitor in Sweden. The Swedish output alone would cover the requirements of the Swedish aircraft industry. Here's my question. Where does the surplus go? The statistics don't really provide us with an answer. Probably some of it goes to England or France. Might you be able to find out something about that?" The gentleman provided no comment, but continued to listen with interest.

"I need not tell you," I continued undeterred, "that we are perfectly aware you cannot officially inquire regarding this. But perhaps the possibility exists. Assuming, of course," and at that point, I looked directly at him, "being a German, you have the same feeling of belonging toward Germany as any Englishman would have toward his empire."

I could see his interest was aroused.

"It is no secret that the English report everything they observe when away from home. For the German, this is, unfortunately, not always the case. This has, indeed, deep psychological roots, which, among others, stem from the prevailing negative attitude of government agencies towards the Abwehr and Counterintelligence Service. However, that's no excuse for a well-informed and thinking man. In England it's the reverse, and I believe it's now high time we change our ways. But, I don't want to polemicize here." I stopped since I realized I was getting a little bit too carried away.

The man sitting across from me stirred for the first time and said, "I want to tell you quite openly that I never cared about those things. And, I'll tell you honestly that, precisely because of this general attitude, I have so far painstakingly avoided everything that might slightly take on the appearance—to put it gently—of snooping. But our talk does provide food for thought. The outside world, after all, is always suspicious of us. Why shouldn't we be on the alert? In the future, you'll learn everything I happen to hear and see."

I now knew I had convinced him, but added, "I'd be very happy if you would handle this matter seriously, not as a sort of sport; I'd rather you base your motive on the realization that this cooperation is necessary."

The exporter cleared his throat and said, "I was never a big so-called patriot, but I do see the need. I'm also quite accustomed to snooping around a little bit to keep up to date with my competition." Then, smiling, he asked, "And how am I to communicate with you?"

"In your case, that's very simple. Since you have business here all the time, just let Mr. Lerner know when you have something for us. He knows how to get in touch with us without compromising anyone, and then we can meet as unobtrusively as we met here today."

I took my leave with certainty that I had gotten the right answer to my question and probably even more. The man was initially quite reserved, but eventually, with cordial dialog, I believe he also gained some insight.

Gradually, I sat firm in my saddle and earned a larger office and adjusted to a second secretary. Also, I no longer had to share *The Skipper* with anyone. The original contacts had gone well, but I still did not have my first man in England.

Now, I should tell about our Welshman in whom I had placed so much hope. I was anxious. We had reserved a room for him in the Hotel Graf Moltke. Two of the employees there were confidants of the Secret Police who were subordinate to our respective liaison. In this case, I had also asked for *Johnny* to be monitored from the moment he crossed the border into Bentheim until his return, because we wanted to be absolutely sure he did not have any other contacts in Germany.

Johnny appeared punctually at the fixed hour. I had no personal description of him, and I was surprised when I saw him for the first time. He was unusually short and barely came up to my shoulder. He looked good and made an alert impression with his somewhat pointy face. His hair was blond. He was slim, and in spite of all of his daintiness, had a good shape. He made an intelligent impression and had a winning smile. His clothing was proper. He wore a dark brown suit with matching brown shoes.

While I did not reveal my understandable excitement, this encounter was an entirely new experience for me. Much of my future success depended upon this meeting. This extraordinary man was to be the key in my work against England.

My invitation to him had exclusively concerned batteries, but *Johnny* knew what was really involved. Consequently, I first took him to the battery manufacturer, where I played interpreter and where I made sure *Johnny* was indeed an expert. He ordered two batteries for testing, and after the usual business formalities, we walked to the office on Spaldingstrasse, which Dierks had made available to me.

Now, we could drop our masks. By way of introduction, *Johnny* brought with him a piece of a new alloy for shell casings with the complete description of all details. It was the first report of this kind that I was able to pass on to Berlin, and it turned out later that this alloy was also something new for our experts. It gave me great pride, and I immediately told Dierks and he shared my joy.

The next day, we established contact with the battery manufacturer with which *Johnny*, Mr. Arthur Owens, would function as the representative in Great Britain. That would be a first alibi for his trips to Hamburg and for our meetings; because he did not speak German, I would act as interpreter.

After our first meeting, I was certain *Johnny* was only too willing to collaborate, but I needed proof of his reliability. That is why I gave him some trial assignments. He was to procure certain items of information about the airfield in Northolt and about the arsenal in Wolverhampton. We knew Northolt from aerial photos and from Röder, and we had details on Wolverhampton from another source.

We agreed to meet again in three weeks in Hamburg. When I learned it was easier for him to get a Belgian visa because he had been working regularly in Belgium for quite some time, I told him we could possibly give him an address in Brussels so that he would not have to come to Hamburg as often. The prerequuisite, of course, was that his deliveries would satisfy us.

After three weeks, *Johnny* was again punctually in Hamburg. When I picked him up at the hotel, he showed me his report about Northolt and Wolverhampton. In both cases, he didn't just simply agree with our documents, but he also shared a series of other interesting details.

He had passed his first test. The Secret Police, who as a precaution had asked once again to watch him, had nothing but good to say about him. Except for us, he did not seem to have any acquaintances, nor did he appear to have any further interests in Germany. Whenever I was not able to meet with him, he mostly stayed in his hotel room, or he drank a glass of beer around the corner at Nagel. He seemed to have an eye for women, but he did not get involved with them.

Now and then I would step out in the evening with *Johnny* and amuse myself as he, quite contentedly, drank a glass of beer and enthused about the loud merriment in the Zillertal as the cheerful guests in the Hofbräuhaus sang and linked arms, swinging side to side late into the night.

One evening, he accompanied me to a café that was on the both famous and infamous Reeperbahn. Every table had a number and a telephone. Each customer could telephone a girl, sitting all by herself, from his table and could ask her to join him at his table. To test *Johnny*, I urged him to call a girl. Since he did not speak German, he asked me to initiate the contact for him. He had already picked No. 3. All of these girls spoke fragments of some language, and the girl at No. 3 confirmed to me that she spoke English. I invited her to join us for a drink. *Johnny* chatted with her as best he could, but he didn't ask her to dance or make any attempts to get closer to her. We left the place together, and I took him back to his hotel. *Johnny* told me he was married and asked if I had any objection to him bringing his wife with him to Hamburg someday. I had no objections. It was not unusual for businesspeople to bring their wives along, and besides, it would certainly be interesting to get to know her.

At that time, if I recall correctly, I gave *Johnny* twenty English pounds. I was always rather reluctant to part with money. If at all possible, we paid the correct value for the deliveries, and *Johnny* rarely received more than fifty pounds, in other words, between about 500 and 600 deutsche marks. Among other issues, money was also a security measure. If at all possible, no one should receive more than would be in line with his standard of living. Too many people have been spotted because they suddenly lived beyond their means.

Meanwhile, *Johnny,* in addition to his cover name, had received his number, like all the other agents who worked for us. The first two digits indicated the section for which they worked. My agents, those at Hamburg I Air, were given numbers that began with 35. Mr. Lerner was number *3503. Johnny* was number *3504.*

Johnny became a steady and diligent associate. He always delivered his information to me personally at a previously designated place and date.

One day, as we sat in my office in the city, he pulled a minute, flat package of cellophane out of his pocket. It contained a tiny piece of paper bearing all kinds of hieroglyphs.

I was baffled and somewhat annoyed because he was so careless in carrying secret notes on him. "What's the meaning of this?" I demanded.

"That's alright," he said, trying to calm me down, and pointed at his teeth. "I glued the cellophane paper under my dentures." I had to laugh, but I did caution him.

In the beginning, *Johnny*'s reports did not contain anything sensational; but they did contain information of which we had no previous knowledge, and they were remarkably accurate. Most of the material was based on his personal explorations. Some he received from contact men whom he had gradually gathered around himself and whose identity he disclosed correctly and without hesitation. Some were in the Air Ministry, and two were in the RAF depots. Those were his subagents, as he called them. Most were Welshmen like himself. The evaluations we received from Berlin on his reports were good throughout. I was well satisfied with the success of my first agent in England.

5

Orders from Admiral Canaris

On a hot July afternoon in 1937, completely exhausted after processing an agent, I returned from beautiful Budapest. I drove directly to my office from the airport. On my desk, I found a pile of mail and file entries; but before I could settle down to work, the officer on duty gave me some "top secret" papers.

I was countersigning mechanically when I noticed the personal signature of Canaris. I knew immediately this was something extraordinary. Quite generally, letters from Berlin were signed by a group chief; Canaris signed letters personally only in special cases.

Then I read the few lines. Without introduction or explanation, it ordered: EFFECTIVE IMMEDIATELY, THE INTELLIGENCE SERVICE IS ALSO TO COVER THE UNITED STATES ARMY AIR CORPS WITH RESTRICTION THAT OUR RESEARCH IS TO EXTEND FIRST AND PRIMARILY TO THE UNITED STATES ARMY AIR CORPS ARMAMENT INDUSTRY.

I leaned back in my swivel chair and stared at the order, at these few sobering words. It took me a long time to think clearly. At first, I felt almost paralyzed. I had a feeling that this meant I would have to tackle a new and heavy responsibility. I had lived too long in the United States not to know what kind of difficulties I would have to grapple with there.

I began thinking of the time I had lived in the United States. It had been fourteen years earlier, when at age twenty-four, during my storm and stress period, I had gone to New York for the first time. Life was wide open before me. All that was left for me was regaining something I had lost as a result of World War I: my youth, my career as an officer, my country, which I never really had a chance to know, and my future, which during my childhood had seemed laid out before me so brilliantly and securely.

After the war, while employed with the border guard, I had been billeted with a wealthy textile manufacturer in Silesia. I was not just a friend of the family and an admirer of their young daughter, I was also interested in the manufacturing of textiles. My host had told me at that time, "If you ever want to pursue a civilian occupation, you could always work for me, but you would have to start as an apprentice."

As I saw no further opportunity to pursue my career as an army officer, I decided, with a heavy heart, to resign; until my discharge, I studied economics in Berlin for a couple of semesters.

I completed my apprenticeship, and both romance and internship came to an end. After successfully earning my diploma from the Preussische Höhere Fachschule für Textilindustrie [Prussian Advanced School of Textile Industry] in Sorau, I took my first job as business manager of a textile plant with 250 office employees and workers.

During that time, hyperinflation caused considerable instability in the Weimar Republic. A box of matches, which previously cost two pennies, now, in 1923, cost 10,000 marks. Money lost value day after day. As business manager, I had to physically carry the wages to the factory, which was located outside the city; I tried everything I could to pay the employees as quickly as possible. The German mark dropped to 4,200 million against the dollar. Such a magnitude of paper money had to be transported in suitcases and laundry baskets. One payday, as I was ready to get under way with my suitcases full of money, the manufacturer's wife called me to tell me she needed the car for herself because she had heard women's underwear was available in Görlitz. I could not believe my ears.

"Dear madam," I said, "that is impossible. There are 250 people in the factory waiting for their money. If they don't get the money today, they can't buy anything with it tomorrow."

She did not care, and because she was procurement officer of the firm she was able to commandeer the car over my objection. I was powerless, but, as I had learned while in the army, I waited twenty-four hours before I complained. Then I handed in my resignation. The owner apologized for his wife and asked me to stay, but I had had enough.

I had often thought of emigrating. Now, the time had come. With my father's help, I established contact with a distant relative in the United States, who finally sent me the required affidavit and the money for the crossing, on loan.

And then came the day when I sat in the smoking lounge of the old North German Lloyd SS *Bremen*. I did not even take the trouble to get properly excited about this tremendous change in my life.

On New Year's morning 1924, I took my first look at the country where I would spend the next several years of my life.

Today, I marvel at the insolence with which I found my first job in such a short time despite the still strong resentment against everything German. Every morning at five o'clock, I stood in line to get the first newspapers, and I checked all the want ads. Very often, I was stopped by a sign reading "Germans not wanted" or "Germans need not apply here."

The first manager who at least talked to me was the personnel chief of the

Title Guaranty & Trust Company. He was polite, and my hopes perked up until he suddenly said he did not have anything for me at this time.

Two days later, I tried the same company once again with the same result. When I turned up the third time, he said, "You are damn stubborn. Didn't you catch on that I don't want you because you're a German?"

"I am German," I confirmed, "but you didn't tell me that this would be the reason for you turning me down, and I couldn't imagine that a man such as you would make me personally responsible for the war."

As I started to take my leave, he stopped me and said: "You're right. Tomorrow, you come to our branch in Jamaica, Long Island, New York."

That was a beginning. After that, I had a series of other jobs, until I finally found my niche with Mallinson Silk Mills in Astoria, Long Island. I started as a weaver; then after a short time, due to my specialized skills, I was promoted to the technical chief of a department with sixty looms. When I felt secure enough, I thought I was entitled to ask for a pay raise. When they refused, I left. After two days, they reconsidered and asked me to come back with a raise in pay. But when I tried the same trick the second time, it did not work.

When that job ended, I was miserable for a while. I worked as a handyman in a nighttime printing firm, as dishwasher, painter, locksmith's helper, parquet floor installer, and in some other jobs. When I was still a student, my father had sent me regularly to intern in handyman occupations, which benefited me in securing these positions. I had received training in carpentry and had also learned the rudiments of locksmithing while I waited on my American visa.

Sometime later, I started driving through the United States with several friends in an old Dodge. Near Lake Superior, hurricane-force winds ripped the top off our car and almost swept us into a ravine. We received all of $10 for the scrap, and in the end, we had to work as busboys in the Plankinton Arcade in Milwaukee.

After that, my friends and I earned money as carpenter's helpers, and for days on end, we were the guests of the Indian chief Reginald Oshkosh on the Wisconsin Menominee Reservation. The chief was pro-German because a German professor had studied the customs and habits of his tribe for two years on his reservation. He had smoked a peace pipe with him, and after that the professor's kin continued a friendship with the chief.

Finally, after a ride across the Great Lakes, we somehow managed to get back to New York and return to our respective occupations. By now, our youthful enthusiasm had waned. That time in my life was followed by steady hard work, with routine promotions all the way to the position of managing director in a weaving mill. I also had friends among influential people in New York and

Nikolaus Ritter. From the editor's private collection.

Washington; I was a visiting member of the University Club; I had a permanent visitor card for the Senate and the Congress. I was married to an American teacher. We lived in a cozy apartment with our two children, and I finally felt at home.

I had seen a lot and had learned even more, and everywhere I had tried hard to contribute to a new understanding between young, victorious America and the beaten country of my forefathers. But one day, the urge to go home became overpowering, just as years before I could not resist the call for distant adventure. I wanted to go back to Germany, and I hoped to have a future in my homeland like I had dreamed of during my childhood years.

And yet, everything turned out differently.

With a jolt I jumped back to reality. I stood up, picked up the top-secret document, and went to see my good chief, Lieutenant Commander Burghardt. The little, roundish commander was seated comfortably in his outmoded leather chair, the single piece of luxury furniture in this barren office. As was his habit, he pulled on the tip of his nose with his thumb and index finger to bring it down upon his raised lower lip whenever he was deep in thought.

As I stuck my head through the door, his index finger slipped between lip and nose, he put both his fingers back to their starting position, and in his brash but kindly manner, he said, "Come on in, man, and have a seat. I know all about it. I've wanted to take this matter up with you for quite some time."

"Yes," I said, closing the door behind me and sitting down. "I feel a little uneasy about this. You know I lived in the United States for many years. I have a great number of friends overseas, both Americans and Germans." I paused and then continued, "I'm well aware of how imperative systematic work is for them. I also know this cannot be done from here. This is only possible on location. But please understand me correctly when I say that I have my own, purely emotional, ideas on that score."

"OK, I understand. I understand, but if by 'ideas' you mean feelings, then that's of little interest to me. On the other hand, if you really have ideas, then you shouldn't be subjected to any binding regulations. How you're going to accomplish this job is left entirely up to you," Burghardt said. "But, I think we have to move fast. Sometimes, I get the impression that our people in Berlin underestimate our brothers on the other side."

"I think so, too. But whom do we have, at least in our own country, who really knows the United States? Most people know it just from books, some also from so-called study tours. When I even hear those words, I see red, and there are hardly more than one or two people who actually lived over there. And they have nothing to say. The others are overbearingly arrogant and think that they know everything better than those of us who have been to America. It's true, after all, that the Americans, from time to time, are quite presumptuous toward us. But, you have to understand that in context, so you won't draw any wrong conclusions."

"Clarify that for me in a little more detail," the commander grumbled.

"For you, gladly; I gave up trying in Berlin. You see, when you come from Europe across to the other side, you see everything first through European eyes, and most Americans seem overbearing, especially to us Germans. But later, with eyes wide open and good common sense, you see you can't measure an American giant with a German yardstick. When you learn to use the local yardstick, then suddenly everything looks entirely different."

"What do you mean by that?"

"The better you get to know the Americans, the less they seem like primitive robots, which is what many people believe. Their history is still so young that even the earliest beginnings have not yet become a part of their living history. One begins to understand the natural chauvinism with which the average American is ready 'to show those damn foreigners where to get off'—to show the cursed foreigners where they belong. You also understand that everything American is the 'biggest' and the 'best,' and why the American girls are always referred to as 'your majesty' and the like in advertisements. But these are eruptions of chauvinism that are as necessary as the artificial wormholes in the replicated Louis Quatorze furniture. Then you can also understand the respectable gentlemen who today, with full conviction, join your cause and who tomorrow, with the same conviction, adopt a different opinion."

"You see," Burghardt agreed with me, "that is precisely what so many Europeans haven't yet grasped. However, in the meantime, the American has fallen in step with the Old World and in some ways, here and there, has even surpassed it. And whoever doesn't get it, that's just too bad. But once more, let's take a look at your new assignment. Do you believe that America would go to war against us again?"

I hesitated a moment, and then said, "Unfortunately, yes! We must not fool ourselves. There are many people in the United States, including leading personalities in the veteran organizations such as the Veterans of Foreign Wars, the American Legion, and others with whom we German war veterans have become friends. These people repeatedly assured me they would never again go to war against Germany; they were certainly sincere about that, and their organizations play a very large role there. But, the American has the unusual quality, which in their case is far more pronounced than it is with others, and which we must not underestimate. He himself calls it 'gullibility.' That is difficult to translate. It's almost like an addictive credulity to take everything that is in print at face value, especially when it comes to sensationalism."

"The individual certainly does not want war," I continued, "certainly not against Germany, but when his government and the people behind the scenes consider it necessary, then a short propaganda campaign suffices, and then they write the word Propaganda with a capital P, and everybody sounds a call to arms. A herd mentality takes over." I had gotten myself quite worked up, and Burghardt tried to calm me down.

"Well, now," he chimed in, "things are not going to be as bad as all that. At any rate, surely you yourself have decided that a stepped-up investigation overseas is absolutely necessary."

"Naturally," I sighed. I had already arrived at this conclusion a long time ago.

"Well and good," the commander concluded our talk. "You now must consider every detail. All necessary resources will be made available to you." He looked at me very seriously. "It's my opinion that you yourself should go there, and that you personally should try to build up an organization on the spot."

I was not particularly astonished. I had been thinking along those lines for quite some time. Nevertheless, I asked, "Does it have to be that way?" The answer was quite clear. I was discharged with a brief nod.

Slowly, I walked along the long corridor back to my office. I stopped in front of my desk, and I knew I could not do anything else right now. I was too roused. I had to distance myself from the entire episode.

I scooped up the papers on my desk and locked them in the safe. Then I put my hat on and went to the little café I had visited with Dierks quite some time ago, and I sat down at an empty table in a corner. I had to be alone; I had to get my thinking in order before I could go back to work.

Naturally, I had to go myself. I knew that. My personal feelings did not play any role here. I was the only one who could be considered for this assignment. In view of my knowledge of the land and the people, I could accomplish more in two months than any neophyte in two years.

My biggest worry was regarding new contacts. I had to locate new investigators who would find good contacts for me. German and foreign vessels had to be combed through for suitable couriers who could carry information and material back and forth. New routing stations had to be set up. No one should know the other. I also had the feeling that we must avoid direct correspondence between Hamburg and the United States. The routing stations must fit into business and private correspondence. If at all possible, they should be located in neutral countries.

The postage stamp dealers had to go into action and again procure the necessary stamps from all countries. Traveling businessmen were asked to bring stationery from every country. A letter, for example, that was sent via a routing station in Sweden to the United States had to be typed in Germany on a foreign typewriter using Swedish paper and put in a Swedish envelope with Swedish stamps, and sent ready for mailing to the Swedish routing station, which then simply had to stick it in the mailbox. My head was spinning. There were so many details that must be considered. Of course, I had my associates for a large portion of the detail work, but everything had to be planned, and all procurements had to be timely.

How much easier the work was in other countries from which we were not separated by a large body of water. There was always a green border. The smuggler trails were easily used with the help of the customs service. There was no green border between Germany and the United States. There was just an ocean.

Gradually, the plans took shape. I felt free again, and the appeal of the new task had already pulled me completely under its spell.

My cigar was puffing at full throttle.

I took a couple of coins, which according to an old American custom, I always carried loose in my pocket, put them on the table and went back to my desk. *The Skipper* was waiting for his instructions.

"See what you can assemble for the USA with the help of the Chamber of

Commerce or in some other way with the help of suitable textile agencies," I said. "At the same time, place an ad reading roughly like this: 'Textile merchant, cotton and rayon, will accept orders of all kinds for three-month travel throughout the various states'—or something to that effect."

"Excuse me, Chief," *The Skipper* interrupted. "You haven't yet told me under what name you're going to travel."

"Under my own," I answered dryly.

The Skipper looked rather baffled, which was a rare thing. "How come?" he snapped in astonishment.

"How come?" I laughed. "Because I consider that the safest. First of all, I will be in this location for just a relatively short period of time, and I hardly believe that American intelligence has already gotten on my trail. Besides, you must not forget I lived there for a good dozen years, and I have many friends and acquaintances there—mostly, in New York and Washington. Although I don't have plans to contact any of my former companions, Broadway, New York, is exactly like Unter den Linden in Berlin or the Jungfernstieg in Hamburg. You're very likely to run into the person you are most eager to avoid. Although I hope to engage in routine business deals, I'd like to refrain from unnecessary complications. You know as well as I do, coincidence plays an excessively big role, especially in our business. It can mean good luck, but also defeat. It's wiser to leave as little as possible to chance."

"Are you going to visit anyone you knew in the old days?" *The Skipper* wanted to know.

"There is only one fellow," I said, "a man by the name of Fritz Duquesne." I was not concerned about establishing contact with him. He had previously worked in Germany, and knowing him very well, I was certain he would need money. Except for him, I had no intention of contacting anyone else I had known before. If, by coincidence, I should run across someone along the way, the fact that I traveled under my own name would certainly remove all possible complications.

What we needed was immediate exploration results. It was not my task to establish any particular organization in case of a future war. The Luftwaffe had to know now what was going on in the US Army Air Corps and in the aircraft industry.

I was determined not to bring any of the new agents I might sign up in the United States into contact with any of the established ones. Everyone should work alone and send his report directly to one of my routing stations.

My plan was based on the fact that Germany and the United States were not at war with each other, and I could, therefore, use routine means of communication and travel. I had no reason to concern myself about what would have to be done if the borders were closed and travel connections interrupted. In any case, I wanted to set up an alternate route, not just across the Atlantic, but also across the Pacific. Our interests were primarily focused on technical matters; it was therefore not so important whether the information took a couple of days longer before it reached us. If there should be a war, then all normal connections would, of course, be broken off. Then, we would have secret relay stations in England and the United States. Right now, we were still using ships and the post office.

"You have to start right now to line up as many couriers as possible," I told *The Skipper.* "Also, please try to get contacts with the Far East through our Chinese consulate and through the Chamber of Commerce. I'll take care of my own visa."

"Miss *Busch* is to take care of the ship ticket," I continued, "but please, under no circumstances, first class, as proposed by Berlin. I want a good cabin amidships in the tourist class on the *Europa*. I have a good reason for this action. All first-class passengers, just like in our country, are listed publicly in the newspapers, and I do not wish to publicize my arrival in the United States. Once all the particulars are clear, I can assess whatever I need in the way of money. Tomorrow I'll go to Düsseldorf to pick up some textile samples and business stationery. That, I believe, is enough for a start."

"Okay, Chief," *The Skipper* confirmed after my long speech. "Everything will be taken care of." In the process, he rebuttoned his jacket for the hundredth time. "Everything will be taken care of," he repeated. "But how are we going to deal with *Johnny* and *Lady May* while you are gone?"

"You have to handle *Lady May* yourself," I said. And then I added, somewhat suggestively, "You wouldn't mind, would you?"

The Skipper had been there when I invited the rather nice-looking Lady Erikson. The old gentleman was obviously quite taken by this lady. I knew his weakness for her, but I also knew her private interests were in Stockholm.

The Skipper cleared his throat and twice buttoned and unbuttoned his jacket. "Well and good," he said somewhat embarrassed. "Have you any special instructions?"

"Make a date with her the next time she is in Stockholm." I had a special assignment for her in England.

"And *Johnny*?"

"You have to handle him this time. Take Miss *Busch* along with you. She knows all the little tricks!"

That was the end of our conversation. I sat down at my desk. My head was spinning. It was full of endless details and plans on which success or failure in the United States would depend.

Basically, it was not permissible for intelligence officers to visit the country against which they were working. But Burghardt and I agreed that in this case an exception had to be made. Of course, some German agents were sitting in the United States, but they worked for other departments. At that time, Abwehr I, Luft Hamburg had no contacts in the United States. It had to be handled quickly.

At first, Canaris was not particularly enthusiastic about the idea that I should be the one to go overseas. It was a bold precedent that entailed a big risk. Personally, I had no doubt I could play my role as a traveling businessman without difficulty. The United States was not at war with anyone, nor was there any talk of war psychosis.

At that time, the general mood among the population toward National Socialist Germany was absolutely neutral, partly even friendly. In some circles, however, mostly in Washington and New York, people were openly hostile toward Hitler's Germany.

As for the rest, all recent experiences suggested that the American Counterintelligence Service was not particularly active. A recent incident at that time indicated the United States was not focusing its attention on foreign spies. It so happened a German agent by the name of Lankowski had been caught in the act as he was transporting plans for a new American aircraft in his violin case. Nevertheless, the American agency let him go without further pursuing the episode.

In Berlin, I reported directly to Canaris to brief him on my case and to explain Burghardt's and my plans. Canaris concurred after initially hesitating. Prior to my departure he expressly forbade me to establish any kind of contact with any official agency of the German government. "Under no circumstances are you to report to the military attaché there. General von Bötticher has no concept of what the Abwehr is all about. He thinks he could do it better all by himself. Stay away from him and all German representatives."

I regretted that very much because I knew General von Bötticher personally and thought highly of him, but perhaps Canaris was correct. Despite his claim, the general could not obtain many things that were perhaps easily accessible to the Abwehr. Besides, there was a general order requiring every officer, when traveling abroad, to report to the local military attaché.

Much was yet to be done. Lying in bed in the evening, I reviewed all details. Some things appeared secondary and unimportant. And yet, if just one little stone were missing in my mosaic, it could mean the end of my mission and my very own demise. That would be a big scandal if the Americans were to catch the section chief of a German intelligence station in the process of doing some spying!

My trip was scheduled for the first week in November. That gave us three and a half months to make all the necessary preparations. Just two weeks before my departure, a steward of the SS *Reliance,* Hamburg American Line, brought a little package. This steward was working for our substation in Bremen. The tiny package contained two small aluminum stabilizer fins for bombs and two mysterious technical blueprints without any accompanying text.

This package had been sent by a man in Brooklyn, New York, who, in a brief note signed with the cover name *Pop,* informed us that he absolutely had to get us together with the supplier of the technical blueprints and that there was much more where that came from. He assured us the blueprints were of the utmost importance, and that it would be well worth our effort to send someone over to establish personal contact with his friend.

Carefully, I looked at the blueprints, but I could make no sense of them. Then I showed them to our Chief Air Engineer, Dr. Nautsch. He could not explain the many circles and dotted lines either. Finally, we passed the material on to the technical analysis station in Berlin.

We had our answer a couple of days later: The experts could not figure out what this was all about. They simply stated that the blueprints were worthless. Could these be forgeries? I doubted that. I decided after my arrival in New York to immediately establish contact with *Pop.* I wanted to get to know this mysterious new man in America.

6

Departing for America

Now my operations covered two major areas: Great Britain and the United States. My USA file, with plans, notations, names, and addresses, became ever thicker, and my exploratory activities against England were in high gear.

Collaboration with *Johnny* had started off well; I insisted he not send any written reports and that he not come to Germany too often; therefore, I would instead meet him at intervals of three to four weeks in Belgium. Then I decided to have him come once more to Hamburg. In view of the increasing preparatory work for my trip to America, it would save me a couple of days. *Johnny's* wife would come along this time.

Meanwhile, I had my regular meetings in Hungary, Belgium, and Holland. It was not a good idea to have all agents come to Germany regularly. Moreover, at that time, there was still no danger that I was being followed.

Since I would be traveling under a different name in each country, I had formed the habit of talking to myself, using my particular cover name so I would be armed against surprises from any direction. When I was a young soldier and drilled for tough challenges, I would handle them in a similar manner by putting myself into a kind of self-hypnotic state before falling to sleep. In the event I would be suddenly awakened, I would automatically be able to speak in keeping with the relevant situation.

All my various passes were accurate, and the pertinent entries could in each case be verified at the local resident registration bureau. The personal data, however, could vary on certain specific points. The birthdates and birthplaces were different. The passport photos were always taken from different angles. One would be brighter, and the other one darker, but all looked sufficiently like me to prevent arousing suspicion at the passport and customs control checkpoints.

I therefore avoided anything that would provoke attention; disguises, blue spectacles, wigs, or moustaches were not my style. Occasionally, I would simply exchange my spectacles; I wore either my German or my American eyeglasses, or no eyeglasses at all.

Naturally, I did not carry a revolver, and it would have been foolish to allow myself to be pulled into any kind of armed confrontation. Playing Sherlock Holmes or James Bond generally would not fit into the tasks of an intelligence officer. *Dr. Rantzau, Dr. Renken,* and all of their "colleagues" looked like ordinary businessmen who busily pursued their work. "They" were polite, well mannered, and instilled with confidence, and they avoided all loquaciousness. "They" were dressed conservatively, and "they" did not in any way differ from any other businessman in Europe or America. Just the umbrella cane would differentiate them from one or the other, especially in the United States.

On my right hand, I wore a simple golden ring with a smooth blue stone, which had been a good luck charm for me since my first days in the United States, and which often served as my "spy." When I would put my elbow on the table, I could quite imperceptibly observe everything that was going on behind me by its reflection in the stone.

While traveling, I always stayed at the same hotels, and the personnel knew me well by my particular cover name. As for the rest, everyone would greet me with *Herr Doktor*. Just once, when I met two informants in Brussels, it so happened they knew me under different names, but since both addressed me as *Herr Doktor*, everything went well.

In the hotels, we never locked suitcases or handbags. I had learned that from Dierks. If anyone wanted to snoop around, they would find everything open and accessible. There were no secret papers to be found. My baggage, as a rule, consisted of a good, but not too new, dark-brown suitcase with the usual travel items, shirts, socks, neckties, and so forth. At home, I always had two packed suitcases ready, one for three days and the other for somewhat longer journeys, because often between trips, I did not have the time to go home, and I had to send someone to pick up my suitcase for the next trip.

My briefcase contained the usual business papers, correspondence with names of companies I was to visit. Frequently, it also held advertising material. I had no reason to fear anything when passing through a specific security checkpoint.

In the various countries, I spoke mostly German and English, but also French, Italian, or Spanish. In spite of the risk, occasionally I could not avoid making notations; I usually did so in my altered shorthand, which only I could read. That would not look as suspicious as the Greek, Hebrew, or Cyrillic-looking letters that some agents used.

When I was in Antwerp, I usually stayed with my new friend, Helmut Thimm. He was a well-known ship broker, and no one ever took note of any of his guests. Hotel doormen, who were frequently working for some intelligence service, undoubtedly, now and then, reported the visit of a *Dr. Rantzau* or even *Dr. Weber*, but neither my baggage nor my person exhibited the slightest justification for special attention.

It was always amazing how much valuable information could be drawn from mere business contacts without having to pay for it. For example, we had tried for a long time to determine the personnel strength of various British garrisons in the Near East, but we never obtained precise figures. One day, I was chatting with the general manager of a large tobacco firm, whom I had met with for an entirely different reason; he had business dealings in Romania and Turkey. Quite in passing, he mentioned that the settlements in the Balkans provided all cigarettes for certain British units in the Near East. We knew the cigarette ration for each soldier, and by means of some simple arithmetic based on the deliveries, we were able to determine the personnel strength.

Another time, through a diamond drill maker, I received another report that was as interesting as it was important. The manufacturer was very accommodating and, in contrast with others, considered it his duty to collaborate with us. In the beginning, of course, he thought nothing much would come of it. One day, I had talked about him with Dr. Nautsch, our technical expert. His ears perked up immediately, and he said, "Ask your friend who in England buys diamond drills. They also use them there for armor plates."

I immediately spoke with the manufacturer and told him quite frankly why we wanted the information. When he returned from England the next time, he reported, "I believe I have something very interesting for you this time. My business friend in the United States, who has been buying drills from me for many years, urgently needed a stronger and longer drill from me. When I asked him what it was to be used for, he was somewhat evasive and simply said, 'Oh, just for experiments.' That made me suspicious. I invited one of his associates to dinner, and in the course of the conversation, he revealed that my customer had received an order for new armor plates from the Royal Navy."

To our Naval High Command, this meant that the British were working on using stronger armor plates, a secret that had fallen into our hands without any major effort and without any treason. That again did not cost us a single penny.

About the same time, Mr. Lerner asked me whether I was interested in a former merchant vessel captain who was looking for a job, and whom I perhaps could use against Britain.

"That's a funny question," I replied. "Naturally, I'm interested in anyone, especially for my work in England. If you believe that he's suitable, then I have to get to know him. And since you say that he's very reticent, I might check him out without his knowledge."

"That can be done," said Lerner. "I'll invite him to a little snack in the first-class waiting room in the railroad terminal. You come at the same time, and sit down at any table. I'll tell him that he should walk slowly through the premises as if he were looking for someone. He does not know you, but I will tell him that he's being observed by someone who perhaps has a job for him. If you think that you can use him, then you might, quite by accident, pass our table and say hello to me. Then I'll introduce you to each other. If you don't think you can use him, you simply keep walking."

"That's a good idea," I agreed. "Schedule an appointment with him."

Some days later, Lerner called me. On the next day, I was sitting in the first-class waiting room at a little table, staring at a glass of Moselle wine. I spotted Lerner entering with his guest. They sat at a table in the opposite corner. After a while, the other fellow stood up and walked around the large restaurant. Since almost all tables were occupied, it was hardly to be expected that he would focus his attention on me. I was drinking my wine and puffing on my cigar, looking as if I were not the least bit interested in my surroundings, while keeping a low profile; but, in reality, I was scrutinizing him carefully.

Before he passed my table, I was already impressed by his bearing. His gait was light, relaxed, and unhurried. He made an alert, circumspect, and thoughtful impression, but without being conspicuous in any way. As he passed directly in front of me, I took a good look at his facial features; I knew he was the right man for me. He was slightly over six feet tall, slim, and rather wiry, and I figured he was in his mid-fifties. He had a well-shaped head, and he was smoothly shaved. He had a strong chin and looked furrowed by wind and weather. He was the man I needed. I paid and walked toward Mr. Lerner.

"This is *Dr. Rantzau*, Simon," Lerner said. "He's the gentleman I told you about who might have a job for you."

"Good day, *Herr Doktor*," said Walter Simon politely but without servility. "I'm at your disposal. What can I do for you?"

I sat down and ordered a cup of coffee.

"First of all, we have to find out who you are and what you can do," I said with a smile. "Tell me something about yourself."

To some, such a direct approach might be cause for concern, but not him.

"Good," he said, relaxed. "I'll start with my birth. I was born in 1881. Ever since I was a boy, I always wanted to be a seaman and get to know the world, but my father did not approve. So, I left my home at the age of fifteen, and all my father could do was bless me. I started as an apprentice seaman and gradually worked my way up; I passed various tests and examinations and ended as captain of a freighter."

"So, do you also speak English?" I interrupted him.

"Certainly," he replied in German.

"Then let us continue our conversation in English," I suggested. "Do you speak any other foreign languages?"

"French and Spanish," he replied, as if this were quite natural, and continued with his life story in fluent English. During World War I, he had been interned in Australia. He had been discharged after the war and had returned to seafaring.

There was something that bothered me about his speech. It was not his English. It was something else, which at first I did not really become aware of until I noticed that his voice sounded unusually rough and atonal.

"What's the matter with your voice?" I interrupted him. "It doesn't sound like an ordinary cold."

"It isn't," he said. "Before the war, I had to have an operation due to a serious larynx disease. It severely attacked my vocal cords, and the situation has been getting worse over the past ten years. This is why I've had to accept low-paying jobs in recent times, because I am not able to issue commands anymore. Because of this, I'm looking for another job."

His vocabulary in English was as voluminous as in German. That was a big plus. But his voice could, under certain circumstances, become a serious obstacle, because it was just too noticeable for an agent and could endanger his security.

"I'm sorry to hear that," I said, "but tell me more."

"Well, that's about all," he replied courteously, "but I hope my voice won't cause you to drop me."

"No," I said, somewhat hesitantly, but then I added quite reassuringly, "I don't really think so."

I had the feeling that this man could be valuable to me, but first of all, I had to have him checked out. Our talk was enough for me. I told Simon he would hear from me within the next week.

Lerner ordered another cup of coffee for Simon, paid, and left the place with me. "He's my man," I told Lerner. "I'll find something for him."

"Well," he said quite simply, "you played your role well, *Herr Doktor*. After our chat in the waiting room, I had expected anything but that!"

The investigation confirmed not merely everything that Simon had told me, but also revealed that he had been too modest. On the basis of his curriculum vitae and my observations, I was certain that, to a great extent, he was still an adventurer, and I resolved to approach him on that basis.

I decided to send Simon to England. A man such as he, who might have passed for a British seaman on the basis of his perfect English and, moreover, was alert, intelligent, and a keen observer, could certainly be successful as a loner. I had no doubt that he would be sufficiently skillful and resourceful to be able to untangle himself from any difficult situation.

His training would be done by me, exclusively, but since I was about to go to the United States, I was not able to begin right away. Besides, I had selected him for a task he could accomplish better in spring than in winter. The weather should provide a calm journey through the English countryside. Simon was looking for work to make a living. I helped him.

We agreed on a monthly salary, and I temporarily put him "on ice" for myself until January. By then, I hoped I would be back from the States with some positive results. My preparations for my trip to America were nearly complete.

When *Johnny* announced his and his wife's arrival, I invited Miss *Busch* to come along and shepherd his wife. Miss *Busch* frequently had to be present when I was briefing agents, in order to record conversations and reports, and her observations were often valuable supplements to mine. But for some reason, she could not come this time, and I received the couple alone.

I was able to see at first glance that the relationship between *Johnny* and his wife was not particularly good. His wife was a small, blonde Englishwoman, who outwardly might have been a good match for him but certainly was not in terms of her essential character. She participated little in our conversation and acted completely disinterested. I was therefore hardly surprised when *Johnny* told me a year later he had separated from his wife and that the next time he would bring along his girlfriend, Lily.

In the meantime, the date of my trip to America was drawing near, and I was becoming increasingly nervous. Any slip-up could turn out to be fatal. I therefore tried to prepare myself for any and all eventualities.

I had insisted on traveling under my personal name. That could create a challenge, but it seemed to be the safest solution. The textile engineer and businessman Nikolaus Ritter, of course, had his home in Germany, but he also had every reason for going to the United States. On October 29, 1937, I obtained a visitor's visa for departure on November 5.

On the basis of the advertisements that *The Skipper* had put in the newspapers, I had scheduled various assignments for the United States. I had addresses and invitations from companies I needed to visit.

Next, my interest was focused on meeting the man who had sent us the blueprints, in order to perhaps penetrate the aviation industry and receive continuous information about new developments.

Our Bremen substation already had some good agents in the States, but they were working mostly for the Navy. Bremen was nice enough to make available to me the best courier, who was traveling back and forth between Germany and the United States on the *Bremen* ocean liner, until I was able to hire a courier.

Meanwhile, I had taken up microphotography so that I might brief suitable agents in that field. This would provide a means to reduce the size of one typewritten page to less than that of a postage stamp.

Furthermore, our photographer and secret ink expert taught me the skill of simple wax writing. Only later did I learn that this cipher script was a primitive method, otherwise I probably would not have concerned myself with it at all. It was an old trick that has been used in many countries by intelligence services. You put a wax sheet between two sheets of paper. The message was written on the top sheet and pressed through the wax sheet onto the second piece of paper. The first sheet with the visible script was destroyed, and the bottom page, with the imprinted wax script, was an invisible letter with the same content. The recipient would spread a fine graphite powder on the wax page of this sheet, which made it legible.

Lt. Commander Burghardt ordered me to submit my first report as a personal letter to Miss *Busch* by this process. Later, I learned that the laboratory was carefully scrutinizing my letters to Miss *Busch* and tried to decipher not just the wax script but also wanted to read between the lines. Although privately Miss *Busch* was reserved, socially she could be affable and at times quite jolly. In the office, she lived strictly for her work. Left to myself in America, I privately hoped someday I would mean more to her than just an associate. I had noticed that in recent times she met Dierks less frequently, but they had remained good friends. Besides, Dierks knew plenty of other women. He made no bones about it, and the special attraction which he held for ladies was to play an important role in our work later on.

As for baggage for my long trip, I did not want to take along more than I would usually take when traveling in Europe, in other words, just an ordinary suitcase. Of course, this time, in addition to my briefcase, I also took along my umbrella cane. Nothing in my baggage would hint that I was a Luftwaffe officer or a member of the Abwehr.

As for the money I would need, I had some cash in addition to a letter of credit to the National City Bank in New York, where I could withdraw the required local currency.

At six o'clock in the morning on November 5, the driver rang the doorbell. I gave him my suitcase. I carried the briefcase and the umbrella cane. Lt. Commander Burghardt, who was a crew mate of the *Europa*'s captain, wanted to take me aboard personally and had gone ahead in another car.

The sky was gray in the early dawn. A cold wind blew through the empty streets. I sat in the back of the car. I wanted to be alone with my thoughts. Normally, I sat next to the driver and chatted with him. Today, I did not want to talk. The haste of the last month had not left me any time for my private thoughts. I had often eagerly looked forward to the day when, aboard ship, I would have a brief period of rest. Building up my subsection and preparing for this trip had placed me in a relentless state of tension. Now, I was to be alone for six days: I was not to meet anyone; I was not to make any hurried side trips; I was not to answer the phone; I was not to dictate any file entries; I was not to draft any messages; and, furthermore, I was not supposed to train anyone. I could have

Nikolaus Ritter, left, ready to board ship for New York, 1937. He is accompanied to the pier by Captain Joachim Burghardt. Originally published in *Der Stern,* March 15, 1953, page 13. Picture taken by American intelligence.

breathed a sigh of relief, but when the car door snapped shut behind me, I just slumped into the seat, exhausted.

Previously, I had always felt free and without worries for days on end before any ocean voyage. Today, I felt a great emptiness inside of me. Involuntarily, I began to doze off, and finally the soporific effect of the monotonous hum of the vehicle put me to sleep. I did not wake up until we were at the pier in Bremerhaven.

7

New York

I had not yet fully realized how exhausted I was. Miss *Busch*, however, seemed to have noticed. The day before I left, she had urged me to take along a roll of Recresal tablets.

I took my leave of Burghardt and the driver, quite mechanically went through customs and passport control, and headed directly for my single cabin. I did not even take the trouble to stash my things in an orderly fashion. I threw myself onto the bunk and was asleep even before the repetitious pulsing of the ship's turbines penetrated my consciousness.

The ship cast off at eleven o'clock. Southampton would be the first stop. As I stood up to go for some coffee, I suddenly noticed I had the shivers. I had to stay horizontal, and I was hardly surprised. The reaction was inevitable. For months I had been running in high gear, and now I had to switch to idling without any smooth transition. Even the best engine could not tolerate such an abrupt shift. That confronted me with a new problem. My name must under no circumstances be put on the sick list, because that list was given to the health authorities upon arrival.

I knew the steward had to report any sick persons to the ship's doctor. I rang the bell. When the steward turned up, I calmed down because he was a round-ish, jovial German-American. I asked him to bring me some hot tea with lots of lemon. "I'm a little bit under the weather," I said, "but please, do not report this to the doctor. I don't want to make any trouble for you." I gave him a hefty tip; he thanked me politely and returned with my tea after a short time.

The next day, I didn't feel better, but I forced myself to go to lunch so as not to be conspicuous by my absence. For the rest of the day, I was cared for by my steward, Fred, and I tried to become friends with him. When he told me that he had a German girlfriend in New York, who was working as a manicurist in a beauty shop, I forgot my holy oath that I would refrain from talking about any-thing official during my crossing. I could not pass up such an opportunity.

For an agent who is supposed to exchange material, there can be no better middleman than a manicurist in a beauty shop, where everybody can come and go without being noticed. And so, even before I landed in New York, I already had a new and willing reliable courier.

On the third day, I received an invitation from the captain (which Burghardt told me to anticipate). I declined courteously with great regret. I did not want to appear as being privileged in any way, but I let him know I would gladly accept his invitation on my return trip.

After Cherbourg, I wrote my first letter to Miss *Busch*. I informed her a number of prominent English guests had come aboard in Cherbourg, among them the Duke of Windsor, the former Prince of Wales, and I asked whether I should try to sign him up for us right away.

We arrived on schedule in New York six days later. As we sailed into the Hudson, I joined other passengers along the railing and admired the always breathtaking silhouette of New York. I was worried a little bit about the coming entry formalities. I was using the right name, and I arrived due to normal business affairs. But obviously I did conceal the true purpose of my trip and, above all, my real occupation; otherwise, I would have made myself culpable to both international legal regulations and American law.

Of course, I kept telling myself that the American Secret Service certainly did not have my name on its list and that, therefore, nothing could happen. Nevertheless, it was not that easy to preserve an outward calm. I was not exactly superstitious, but when I stood in the long line in front of the immigration officer's table, I suddenly, again, remembered the twelve priests and one nun, thirteen in total, who had gone up the gangplank directly ahead of me in Bremerhaven. The driver, who had carried my suitcase, had, moreover, been harping on about the number thirteen. As a strong man, I did not like to admit it, but I had to swallow hard a couple times as I stood in line.

The immigration officer took my papers, and when he saw my reentry permit, he was particularly friendly. I replied with equal courtesy and friendliness, and I was happy that I was able to come up with a couple of good, humorous American figures of speech.

I held my breath when he stamped my passport and wished me good luck. Then I thanked him briefly and, as calmly as possible, put my papers back in place. I had passed the first obstacle, and I felt greatly relieved. At that time, entry formalities were always unpleasant. Not much could get overlooked at customs check. Then, as I headed toward the exit, I suddenly heard my name being called out in a loud voice, "Ritter!"

Now they've spotted me, it shot through my head. Now they'll take me to Ellis Island. I pulled myself together and turned around. Nobody was paying any attention to me. The immigration officer was processing other passengers. Perhaps I hadn't heard right? Relieved, I took a deep breath and continued toward the exit.

"Mensch, Ritter! How come you're here?" someone right next to me said. He was a reporter for the German-American *Staatszeitung*, whom I knew well.

I was very happy to see him again, and as we shook hands, he continued talking loudly.

Good grief, I thought. I had prepared intensively for any surprises, but this was not anticipated, and before I could interrupt him, he continued, "I thought you might be a captain with the German Luftwaffe!"

I had to restrain myself from turning around to see whether anyone had overheard us. "No," I said to him equally loudly. "Unfortunately, only with the reserves. Otherwise, I would hardly be here." As I anxiously kept talking, I linked arms with him and pulled him away from the vicinity of the officer and quickly tried to get rid of him.

"Did anybody important arrive? Otherwise, you would certainly not be here," I said, quite randomly.

"Sure," the reporter answered and unfortunately let go of my arm. "The Prince of Wales. He's going to be giving a press conference."

Finally, I was able to go through customs control unperturbed. The officer was very thorough, as they usually are in New York. He rummaged through my suitcase and then spotted my business papers. Some were written in German, and he randomly translated them. Then he spotted the Recresal tablets that Miss *Busch* had given me. He thought he could smell opium.

"What is that?" he questioned.

"It's a sedative," I replied, "for nerves."

"That's a drug," he ruled. "You can't take that with you." I was in no mood to get into an argument with him.

"Okay," I agreed. I wanted to get through this entire exercise and leave, but the officer was not ready. He had someone translate the identification label of the tablets. Then, after he was convinced my German papers were genuine, he returned them to me. I was now allowed to close my suitcase again. The officer put a chalk checkmark on the suitcase and the briefcase, and a porter carried them to the barrier.

I was almost outside when I again heard, "Mr. Ritter." Astonished, I turned around.

"What is that?" the customs officer shouted and pointed at my umbrella cane. Such canes were not at all well known in America at that time. I returned to him and took the casing off.

"This is an excellent hiding place," the customs officer said and took a close look at the casing. I observed him, rather amused. He was not able to find anything.

"I'm sorry I have to disappoint you," I said, laughing, but in reality, he was right. I had never thought of that.

"Okay," he said and returned my umbrella.

Finally, it was all over. I took a deep breath and had the porter hail a cab for me. "Hotel Taft, please," I said. The Taft is a large hotel on 7th Avenue and 50th Street in the heart of the city's energy, always crowded with tourists of all varieties from all over the world. One more or less will not be noticed. I was lucky to get a room.

I had already outlined my agenda on board. First, I had to carry out the business part of the trip, which served as my camouflage. That meant visits to various firms, and it took about three or four days. During that time, I visited my old wartime buddy Brandts-Sobieski, a painter and sculptor, who lived on 179th Street. I told him I was in the United States on business and would like to have lunch with him in the next several days, and that when I returned from the Midwest we could meet again. I did not hint anything about my true intentions.

During the interim, I made my business visits. I scheduled my appointments by phone, usually not from my room but rather from a phone booth in the lobby. There, in a loud and distinct voice, I gave the porter the addresses and asked him to have me connected.

Since I would need all my clothes for my trip to the Midwest, I would have everything laundered beforehand. In that way, I would assure that all my clothes, including my shirt collars, had the same American markings. I threw the dirty laundry on the bed and rang for the laundry boy.

A friendly Chinese turned up. "Good molning, Mistel Littel," he said and made a deep bow as he tried to get as close as possible to the "R" sound.

"Good morning," I said and pointed to the dirty laundry. "When can I get it back?"

"Tomollo molning, Mistel Littel," he said. "I will bling it to you as ealy as possible."

"Okay," I said, and tipped him. As I looked at the Chinese, rather amused, I suddenly spotted a sewn-on military label on the collar of a blue shirt. I snatched the shirt and flipped it under my arm and said, "That does not belong here."

But the little man did not pay attention. He took the remaining laundry, bowed, smiled, and disappeared. After he had closed the door behind him, I took a close look at the label on the shirt and shook my head. In large, bold letters, the label read, "Luftwaffe Sales Department"! I removed the label with a razor blade and burned it in the ashtray.

In the evening, I promenaded down Broadway and, from a drugstore, called the Wellington Hotel on 7th Avenue between 55th and 56th Streets and reserved a room for the next day for *Mr. Landing*. Then I returned to the Hotel Taft and, on an open postcard, wrote a couple of lines to *Mr. Landing* at the Wellington Hotel, informing him I could not visit him over the next two to three days.

Using the Hotel Taft letterhead, I wrote a letter with a similar content, likewise to *Mr. Landing*, but I addressed it to the main post office on Lexington Avenue, general delivery. Then I took the elevator down to the hotel lobby, checked out at the reception desk, effective the next morning, and ostentatiously took my leave of the clerk at the reception desk.

The little Chinese kept his promise and brought my laundry even before breakfast. I packed, paid my bill, and ordered a cab. Then I had myself driven to the Wellington Hotel via a circuitous route. I checked in at the reception desk: "I am *Mr. Landing*. I ordered a room yesterday."

"Oh, yes, *Mr. Landing*," the porter confirmed. "We already have some mail for you," and the porter gave me the postcard, which I had written to myself yesterday evening addressed to *Mr. Landing*.

I settled into my room. Then I went to the main post office and asked for mail for *Mr. Landing* at the general delivery window.

"Do you have any identity papers?" the official asked. I showed him the postcard I had received at the Wellington Hotel. He saw the name *Landing* and gave me my card back. He found my letter which I had written to *Mr. Landing*, and he handed it to me.

That was everything I needed to take care of for the next several days in order to be able to identify myself. I went uptown, to 90th Street, and walked to the nearest City National Bank. There, after showing my letter of credit, I withdrew a considerable amount of cash. I rented a safety deposit box and put all of my papers that bore the name Ritter in it, including my passport.

I then met Brandts-Sobieski for lunch. As we took our leave from each other, I gave him the keys for my safety deposit box and told him I had deposited a number of items there that I would not want to take with me on my trip to the Midwest.

That meant that textile engineer Nikolaus Ritter had ceased to exist until further notice.

Now, I was *Alfred Landing*, looking for agents.

8

Herman Lang and
the Norden Bombsight

I scheduled my first visit as *Mr. Landing* for the following afternoon between five and six o'clock. I assumed my esteemed mysterious one would then be at home.

The weather was pleasant and, because I had lots of time, I went to the Metropolitan Museum of Art on 82nd Street and 5th Avenue. I walked into the Egyptian exhibit again, which had made a great impression upon me earlier. Shortly before three o'clock, I left the museum and flagged a cab: "I have to go to Brooklyn," I told the driver. "Do you think you could find 248 Monitor Street in Brooklyn?"

"Well, let's see," the driver said. "Get in."

I was wearing the same gray overcoat that I wore when I left Hamburg, but I had bought a new felt hat on Broadway and wore my American nickel eyeglasses.

When we arrived, I discovered 248 Monitor Street was an ugly, gray crate of a building. I asked the cabdriver to wait a moment, stepped out, went to the entrance, and studied the name tags. "That's it," I said, as I returned to the driver and paid him. Then I disappeared into the house. After I made sure the taxi had left, I came out again and went around the corner to house number 262. It was a rather large apartment building, and it made a far better impression.

I was particularly cautious; as my instructors in World War I used to say, "One can never imagine anything as stupid as it might be!" I took my eyeglasses off, put them in my coat pocket, and climbed the stairs to the fourth floor. At the door was a business card reading "Heinrich Sohn." I rang the bell and waited tensely. The door opened a moment later.

A stocky, middle-aged man in shirtsleeves opened the door and asked suspiciously, "Yeees?" According to the description I had gotten from the courier on the SS *Reliance*, I immediately recognized *Pop*.

"Herr Sohn?" I asked politely. "I am *Mr. Landing*, and I'm to bring you greetings from Roland in Bremen."

"Please?" he said, still somewhat hesitantly, and stood there, still holding onto the door.

"*Pop*?" I asked softly.

He smiled, relieved, pulled me in, and closed the door behind me. *Pop* was the cover name he had used in signing his report. "So, here comes another one," he said. "Make yourself comfortable. I had become disgruntled and disappointed. I thought nobody else was going to come. No one has contacted me. I thought, 'probably the gentlemen don't consider me good enough.'"

Pop led me down a long, narrow hallway, the kind we have on express trains, with many doors along one side leading to small rooms, into a larger living room. He called a name I did not understand. Thereupon appeared a pleasant, roundish teenager, and *Pop* sent his daughter into the kitchen to fix a cup of coffee. His wife was at the movies, he said.

"Yes," he continued, "I was thinking you people in Germany are too snooty. They simply know everything better!"

I had to laugh. "Well, things are not as bad as that, *Pop*. Otherwise, I wouldn't be here. On the contrary, we appreciate everything you sent us."

Pop beamed. "I thought you might be able to use something like that, like those two stabilizing propellers that I sent you. You can believe me, it's not so simple to spirit such a thing out of the factory. By the way, the drawings were made by my friend."

I nodded, appreciatively. In reality, the propellers did not mean much to us. Besides, I was not so much interested in the contact with *Pop*, but I did not want to disappoint him.

"You're building a new Luftwaffe now," he continued, "and I thought, as a loyal German soldier, I should also help."

"Naturally," I said. "Now, look here, that propeller is a finished product. You can tell right away what you are dealing with. However," I continued, "perhaps at some time I could meet your friend from whom you received these drawings."

Pop was proud of his middleman role. He said, "*Paul* actually wanted to stay in the background, but if I tell him that you came all the way just because of him."

"Well, that is not exactly true," I interrupted him. "I didn't come just to meet him, but at any rate, I did want to get to know him."

Pop looked at me with his wily eyes. "I'm quite sure that you would have come if you had known what *Paul* has constitutes the most secret and most important invention of the US Army Air Corps."

"What do you mean?" I perked up.

"The Norden Company, where *Paul* is working, is building a bombsight."

A bombsight! Now it was my turn to get all excited. I knew our own bombsights did not meet expectations. High-altitude bombing was a particular problem, because pinpoint accuracy was difficult to achieve, and that caused destruction of unintended landmarks. Everyone was feverishly working on improvements for the aiming instruments. So far, no one had solved the problem successfully. Might this be the solution that all bombardiers were looking for?

"*Paul* actually wanted to remain in the background," *Pop* repeated and paused. He did not need to know how much his disclosure excited me. "But he can never come on any day except Sundays," *Pop* continued. "If you tell me that you can be here next Sunday, I'll see to it that he comes."

"And?" I nodded in a questioning manner toward the kitchen.

"I'll take care of it," *Pop* promised. "My family will not be here Sunday afternoon."

"OK, let's say at 1500 hours." I arose and took my leave.

It was Friday. I had two days. I had other matters to take care of in New York; I hoped that something would come of it, but I preferred not to mingle the various projects. *Paul* was entirely too important!

I sauntered down to the Bowery, where I found a secondhand American portable typewriter in an antique shop. I was happy to have haggled down the price to all of $25. I had handwritten the first letter to Miss *Busch* aboard ship. That was something I wanted to avoid in the future as much as possible. Besides, a typewriter was more effective for the invisible wax imprints.

In my hotel room, I wrote a letter to *Mr. Landing* addressed to another rather small, nearby hotel. If at all possible, I did not want to use the same name in the same place and in the same hotel for more than two, or at most three, days.

On Sunday afternoon, my second Sunday in New York, I arrived punctually at *Pop*'s. He invited me into his apartment. His family had already left, and *Paul* was already waiting for me.

Paul was about thirty-five years old, rather tall and slim, with a full head of dark blond hair, pleasant facial features, and blue eyes that exuded so much openness that, when I shook his hand, I involuntarily felt well-disposed toward him and, in spite of my fundamental Intelligence distrust, was also ready to trust him. His real name was Herman Lang. He had been born in Germany and had become a naturalized American. He was an engineering draftsman and, as he told me, lived with his wife and daughter in Glendale. He had made his decisions based on his innermost convictions and out of love for his fatherland.

"I really didn't want to listen to *Pop*," he said rather modestly, "but now I'm glad I came." Without any further ado, he pulled a big, folded sheet of paper out of his pocket and said, "This is the continuation of the first drawing that *Pop* sent to you."

Without understanding, I looked at the circles and the dotted lines, which meant as little to me as they had during the first transmittal. "Is this really a bombsight?" I asked him. He nodded. "How do you actually obtain these things?"

"I'm an inspector at Norden," he said modestly. "Those are just partial drawings. I didn't know whether I would ever be able to get copies of the entire instrument. It's so secret that it's produced in fourteen different factories, but I will certainly be able to deliver enough so that your experts can reconstruct the missing parts." He smiled. "This is the newest and best bombsight the world has ever seen."

I had met *Paul* just a few minutes earlier, but I was already prepared to believe every word he said. "How do you have access to these drawings?" I asked once again, and then I added, "And how did you arrive at the idea to offer this to us?"

"That's easy to explain," *Paul* said. "I am a German, and I love Germany. I know that Germany is trying to build itself up to be free and strong again. I know it's industrious, and I also know that it's poor. In the same sense I realize it needs such a device for the Luftwaffe, and that just the development alone of such an instrument devours millions and is very costly in time. As these drawings came through my hands, I said to myself, 'If you can bring this kind of instrument to Germany, it will save millions, and many research hours. And then you have also done something for the land of your fathers.'"

I sat perfectly still, and as I looked at *Paul,* I knew I was facing an idealist, the type you rarely meet. I wished we had more people like him back home who thought about their native land the way this man did. It was quite obvious, as regards his new country, that he was ready to engage in treason, but what he wanted to provide for his native country was simply incomprehensible. He did it out of genuine conviction.

When I mentioned something about possible payment, *Paul* looked at me, astonished. "I hope that this is just a figure of speech," he said calmly, "and I hope you'll find a sure way of getting those drawings to Germany. Your experts will then know what they're dealing with." Then he added, with assurance, as if the mention of money had been an insult, "Don't worry about me."

What was I to answer? I was almost ashamed. It would perhaps have been easier if he had taken money. I simply changed the topic to get out of this embarrassment. "And how do you make the copies?" I asked.

"That is comparatively simple. I'm an inspector in the assembly department. We are now in the process of assembling the first complete units, but that doesn't mean that they are being issued to the shop. For the assembly of such a complicated device, we need the drawings for each individual part. Tomorrow, I'll get the blueprints, and I'll distribute them. Whenever a part of the instrument is completed, the relevant copies must again be returned to the original maker. Sometimes we need the drawings for several days. Then it is my job to lock them up in the safe in the evening, but instead, I take one or two copies home with me. On those evenings, I insist we go to bed early. Then I wait until my wife is asleep; I get up secretly, and I go into the kitchen at the other end of our apartment. That's where I make copies of the drawings. Sometimes it takes a very long time. As far as this one here is concerned," and he pointed at the drawing that I still held in my hand, "it took until five o'clock in the morning. Then I'll go back to sleep, and I get up at seven o'clock in the morning with my wife. By 8:30 the next morning, the monitor has the drawings again on his desk."

What nerve that man must have to be able to move such drawings in and out of a plant that is so strictly controlled, I thought. At any moment he could be caught, and his freedom and his very existence were at stake. I continued staring at the drawing in my hand. My situation was different. I did not need to fear that I would be searched, something that could happen to *Paul* at any time, but he did not seem to think of himself or the big risk he was taking. He was satisfied to have placed these drawings in my hand, and to know that his action was appreciated.

"When can you give me the next drawing?" I asked him.

"Next Sunday at the same time," he replied.

Carefully, I rolled up the drawing and inserted it into my umbrella cane. Then I took leave of *Paul* and *Pop*. On Tuesday, the *Reliance* was to put into New York with our steward *Oskar* on board. I would give him my umbrella cane with the drawing so that he could take it to Germany.

In the meantime, I had a week before I saw *Paul* again. Therefore, I decided to arrange other meetings. First of all, I wanted to get together with my old acquaintance, Duquesne. I remembered his private number, but to make sure, I checked the directory again. He lived with a Miss Lewis, a charming American, in an apartment on 57th Street West. I called him from a phone booth, and he answered the phone. We would meet the next afternoon for a glass of whiskey in his apartment.

Duquesne was very happy to see me, and when I told him what I wanted, he immediately agreed. As always, he needed money. I gave him a down payment of $100. He did not require any lengthy explanations or instructions. I had met him in 1931 through my friend Colonel Uldric Thompson. Uldric Thompson Jr. was a well-known inventor, who, among other things, had designed special apparatuses for loading high explosive devices. He was a member of the University Club and had introduced me there. During Prohibition, both of us had frequently downed a prohibited little glass in the Alpha Delta Phi Club or in the University Club.

Thin and agile, in his early thirties, with a narrow, intelligent face and an aristocratic nose, wavy, salt-and-pepper hair, and gray eyes, Duquesne made the impression of being not just a distinguished man, but also an adventurer. He never had money, but he had excellent social contacts. He earned his living by occasional lectures and by writing short articles for various dailies and technical periodicals, and sometimes he also engaged simply in economic espionage.

Duquesne was a go-getter with iron nerves, and he got what he wanted. When, for example, in the newspaper he read an item about a new cartridge casing, he would, without hesitation, drop in at the office of the general manager of the company and boldly assert that he needed details for a lecture about future American weapons. He was rarely turned down, and his information was promptly passed on to Germany. Sometimes he also, without advance notice, dropped in at a factory and quite calmly demanded to see a certain product. Here again, he was mostly successful.

He was a Boer, and when he had been a little boy, he had had to watch his mother perish in a British concentration camp. He hated everything British. He was particularly proud of his acts of sabotage against England during World War I. With satisfaction, he showed me a photo of himself in 1916 on board the flagship of Admiral John Jellicoe, which he wanted to sink. As a world traveler and an entertaining charmer, he was an especially popular lecturer in women's clubs.

I enjoyed his company and listening to his adventurous experiences. However, we never became close friends. Back then, I could not imagine he would ever become particularly important to me. Now the time had come!

I wanted to make sure that Duquesne was working alone. His contact man was to be our chief courier, Karl Keitel on the *Bremen,* or my brother Hans, who lived in New York. As long as there was no war, everything could proceed without difficulty, but when war started, it would be impossible. I had to get Duquesne connected with other agents, but for almost two years, he was a constant source of secret information without ever being suspected.

Through my brother, I also learned about Elsa Weustenfeld, who was a secretary for the attorney of the German Consulate-General in Battery Park. She was prepared to act as a routing station for letters that she would forward to an optician in Hamburg. She believed that these were business letters that, for some personal reason, could not be sent to me directly.

On schedule, Tuesday, the *Reliance* put into New York. It was a gray, unpleasant autumn day. Along with many other people, I waited and watched the docking maneuver. I had hung my umbrella cane over my arm. I was standing next to the tourist class gangplank so I could get a good look at the stewards who were carrying the baggage of the passengers to the pier on a catwalk underneath. As I spotted *Oskar* coming down with a big suitcase, I waved to him and indicated to him that I had something for him.

"Okay," he said, "as soon as I get rid of the baggage."

After he put the suitcase away and returned, I wanted to give him my umbrella cane. "Impossible," he said firmly, "I'm not allowed to take anything on board now."

I had been afraid of that. "Try somehow to twist your ankle," I said quickly. "Try to find a cane on board, and then this afternoon, you can waddle into the city. When can you come?"

"1600 hours."

"Okay, Whelan Drugstore in the Astor Hotel, Times Square." I took my leave conspicuously and pushed my way through the crowd outside.

At four o'clock in the afternoon, I was sitting comfortably at the soda fountain in the drugstore in the Astor Hotel, enjoying an ice cream soda. *Oskar* turned up five minutes later. He was hobbling and leaning heavily on his umbrella cane. A thick dressing bulged out of the cut-off tip of his left shoe. He saw I had to restrain myself.

"Well, here it goes," he said. "I was not able to find a cane on board. So, I finally bought this umbrella cane at the shipboard store for a lot of money."

Once again, a couple of dollars more, I thought. "Let's go to my hotel," I said. I paid and put my arm under *Oskar*'s arm. As we were on our way to the subway, I suggested, "It's best if we exchange those canes right now."

"That won't work." *Oskar* shook his head. "They look entirely too different. People might wonder if I suddenly come back with another cane." Then he added, "Why all of this hullabaloo? Letters and so forth I simply stick in my pocket. Nobody has checked on me. Everyone knows me."

By then, we were sitting on our train and no one in the crowd was paying any attention to us. I pulled the casing of my cane far enough back so he could see the edge of the large drawing.

"Well, that's something else," *Oskar* agreed.

In my hotel room, we cautiously pulled the drawing out of my cane, and put it just as cautiously into his umbrella casing.

"I just hope the customs people don't get the idea of pulling this thing apart," I said.

"Don't worry about that," *Oskar* said. "As I was hobbling off the ship, I chatted for quite a while with the official, and I told him all about my accident so he certainly won't stop me on my way back."

"Lots of luck," I said. "I'm sure everything will go well this time, but we can't try the same trick a second time. I'm already contemplating how we should handle the next drawings."

"Think about it and talk it over with *Pop* later," *Oskar* said. "Perhaps he will have a good idea."

Among *Paul, Pop,* the steward, and me, we finally agreed that in the future we would separate the drawings into numbered strips as inserts in newspapers, as adhesive strips, or, if possible, we would try to send them across the ocean in one piece again. The first complete set sailed with *Oskar* on the *Reliance* back to Bremen on November 30, 1937. Before I left New York for my trip throughout specific areas of the United States, a second set of the bombsight drawings, subdivided into strips, was on its way to Hamburg and, from there, to Berlin.

9

Contacts in America

At our last meeting, I said goodbye to *Paul* and *Pop,* and we all crossed our fingers. Then I started on my planned trip to the Midwest. My first stop was a little town in the vicinity of Philadelphia on the Delaware River. It was the home of a man who, some years earlier, had once worked for Lt. Commander Burghardt. Burghardt wanted to know what had become of him.

I did not particularly like the idea, because in a little town, every outsider is immediately noticed. I also had no idea if or how Burghardt's former acquaintance would receive me, but I couldn't very well ignore the request.

I took the train all the way to Philadelphia, and then I took a bus to Doylestown, a little town with about a thousand inhabitants. I asked as few questions as possible and found the house without anyone's assistance.

Just the wife was at home. In her friendly Quaker style, she welcomed me, and she offered to drive me to the factory where her husband was working. "This happens to be lunchtime, and you can meet him in the little lunchroom opposite the factory," she said.

"What kind of a factory is it?" I asked.

"They are building flying boats for the Navy," the woman said.

Flying boats! I thought. "Is just anyone allowed to drive in there?" I asked. I could not imagine that one could so readily visit a factory that was building flying boats for a military service.

Astonished, she asked, "Why not?" I realized I had been careless. Why would a harmless traveler get that idea? But the woman continued driving without having suspected anything. "If you have time, I'll drive you to the lunchroom, and just pop in to let my husband know you're here."

Of course, I had time. If you meet an acquaintance wherever you go, then you're simply not a stranger. We stopped in front of a little snack shop. She took me in and introduced me to the female owner. She told the owner I was a friend of her husband's, and that I would like to wait for him there. Then she said proudly, "My husband is the technical assistant here, and he's the right-hand man of the technical manager."

The friendly lady took her leave, and I ordered a cup of coffee and my usual piece of apple pie. I was the only diner, and the rather plump hostess was happy she had someone with whom she could chat. "Are you a stranger here?" she asked, as she put the apple pie in front of me.

"Yes," I replied simply, yet tried to act as friendly as possible.

"You're not from around here?" she prodded.

"No."

She leaned on the bar, intent on continuing our chat. "I thought you were one of the new designers from the Navy."

"Unfortunately, not," I replied politely. "Is the old one gone?"

"No," she continued undeterred, "but they do intend to build new coastal patrol boats for the Navy. And for that, they need a new man."

Now I listened up. I wondered whether it might be wise to show some interest. I decided to display no interest. I knew the most important thing now without even having asked. As I tried to switch to another topic, a short, lively man in shirtsleeves came in, saw me, sat next to me, and greeted me in German like an old acquaintance.

"You are *Mr. Johnson*? Glad to see you. It's been a long time since I've had one of my compatriots here." Without waiting for an answer, he ordered a couple of sausages. Then he turned again to me. "Have a couple of franks with me. That's my daily lunch."

I had not been able to say a single word. Finally, I managed to ask, "How do you know I am a German?"

"All the people who visit me here are German." He laughed. "At least once a year some fellow shows up. Yes, where do you come from?" he asked, as he suddenly realized he did not know me at all.

I delivered regards from *Kurt* in Hamburg, and I told him that *Kurt* was wondering why he had not heard from him for such a long time.

"That's just like him." The little fellow laughed. "Well, we did not have anything for him in the past two years."

I was beginning to feel uncomfortable. The man talked openly about things that should have been secret. He made fun of my dismayed expression. "Calm down," he said, and pointed toward the hostess. "Annie here can listen in on everything. First of all, she doesn't know a word of German, not even Pennsylvania Dutch. And besides, those women always know more than we know."

Then he saw that my plate was empty. "Come on," he urged me and put three ten-cent coins on the tray. "Let's go over, and I'll show you the shop."

I had to gasp for air and went along with him. But actually, he was quite right, I was thinking. I was on a routine business trip, and I had simply taken a side trip to say hello to him from some old friend. It was not unusual for him to show me his factory.

The factory was an old, not at all modern, shop. The little fellow saw how disappointed I was. "Don't worry," he said. "Now everything is being modernized. We have a big order from the naval air arm. Let's get over there and take a look at the model boat."

A brand-new flying boat was hanging on a crane in the yard behind the building. I was sorry I was not technically trained, and I said so quite openly. He calmed me, putting his hand on my arm. And now he looked around for the first time to make sure we were alone.

"They're all at lunch," he said, and then he added softly, "I take care of everything! All I need is a reliable routing station, but, if at all possible it should not be in New York. I have no contact at all with New York, and it would be quite unusual in this little town if I were now suddenly to write letters to New York all the time. Here, everybody always knows everything about everybody. I would prefer the Midwest."

"How about St. Louis?" I asked. "I have a contact there."

"Great, afterwards I'll take you wherever you want to go. Then you can give me the address." Without waiting for confirmation, as we sat in his car, he continued, "I have just one condition: If I see that things are getting queasy here, then I'll go to Germany with kit and caboodle, and you have to find me a place there."

I could agree to that without hesitation. Many technicians had returned to Germany over the past two years, and they had been received with open arms. That included so many experts that American industry had become concerned.

While I was still thinking, my escort continued, "One fine day, all hell will break loose here. You can be sure of that."

I let him talk. Then I said, "Well, you'll get your re-routing address as soon as possible, but to begin with, we must do a careful trial run. First, just write two harmless letters so we can see if everything is clear. Then, we can begin with your confidential reports."

"How am I to send them?" he asked.

"Via microphotography."

"What is that? I've never heard of it!"

"You'll soon find out. I'll send you an agent who will initiate you into the mysteries of microphotography, and from then on, don't use anything else for your reports."

"Understood," he agreed.

From Philadelphia, I reboarded the train to St. Louis, Missouri. My first stop from the train station was at the post office to pick up my letters. In St. Louis, I had two good business addresses, and I had sent the necessary papers ahead, general delivery, using my correct name. As for the two business visits I wanted to make and for the "covert" personal visit, I figured I would need two days.

With my papers in my pocket, I took a room under my name in one of the larger hotels. Then, I scheduled my appointments by phone, and I visited the two firms. To my astonishment, I almost landed a major textile deal with one of the shops. I could not have had a better alibi.

On the second day, I moved out of my hotel room and stopped in a little boardinghouse in a good residential area—again, using my own name. My business papers once more preceded me to Chicago, general delivery. My particular task was to set up a routing station here in St. Louis for my informant in an aircraft corporation on the Susquehanna River. I wanted to avoid having all agent mail going only via New York.

The man I wanted to visit was not German nor was he of German ancestry. He had no reason whatsoever to assist with anything for Germany. I had no intention of talking about this with him. He was a stamp collector, and for many years he had corresponded and exchanged stamps with a philatelist in Germany whom I used as a routing station.

When I delivered greetings from his German postage stamp partner, he was not particularly impressed. With a surly greeting, he appeared as if he wanted to dismiss me and made no attempt to offer me a seat. It was an embarrassing situation, but I had to at least try.

I carefully took a stamp out of my briefcase and held it under his nose. He looked at it briefly, and then offered me a chair. Then, he took a magnifying glass out of his desk and closely examined the stamp. It was a rare 1916 "Kamtschatka."

After a while, he shook his head, gave it back to me, and said, "I have it already." I was annoyed. Who foisted this situation on me? But I didn't let on, and took another stamp out of my briefcase. This was a "Cap-Verde-Inseln" dating back to 1877.

The man took it to the window, took a magnifying glass, and studied it for a long time. This time, he seemed to be satisfied. I was pleased, and I gave him a third stamp: an "Antigua" dating back to 1862. Again, he took his magnifying glass to the window, and now, life came into the old fellow. Now I have him where I want him, I thought. "Do you like it?" I asked politely.

"How much do you want for it?" he asked, and I noticed he was ready for a deal.

"They're not for sale," I said, "but I thought you might be interested."

"What do you mean," he demanded. "Do you think me a fool?"

"I certainly don't," I laughed.

"So, what do you want?" he asked.

"A favor from you," I replied. "I have a friend in Doylestown. He's a German, and he's working there in a factory that employs only Quakers. During his last visit to Germany, he met a girl he'd like to marry."

"What do I care?" the old man impatiently interrupted me.

"Hold on," I cut him off. "This friend would like to remain in contact with the girl, but it's difficult to correspond with anyone in Germany from such a small American town. There are always people who are curious and suspicious, and he's afraid he might run into some social issues." Understanding, the old man now snickered. Perhaps he was thinking of an old love or maybe a proverbial small-town gossip.

I kept talking. "He asked me to help him. And because I had business here in St. Louis, and because I was also supposed to pass greetings on to you from your friend in Germany, I thought this would be a good opportunity. You correspond regularly with Germany anyway, and it certainly would be no trouble for you to forward letters he might send you."

I pointed at the stamps and said, "He gave me these stamps and said I should just give them to you, provided you agree to forward the letters to his betrothed."

The old man looked eagerly at the stamps. "For those, he can send me as many letters as he wants and as long as he wants."

"Very good," I said, "and into the envelopes you will receive from Doylestown, he will post letters to his intended bride, ready and addressed, and all you need to do is drop them in the mailbox."

"Okay," the old man said and extended his dry, bony hand to me.

With these words I left him. I knew I had a good routing station here. Even if the old one should one day become nosy and open a letter, he would merely find a foolish love letter. Neither he nor anyone else would find any classified information in there.

We were lucky. Our man in Pennsylvania quickly absorbed the secrets of microphotography. It was not that simple and was not suitable for every agent. The prerequisite was a basic understanding of photography and a certain amount of experience. Many lacked the technical understanding of this unique equipment. Moreover, the apparatus not only required special treatment, it also differed in many ways so significantly from ordinary photo devices that it would arouse immediate suspicion among anyone not familiar with it. Under certain circumstances, this could betray all.

Today, microphotography is used everywhere in science and industry and plays an inestimable role, especially for archives. The procedure itself was known about for many years, but the German Intelligence Service was the first to use it for the transmission of secret information. It was perfected by German specialists between 1935 and 1936. It called for highly skilled training, mastery of an unconventional camera (we used the Leica), a particular lens that was not available everywhere, and a precise frame that made it possible to set the camera to the shortest distance and to any required angle. The unit also came with a device that developed the film and projected it onto a screen in order to check legibility before distribution.

Our man in Pennsylvania was the only one among the agents known to me in the United States who had mastered the mechanical equipment and the entire process. With utmost skill, he successfully used microphotography for two years for all reports, which he routinely submitted regarding his aircraft factory. At the end of 1939, he had to return to Germany for security reasons.

My brother, Hans, was a representative of the Chase National Bank in New York, and during his vacation in Germany he had been assigned by Captain Burghardt to work for us. Once, at the end of 1938, he was in Philadelphia on business and used the opportunity to pick up a set of larger drawings from our man in Doylestown. The fellow implored him to be particularly careful because he was aware that the Corps of Intelligence Police was surveying the aircraft factory.

My brother stashed the drawings in an old briefcase, took a cab in the opposite direction from the train station to a farm whose owner had befriended him, and buried it there under a hedge. After three days, he returned to the farm via Philadelphia, picked up the case, and delivered it directly to our steward on the same *Reliance*.

All other reports were put on microfilm under the stamps of the love letters via the unsuspecting stamp collector in St. Louis and sent by regular mail to Germany. After I made sure that the old fellow in St. Louis was properly installed, my work there was completed.

My next station was Chicago.

10

Mr. X

The icy wind blew fine snow through the streets of Chicago as I took a cab from the train station to the main post office. There, I picked up my business papers, which I had sent general delivery in advance from St. Louis. I needed them again as an alibi for my visit with a major textile establishment.

In the afternoon, I paid a private visit to a former classmate, who was one of the technical directors at the General Electric Company. Ladislas Trebusch was a Hungarian, and we had been good friends in Germany. We had corresponded occasionally after our paths had parted. As a boy, Ladislas had lost his mother during the bloody Red Terror under Bela Kun in 1919; after that, he was beset with blind hatred against anything communist. He worshiped Hitler, because Hitler was fighting against Bolshevism. I had no objections to visiting *Lazi* and to disclosing to him the real reason for my stay in the United States. He was pleasantly surprised when I called him on the phone.

We spent a happy evening together, and we indulged ourselves with memories of our student days. It was really great to visit with a true friend and to be myself once again.

Lazi wanted to know a hundred thousand things all at once. He was most interested in the war against communism and in the social institutions of Germany. He knew Germany had always been a leader in these fields, and now he wanted information about the latest achievements. I was well informed about both, and could draw comparisons based on my personal experiences in the United States.

Few words were wasted over my real mission. It was quite natural for *Lazi* to let me have all available official and unofficial statistical data on the condition of the arms industry, to which he had access as the technical manager of his plant. He had no objections. Germany and the United States had contacts with each other on a well-meaning neutral basis, and, at the time, no one thought that there would ever be a war between the two.

Most individuals never considered war a possibility. My friend, *Mr. Black*, a senior VFW officer from North Carolina, assured me, during our last meeting in Asheville, North Carolina, that everyone felt they had fought on the wrong side during the previous war and that they had no intention of being drawn into another war with Germany. *Lazi*, likewise, had not heard anything to the contrary, so far.

I gave him a billing station in Hong Kong, which *The Skipper* had been able to set up shortly before I left Germany. It bore the address of a large Chinese import and export firm that received voluminous amounts of mail from all over the world. I had picked China because, among all of the Asian countries at that time, it still seemed to me to be the most neutral.

I was certain from the very beginning that *Lazi* would help me, but he did far more than I expected. I was satisfied, but he had something else for me. "I know someone you really should visit while you're here," he said. "I have a friend in Detroit. If I give you a letter of introduction, he'll receive you there with open arms."

"Actually, I have no business in Detroit, and I'd like to return to New York as fast as possible," I said.

"You don't have to stay there long. Just make a little detour via Detroit for a couple of hours. From there, you can easily catch a train to New York. I promise you it will be worthwhile. He's one of America's leading industrialists."

"Why should he receive me? Is he a German?" I asked.

"No, he's not even conditionally pro-German. But he hates the Russians, and he hates communism, just as I do, and he supports everyone and everything in the fight against Bolshevism."

"All right," I finally agreed. "I'll take you at your word."

I knew only too well that there was a widespread antipathy against communism in America. A series of my friends in the University Club—Commander Riggs, an ex-governor, Colonel Uldric Thompson—were utterly convinced that communism was the greatest threat to America, and on that score, they totally agreed with Hitler's policy.

Of course, I also knew there were individuals who sympathized with the Bolshevists, above all, Mrs. Roosevelt, who asserted that Russian propaganda against the United States was no worse than American propaganda against Russia. That might be. But as my friends argued (and I had to agree with them) why were the Russians, on the one hand, so openly insistent on a clause concerning noninterference in the internal affairs of the United States, whereas, on the other hand, they demanded "diplomatic status" for their trade organizations? My friends were convinced the Russian trade missions in reality were Secret Service organizations.

I wanted to return directly from Chicago to New York because a special business matter was waiting for me there, which I had intentionally postponed until the last moment prior to my departure for Germany. This was a meeting that wasn't just extremely unpleasant for me but against which I had been warned by an inexplicable premonition. On the other hand, *Lazi's* proposal intrigued me, and it provided a good excuse for postponing my meeting in New York for yet another day. I took the train to Detroit early the next morning, and I drove directly to the office of the industrialist, whom I will call *Mr. X.* I gave the secretary the letter of introduction *Lazi* had given me and asked her to announce me. The girl disappeared into the office of her boss, and returning after a while, she asked me to wait. That was nothing unusual for a man of his caliber. Nevertheless, it seemed rather peculiar to me that she gave no explanation for his delay—that he was just in a conference or how long he would be. I began to get restless when the buzzer on the secretary's desk came on, and she disappeared again behind the thick, cushioned door. When she returned, she headed directly for me. I stood up and expected to be introduced.

But instead, she handed me a sealed envelope and said, *"Mr. X greatly regrets that he cannot receive you at this moment."*

I was nonplussed and barely able to get hold of myself. I thanked her mechanically, picked up my hat, and in my confusion made a completely un-American, European bow. I left the beautiful, bright office building, still holding the sealed envelope in my hand. Perhaps *Lazi* did not really know this *Mr. X* well enough? After all, he said *Mr. X* would receive me with open arms.

Now I remembered the envelope. I opened it, and read, "I expect you tonight punctually at 8:00 at my private apartment." I began to suspect something, and I felt a bit more comfortable. I even allowed myself a slice of my beloved apple pie, although I had promised myself I would never eat more than one slice per day. But today, I thought I could make an exception.

I spent the afternoon inspecting the Ford plant. I caught a cab at the calculated time, and it brought me to my destination through a magnificent residential area along the outskirts of the city. Punctually, at five minutes before eight o'clock, the car stopped in front of a massive wrought-iron gate that was wide open.

At the end of a boundless park-like garden, I saw a towering mansion. A wide gravel path led to the house, between tall trees and thick rhododendrons. In the light of the lanterns, fresh snow glittered on the trees and bushes. The way to the brightly lit house was swept clean. I paid the driver. Since I still had about five minutes, I intended to walk in order to savor this fairy-tale world for one more instant and to marvel at the gigantic terrace with the wide marble steps leading to the garden.

On the dot at eight o'clock, very tense, I pushed the doorbell next to the artfully carved doorway. At the same moment, a servant with the typical attitude of an English butler opened the door. He had obviously been waiting for me. Without saying a word, he took my hat and coat and hung them in a cabinet in the immense lobby. With the sovereign mien of an ambassador, he pointed to a marble staircase covered with a thick runner, and with a "please, sir," he guided me upstairs. Here he opened a large, carved door, stepped to the side to let me pass, and announced, "*Mr. Renken,* sir"; then he disappeared without dignifying me with any further glance.

Rising from a high-backed leather chair was a tall, gaunt man, who approached me with extended hand. *Mr. X* looked to be in his fifties. His hair was ash blond, his face was narrow, with a long slightly bent nose, and his eyes were a brilliant clear blue. His entire demeanor exuded dignity and self-confidence, and I felt instinctively drawn to him before he had said a word.

"You probably already figured out why I didn't welcome you this morning," he said with a winning smile.

"Yes," I replied; and I felt as if I were facing an old acquaintance. "After I got over my initial disappointment, I began to suspect something."

"Yes," he confirmed. "After I read the letter from *Lazi,* I immediately called him in Chicago, and when he told me who you really are, I thought an office was no place for the kind of talks we were going to engage in. The less the office staff there hears and sees, the better."

He took me over to the fireplace, where we settled into comfortable chairs. The stiff-necked butler returned and brought two cocktails on a silver tray. "Thank you, William," my host said.

"Very well, sir," William replied; then he bowed and closed the heavy door behind him.

"So," my host said, as he turned toward me, "tell me something."

I was thinking, what does he mean by "tell me something?" and asked cautiously, "What should I tell you?"

"Well, what are things in Germany really like?" my host asked quite casually. "Look here, we always get everything presented here through rose-colored glasses. I am, of course, accustomed to reading between the lines, but rarely have I an opportunity to get eyewitness reports."

I did not feel very comfortable when he said that. I had heard this line of questions often in the past, and I recalled what had happened to me in 1935 when I returned from Germany. That was barely two years after Hitler had seized power, when the German people began to breathe freely because, after so many horrible years of subjugation and unemployment, order and work had returned. When I told my American friends who asked about conditions in Germany what I had seen and heard, I found my listeners became rather embarrassed and began to talk about something else. In reality, they did not want to hear what I had to say. Their questions were almost rhetorical. They preferred to believe what they were reading in the newspapers and what they heard on the radio. And now I was asked the same question by a man of my host's caliber. It was disappointing, but what could be done? I had to respond as he wished.

I said, "My job would be easier if you would mention a certain area you're particularly interested in."

"You're correct," *Mr. X* agreed. "I am not interested in party squabbles and the like. We have that here, too. No, what interests me is the further development of German foreign policy—above all, regarding the East. That is something that concerns all of us." After a pause, he continued: "Well, at least it should concern us! I expect, however, from you that I will not be presented with Joseph Goebbels's propaganda. That I can get here also."

"Regarding the question of communism, one certainly doesn't need Goebbels's propaganda. But I think I can assure you that Hitler has such a large following precisely because the people have seen that he fought communism so successfully in Germany."

In the course of the following conversation, *Mr. X* left no doubt that he considered communism to be a tremendous threat to the entire West.

Then he said without hesitation, "How could it be possible that a man like Franklin Roosevelt, with all the information he has, could deliver such a quarantine speech as he delivered a couple of weeks ago in Chicago, in the course of which he spoke of 'a regime of terror and international lawlessness.' Maybe he could have meant Moscow, but everybody knows he had Tokyo and Berlin on his mind." [In 1937, FDR's "Quarantine Speech" called for a "quarantine" to stem the spread of an "epidemic of world lawlessness."]

"Yes," I interrupted him, "now he will probably have to amend the 'Neutrality Acts.'"

"You see," *Mr. X* excitedly interrupted, "that's where he loses me. Roosevelt maintains his quarantine speech does not in any way conflict with the Neutrality Acts. But please tell me, how can we remain neutral on the one hand, if on the other hand we identify ourselves with a particular group of nations? If we are to be linked to any single group, then it would, of course, be the sort of group that also fights against our enemy, in other words, Bolshevism."

He had obviously become quite stimulated. He made a long pause and for the first time emptied his glass. Then he continued, "If I, as a millionaire, were to go public with this type of warning, then naturally everyone would immediately scream, 'Capitalist!' But they do not realize that in the end the fight of Bolshevism's rise to power is carried out on the backs of the workers and poor." He rose and began to pace.

Suddenly, he stopped in front of me and said, "No, *Mr. Renken*. I'm well aware that we must carefully track the rearmament of your potential enemies, among which, unfortunately, we are also included—yes, do not interrupt me—

and among whom unfortunately we will also belong. On that score, I cannot help you. But please pass on to Mr. Hitler, although I do not really understand some of his measures, please pass on to him that I would outfit an entire infantry division for Germany, personally, at my expense, if he starts an open battle against Bolshevism. And believe me, I'm not the only one. There are a great number of Americans who think exactly as I do."

I said nothing at all. What should I say? I was very impressed. The words spoken by *Mr. X* echoed in my ears for a long time after I left his house late in the evening.

I was unable to understand how such a man this very day could be convinced that Roosevelt would someday join the greatest enemy of his people, in other words, Bolshevik Russia. I began to think about this seriously, and I was afraid. This conversation did not help my direct intelligence work at all, but I had learned what some of the powerful Americans were thinking.

In Berlin, I presented the offer of *Mr. X* to Colonel Hans Piekenbrock, head of Abw I. In the beginning, he acted very dubious, but I finally managed to convince him of the sincere intentions of *Mr. X*. Then he promised me he would see to it that the message would be passed on to Hitler. "But," he added with a note of doubt, "I do not believe that Hitler would accept such an offer. He seems to be bent on doing everything by himself without anybody else's help." Piekenbrock did not add "unfortunately," but the word hovered in the air unspoken. I felt that's what he was thinking.

Mr. X never had the opportunity to outfit a division for Hitler. But he did not abandon his personal fight against Russia, and to this very day, he's still one of the leading anti-communists in America. As of 1970, he was an old man, but his views, his fortune, and his power still play a role in the United States. That could be seen again when he supported Governor Reagan of California.

Then, as I boarded the midnight train to New York, I put my thoughts back in some order again, and was able to prepare myself for the last leg of my American journey. With trepidation I headed directly to New York.

11

A Close Encounter

Two months prior to my trip to America, one of my investigators told me a German-American by the name of Burger was to come to Germany via the North German Lloyd ship *Columbus* to spend his vacation here. He was an engineer working for a big American armament company that made gyrocompasses.

His firm was particularly important to us, especially since we did not as yet have any contacts with the people who made gyrocompasses. I was very interested in meeting this man, and hoped we might direct him to a useful purpose. I searched for ways we could possibly get him to work for us. I was still exploring avenues to approach him when he delivered himself into our hands.

I had persuaded our informant with the Passport Control Office to take me along to the *Columbus* dispatch boat to Cuxhaven and help me establish contact with Burger.

As the passengers gradually passed through the control procedure, engineer Burger was asked to come to the table of our agent. The inspector asked him to sit down and began to question him. The questions related to origin, his education in Germany and the United States, and his emigration to the United States.

Burger answered all of the inspector's questions willingly and calmly until the inspector asked, "Before your emigration were you employed by anyone here?"

Burger was visibly shaken and became pale. "Why do you want to know that?" he asked.

"Purely routine," the inspector replied, seemingly unimpressed. "Does that make you nervous?"

"No, no! Certainly not," Burger stammered.

"Well," the inspector said in a friendly voice, "would you like to answer my last question?"

Burger swallowed and gave the name of an unknown company. The inspector took notes. "Were you in the United States uninterruptedly?" he then asked.

"Yes," Burger said curtly.

"Always with the same company?"

"No."

"And where do you work now?"

"Sperry Gyroscope."

"I don't know what that is," the inspector feigned. "What do they make?"

"Special instruments," the engineer replied. He was visibly nervous.

The inspector was a good observer. He knew he could not ask any further questions now. The man was becoming obstreperous, and in that case, there was no sense in any further questioning. There was also no plausible excuse for continuing the interrogation. But there was something more to all of this, and we had to find out exactly what it was. So, the official tried once again. "Why were you actually not back again in Germany during all those years?" he asked casually.

Burger shifted restlessly back and forth on his chair, and his hands betrayed his excitement. "Because I had no money," he finally blurted out.

"That's a plausible reason," the inspector replied and wondered why that made the fellow so nervous. There was something behind all this. With a severe official glare, the inspector asked Burger point-blank, "And why did you leave Germany at that time?"

Something quite unexpected happened at that point. Burger jumped up, gasped for air, waved his arms, and burst out, "My God! Why do you have to dish all this up here? I thought that was old history. And," he added, quite subdued, "it was really not as bad as all that."

Now the inspector became really curious. At first, he wanted to press Burger further, but then he held back. Burger was in a state in which he would ultimately fully betray himself. He had to believe that we knew more about his past. The inspector acted as if he was about to close his files. "Well, look here." He smiled, half-earnestly, half-amused. "Just let it all out, and then we'll see what we can do."

Burger fell back into his chair, put his head in his hands, and said, "Well, if you know anyway." The inspector nodded encouragingly.

"It was really not as bad as all that. At that time, I had a rather poor salary in a bicycle dealership. Then I had an opportunity to sell a big shipment of ninety bicycles at a higher price. The boss wasn't there, and I decided to handle the deal myself. I had two checks made out, one for the regular price and another one for the extra price I had finagled. I cashed the latter for myself, personally. Finally, I became very scared, I ran away, and two weeks later, I took a steamboat to America, and now the whole thing is coming out again," he added with a note of resignation.

The inspector did not really know what he should do, but he did not want to let his catch go, either. Somehow, he had to convince the fellow that he could offer him impunity, even though he was not legally threatened with any penalty. Perhaps he could arrange it so Burger would feel obligated, and so he said, "Now you really feel better. Too bad that at the time, proceedings were initiated against you. Now, we will have to see how to get you out of this mess."

He paused for a moment and then seemed to think hard. After that, he said, "Earlier you said that you are making special instruments in your company? Personally, I'm not very interested, but I have a good acquaintance who is very much interested in such things. If you come to an agreement with him, then I'll straighten everything out for you."

Burger seemed greatly relieved and immediately agreed. Thereupon, the inspector brought him to me and saw to it that he was quickly processed out. Before I took my leave, we scheduled a meeting for the next day in my city office in Hamburg. Burger provided some interesting data about the type and purpose of instruments his company made, and also promised to supply technical details after his return to the United States. But we never heard any more from him until after my departure for America.

In New York, during my initial meetings with *Paul* and *Pop,* I had called him and was invited to dinner in his home. For my personal backup, I took along my brother, who at that time, however, did not yet work for us.

The conversation was rather stiff, and the evening was unsuccessful as far as I was concerned. I felt somewhat uneasy. Above all, I did not trust Burger's wife, and therefore could not express myself openly. She kept a sharp eye on us at all times, so I finally gave up and returned to my hotel without having accomplished anything. I decided to let the matter rest until my return from the Midwest. I trusted the woman less than before.

She was a Puerto Rican, hot-blooded and domineering. There was something phony in her eyes as she served us hospitably at the table. That made me suspicious and worried. My brother had the same feeling. Now, after my return, I resumed the contact and phoned Burger at his apartment. The woman answered the phone: "Oh, good day, *Herr Doktor*! No, my husband is not here."

"Too bad," I said. "Please say hello to him for me and tell him that I'll call tomorrow around the same time."

"Okay," she said curtly and hung up.

The next day I tried him at the factory. The switchboard told me they could not connect me with him. It was clear I could not call him there again without arousing suspicion. I had to try to reach him at home again.

In the evening, I called his apartment once more. Again, the woman answered the phone. She was so sorry, she said, but her husband was not there, and she added, "My husband does not want you to call him at the factory. He always has trouble when he gets private phone calls."

Burger was obviously trying to avoid me. "How can I reach him if he is not home?" I asked.

She replied in a somewhat friendlier tone, "Why don't you call me tomorrow at my office? Then I'll arrange a lunch for the three of us." She gave me her phone number. I wrote it down and thought carefully about this entire matter.

In Hamburg, Burger had told me more than was necessary. Why was he now avoiding me so stubbornly? I became fully aware now that this entire situation was attributable to his wife.

The next morning, I called her at the office. The woman was kindness personified. She told me her husband was happy she had thought of having lunch for the three of us, and would I please arrive punctually at 1400 hours at Child's Restaurant around the corner from her office. Then she almost outdid herself and said she was very happy . . . and . . . I stopped listening. The politer she became, the more cautious I became. Finally, I said, "Well and good! We meet at 1400 hours."

Instantly, she stopped talking and snapped "Thanks," and hung up.

Now I saw everything clearly. No, young lady, I thought, you do not trap me as easily as all that. I had the opportunity to drop the whole thing, but I still wanted to make sure what this was all about.

At 1400 hours the next day, Mrs. Burger waited in vain. At 1500 hours, she was still waiting. At 1600 hours, I called her again. I could sense that she was getting hot under the collar, and I noted I was correct in my suspicion. I excused myself properly and asked her for another appointment for the next day.

Madame began to stammer. Suddenly, she seemed to have a new idea. Her voice became soft and gentle, and she appeared even politer than yesterday. She asked me for my phone number. "I'd like to quickly call my husband," she said, "and ask him if he could make it tomorrow."

I was thinking: You can call your husband, but my number you don't get. No, unfortunately, I cannot give it out. With all of the politeness I could muster, I said, "Unfortunately, I cannot give you my number. I'm talking from a phone booth. Perhaps you could call your husband right away, and I'll call you back in half an hour."

When I called back, she said, "I'm sorry, *Herr Doktor.* The only time my husband is free is at 1100 hours, and I don't know whether I can get away at that time. But I will try."

"Good," I said. "So tomorrow at 1100 hours."

"Please don't leave me high and dry again, *Herr Doktor.* It was so embarrassing for me, especially since my husband has such a long way to go from the factory, and then you simply did not turn up!"

"But by the way," I interrupted her, "I just remembered, tomorrow isn't good either. Unfortunately, I cannot." I could just about hear how she was seething with anger when I said, "I'm exceedingly sorry if that causes you any trouble, but I really cannot make it tomorrow. You see, I tried many times, always in vain, to set up a meeting with your husband. After all, I have other things to take care of."

"But *Herr Doktor*," she objected on the other end of the line.

"I'm sorry," I interrupted her. "It is really impossible. Today is Tuesday. Perhaps I can visit you in your office on Friday. Then we can have a good talk."

"No, no," she shouted, frightened. "Please do not come unannounced. My boss doesn't like that."

"Well," I said, "I'll call you before I come. Adios, Señora." And I hung up. Now I needed a cup of coffee. I had to think about this entire issue carefully.

While in Germany, Burger had been ready to cooperate. The invitation in New York had come from him. His wife had viewed us suspiciously the entire time. She had not liked me from the outset. Burger was completely under her influence. She hated the country of his origin. She had asked me to lunch, although she detested me; her coolly suppressed anger was the best indicator of that. But as I called her the second time, she had claimed she would first have to call her husband. Then she had said he could come only at eleven o'clock in the morning. That had been a blatant lie. His job made it impossible for him to leave the office at any time during working hours.

But she had also lied about the fact that she herself could not come. Every secretary can arrange to disappear from their desk long enough to have a few minutes' break. Her disappointment over the fact I was unable to come was genuine, not on my account, but for some other reason. That I was not allowed to visit her unannounced was likewise an excuse. She just needed to know the time of my visit to make the necessary arrangements.

No, *Herr Doktor*, I thought. You do not need to be a hero detective. That woman is trying to trap you. That would not merely be unpleasant for me personally, but it would also cause unnecessary international complications. Nevertheless, I felt I had to make one last attempt before I could drop Burger from my list.

My ship was to sail on Friday. No one knew where I was staying; no one knew under which name I was registered. In the eyes of the law, I was the business traveler Nikolaus Ritter from Germany. I had a bulletproof alibi for every place I had visited. Nowhere was there any connection between me and other contacts and the Burger couple. Actually, nothing could really happen. Even if they should interrogate me, at most, the Burgers could voice some suspicions, but they could not prove anything. I was completely calm and decided to take a well-earned rest for the last two days.

On Friday, I left my hotel early and personally took my suitcase for storage at the pier. At ten o'clock, I called Mrs. Burger and set up an appointment with her for 11:30 a.m. in her office.

"Can I be sure that you will come?" she asked. "I'd like to talk to you face to face."

"I will certainly come," I promised her, and without another word, I hung up. Mentally I added, "But not at 11:30."

I strolled down 42nd Street toward Times Square and sat in the movie theater for one hour and watched the up-to-date news. At 11:15 a.m. I went downtown. On the way, I put on my American steel spectacles, which the Burgers had never seen me wear before. Today I was wearing my blue Homburg hat; the new, soft hat that I had been wearing in the United States had already been packed.

I got off at Wall Street and walked to the office building where Mrs. Burger worked. I took the elevator to the fourth floor, went to the other end of the corridor, and leaned against the windowsill. Then I read my newspaper and positioned myself so I could observe the door to her office.

At 11:25 a.m., two men came out of the elevator at the far end. Now, I knew what this was all about. One of them could have been out of the movies. He looked so typical, with his black bowler and his fat cigar. They checked the nametags on the doors and disappeared into Burger's office.

I folded my newspaper, took the elevator down, left the building, and went uptown to see my friend the sculptor. There I retrieved the key for my bank safety deposit box. I went to the bank on 90th Street, took out my normal passport and my private papers, and dropped the key off at the window.

Then I allowed myself some lunch. At 1450, I entered Mrs. Burger's office. Without looking up and without noticing who was standing next to her, she asked mechanically, "What may I . . .?" That was as far as she got. She had recognized me, and she looked frozen.

"I have to ask your pardon again." I smiled obligingly. "I hope this did not cause you any unpleasantness!"

"You . . .," she uttered with the full hatred of a woman who thought she was going to make a hit but now thought herself beaten. "You . . .," she hissed once again, as if she wanted to spit on me, but suddenly she took control of herself. She had not yet given up. "Please sit down, *Herr Doktor*," she said as calmly as she could. Her voice was shaking with excitement. "Excuse me for a moment. I have to take these things to my boss."

I knew right away she would make a phone call. I also knew that the nearest police station was, at most, five minutes away. That was about all the time I had. By the time Mrs. Burger came back, I had already stood up.

"You don't really want to go again?" she asked hastily. "But we haven't talked about my husband yet. Stay for another five minutes, please. I have to run across to the bank for my boss. Then I'll be available to you." While she talked, she nervously shuffled the papers on her desk and, in vain, looked for the bank book.

"You have made a big mistake, madam," I said in a friendly tone. "There is no bank in New York that can process you one minute after three o'clock." I pointed at my watch and said, "It is now 3:10."

At that point, she forgot herself. "You damned German," she hissed at me and did not even try to get herself under control. "I hate you. I hate all of you. My husband told me everything, and he was stupid enough to think I would help. Anybody else, yes, but never a German! You *spy!*"

"Again, you are making a big mistake, madam," I said quite calmly. "You are calling me a spy? On the contrary, your husband is the spy, and he's working against his new homeland. I work for mine, but I thank you for being so frank. And now allow me to take my leave before your gentlemen detectives arrive."

With these words, I closed the door behind me. It was high time. I could not afford to wait for the elevator. If I ran down the stairs, they might receive me at the bottom. I looked at the elevator level indicator; the elevator had just passed the third floor. So, I ran up the stairs to the fifth floor and took the elevator down to the third floor. I did not dare go all the way down. On the third floor, I headed for the first door I saw. I was lucky. It was the waiting room of a dentist with some patients sitting around. I picked up a magazine and sat down. Patiently, I waited for half an hour. Then I again put on my spectacles and my Homburg. I went down the stairs to the next subway station and went uptown.

Now I breathed a sigh of relief. This last run-in perhaps might not have been necessary, but at least I was able to confirm my suspicion. Now, of course, I realized it was not just my nerves. The danger was real. I was glad everything was over. That was the trickiest situation in which I had found myself since the excessively friendly reporter loudly announced my name upon my arrival in the reception area of the *Bremen,* and then added, "I thought you would be a captain with the Luftwaffe."

I got off at 42nd Street and saw a vaudeville show to make the last few hours prior to my departure as enjoyable as possible. After the show, I had a cup of coffee at a Nedick's hotdog stand at the corner of 42nd Street and 7th Avenue, and then I slowly walked toward the pier; next I boarded the *Europa.*

It was Friday, December 13. No ship would put to sea on that day. The lines were cast off shortly after midnight. I felt happy, and I was grateful that everything had once again turned out well in spite of the black Friday, and I felt greatly relieved as the ship finally headed homeward.

12

Reconstructing the Bombsight

It was the deep of winter when my ship arrived in Bremerhaven two days before Christmas. The entire landscape was covered by a thick blanket of snow. It was cold. The driver was waiting in the car. We drove directly to Hamburg to my duty station at General Headquarters. I reported immediately to the Intelligence station chief, Dr. Ludwig Dischler, and to Burghardt, happily greeted everyone else, and sat down at my desk.

Everything that could be done in the meantime had been done. My first concern was the collected drawings supplied by *Paul*. Everything had arrived accurately—the first drawing, which I had transported myself in my umbrella cane, and a number of additional drawings that had arrived in the meantime.

I immediately sent the drawings, with a corresponding cover letter I had drafted on board, to Central Headquarters in Berlin for analysis and evaluation. Eagerly, I waited for a response. The bombsight was by far the greatest and most important coup I had pulled off so far.

Two weeks passed before the answer came from Berlin. I read it and stopped short; I could not believe my eyes. I let the information sink in and checked the copies again. There had to be some sort of mix-up, but the copies matched. The answer from Berlin read as follows: "The drawings that were sent are completely worthless. It is assumed that the informer fraudulently sought financial gain. It is proposed that the contact be cut off immediately."

I was speechless. People topside are crazy, I thought. "The informant is trying fraudulently to get money . . .?" I saw *Paul*'s open face before me. I again heard his quiet and honest voice as he said, "This 'offering money,' after all, was just a figure of speech, and you don't have to worry about me personally." Once more, I stared at the scrap of paper. Then I slammed my fist down on the table so hard that my secretaries looked up, frightened. I jumped up.

"Those damned pencil pushers," I hissed angrily. I picked up the letter, ran out of the room, and slammed the door behind me. Then I reported to Captain Burghardt and showed him the letter. "Look at this, Captain! Those people are not normal!"

"I know, I know," he said. "For heaven's sake, don't bother me with this scrap of paper. I can't change anything."

I had no intention of leaving him in peace. "That is an affront, Captain," I said. "How can our colleagues make such a claim? What do they know about the type of fellow *Paul* is? What difference does it make whether he gets money or not? They don't know that he gets all worked up over the slightest mention of money. I know personally that there are hundreds of drawings for this particular instrument. These drawings are not sheer inventions. I need to go to Berlin immediately and give that idiot analyst a piece of my mind!"

"Now just take it easy, Captain," Burghardt said quite officially, and now I noticed that even he was not totally convinced.

Then I pulled myself together. He was right. After all, I was the only one who knew *Paul* and his motives. Burghardt and the associates in Berlin had nothing but my word to go on, but the captain had worked with me long enough to know that I had both feet on the ground and certainly was not suffering from delusions.

"I had not thought about the fact that *Paul* did not receive a single penny and rejected any offers of payment," he said after a brief pause, "but you are correct. What kind of motive might someone have for going to so much trouble to prepare these drawings? He certainly didn't do it just for fun!"

"I know what these drawings mean, and I know why *Paul* took personal risks so we could have them," I said. "Anyway, I will not give up here without a fight."

"If you are so convinced," Burghardt finally conceded, "then go ahead. But how? What will you do?"

"Tomorrow I'll go to Berlin," I said. I had already put a plan into place. "There, to begin with, I'll talk to the section chief of I Air Technology; he is a most sensible man. Perhaps he can tell me how we can contact a real expert."

"Ok, fine," Burghardt said, and pulled on his nose as he always did when he was thinking hard. "You have my blessings. Good luck."

First, I called Dr. Nautsch from my room. He always had an airplane available for important official trips. "Nautsch," I asked, "can you fly me to Berlin tomorrow?"

"Is it that important?" he asked, astonished.

"Absolutely," I said. "Your colleagues in Berlin labeled the drawings supplied by *Paul* as deceitful fabrications."

"How is that possible?" he interrupted me. "In that case, we fly."

"Thanks," I said and hung up. Then I called *The Skipper*. "I'm flying to Berlin tomorrow. Please let me have all of the documents concerning *Paul*. I would like to take along two copies each of the photocopies of the drawings."

The next morning, according to regulations, I reported to the section chief in Berlin. I told him in a few words what was involved, and then I had a long talk with the chief of the technical section. I explained the entire incident to him once again, from the first drawings we had received via *Pop* to my meeting with *Paul*, and to the last agreements which we had made regarding further deliveries.

I spread the drawings out before him on the desk, and said, "Take a look at that—at least take a close look. Tell me quite openly whether you get the impression that these drawings are mere inventions."

"No," he said without much thought, "they are certainly not. I can barely get a general idea of what they're supposed to show."

That was enough for me. "I thoroughly understand that," I said. "This, after all, is something entirely new, something revolutionary, and because such a thing as this does not exist, there is nothing else to compare it with. Who knows if there isn't a little man in the analysis section who doesn't recognize what is in front of him and therefore simply says the drawings are contrived."

I paused slightly and continued, "After all, in Germany, we certainly have a specialist who is working on the problem of a bombsight. I'd like to show those drawings to that individual."

The aviation engineer looked at me for a moment, and then he laughed. "You are damned stubborn, Ritter, but perhaps you're right. One shouldn't just simply push these aside. In Frankfurt, sits our well-known Professor Wolfram Eisenlohr [Department for Engines and Accessories within the Technical Office, Ministry of Aviation]. He's your specialist. He's number one in this field. Get a positive evaluation from him, and I promise you I'll submit the matter personally to General Ernst Udet."

I could not have asked for more. Ernst Udet was chief of the Luftwaffe's highest engineering bureau, the technical department of the air ministry.

"I wouldn't want to be in the boots of the analyst who wrote you that evaluation," he added.

I had to get to Frankfurt as quickly as possible, and since there were no other flights, I again asked Dr. Nautsch to fly me there.

On that same evening, I sat looking across the desk at the highly accomplished Professor Eisenlohr, and told him the whole story of *Paul* and the drawings of the Norden bombsight. Eisenlohr listened attentively. I made my brief as concise as possible and presented him with the drawings. You could hear a pin drop in the room. Anxiously, I waited, my heart pounding.

The professor bent over the drawings. He scrutinized them very carefully without saying a word. It seemed to me an eternity. Then he arranged them next to each other. Then he added a third one. Finally, he took paper and pen and began to draw. Eagerly, I stared at the sheet of paper and saw how the lines took on shape.

Finally, he looked up and said very simply, "You are right! This is something

Nikolaus Ritter. From the editor's private collection.

really big. Bring me as many drawings as you can. The more we have, the less we have to design ourselves."

I rose, thanked him, and said good-bye. I felt dazed. The same night, I took a train to Berlin. When I brought the news from Professor Eisenlohr, the Luftwaffe engineer said, "My congratulations, Ritter. I will take it to Udet today."

Four days later, in Hamburg, Captain Burghardt summoned me to his office and gave me a new assessment signed personally by Canaris. The old assessment was declared void, and it was requested that an attempt be made, by any means necessary, to accelerate the acquisition of further drawings.

We kept getting more drawings from *Paul*, and he never knew about the original rejection. Six months later, I received a call from Berlin. I was asked to persuade *Paul* to come to Germany on vacation. "We have something we would like to show him," they said. Initially, *Paul* rejected the idea, but when I urged him to take the opportunity, he finally agreed. The fare and a portion of his per diem were the only reciprocation he ever accepted from us.

When *Paul* arrived in Germany, I was first surprised, then disappointed, and finally angry that I was not asked to go to Berlin with him. Much later, I learned from others what had really happened.

In a conference room on Kurfürstendamm, several men stood around a green table and thoughtfully contemplated a rather odd-looking box, the bombsight. *Paul* fixed his gaze on the instrument on the table. He turned chalk white. "So, you already have the instrument," he said, subdued. "Then you don't need me anymore."

On the contrary, he was told. "This device was built on the basis of your drawings." And then everyone congratulated him. Although the drawings *Paul* had sent were never quite complete, they were still sufficient to assemble an intact device and even make some improvements.

The device was quickly built for assembly line production and was already in use by German troops while Americans were still in the experimental stage. When the war broke out, it was used with great success by the German bombers. It was an irony of fate that one of the greatest secret devices of the United States was in the possession of the enemy even before the Allies had their own.

When in the summer of 1940 a German bomber equipped with such a device was shot down in France, the United States gave the plans for construction of the bombsight to the Allies.

Immediately after the outbreak of the war in Europe, we repeatedly urged *Paul* to come to Germany with his family as quickly as possible. We knew sooner or later an aircraft equipped with the bombsight would be shot down and would get into enemy hands. That would expose the secret, and the theft of the plans would inevitably lead back to *Paul*. We had a good job available for him in Germany, but he refused.

At my request, my brother Hans remained in touch with *Paul* until the end of 1940. Once he even met him on board the *Reliance*. The last time he saw him was on Wall Street, right around the corner from his office. At that time my brother already knew the FBI was after him and Duquesne and urged *Paul* to leave the United States. He advised *Paul* to take a detour via Mexico, which he was planning to do himself; and, fortunately, my brother was able to escape at the last minute in January 1942. But *Paul* remained stubborn.

Later, when the war with the United States was about to break out, we made one last attempt; but by that time, it was already too late. His former middleman had betrayed him. *Paul* was found guilty and sentenced to prison.

My role in the history of the Norden bombsight ended with a personal letter of appreciation from Canaris.

13

British Agents in the Abwehr

After the hurdle with the bombsight had been cleared, I was able to focus my attention on other matters. The next most important was to train Captain Simon for his mission in England.

I did not need to say much to him about country, people, and customs, because he knew more than I. We concentrated exclusively on tasks I expected him to accomplish: careful observation of airfields, unit strength figures, aircraft types, testing, defense, construction of new airfields, and primarily, details on specific ammunition and arms factories.

As I had surmised, Simon was a good student. In order to provide him with some comparisons, we visited airfields and factories together, where it was explained to him what his primary focus should be: air traffic, hangars, control headquarters, laboratories, and railroad terminals. He should also scan all local newspapers for relevant information to determine the precise location of new airfields or dummy airfields for target files of the German Luftwaffe. As an experienced navigations officer, the work would not be difficult for him.

On a beautiful March morning, Simon left my office in Hamburg, and I wished him, and myself, good luck with his first assignment in England. He traveled on his own nautical passport, which was full of visas from all countries. I had assigned him neither a target date nor a certain region. However, the territories were specifically defined by the General Staff of the German Luftwaffe's focus at that time in Berks, Hampshire, Surrey, and Sussex.

After four weeks Simon returned. When I received him at my bureau in the city, I took Miss *Busch* along just in case he had any special reports to make, and that proved wise. When Simon calmly pulled out his notepad, we looked at him with astonishment.

"Don't worry, *Herr Doktor*," he said. "Those are just dates, addresses of private people with whom I became acquainted, and some notes that relate to my earlier nautical activity. As for the rest," he said modestly, "I still have an excellent memory."

Clearly and precisely, he dictated details about five new airfields about which we had previously known only that they existed. One of them had just been made operational, another was still under construction, and a third was just beginning construction. On the basis of the map, he indicated the precise location, height, the hangars, and everything else that he knew.

I was most impressed by the number of factories about which, so far, we had known little. In Winchester, he met an employee of an aircraft factory from whom he was able to obtain precise details regarding the factory's output.

Simon's first mission was an obvious success. There was no doubt his reports were correct, but I was not able to confirm that for him until I received the assessment from the Luftwaffe Operations Staff. It was a long report, and each individual entry not only received a good evaluation but also triggered additional orders—orders for *Johnny.*

In the meantime, more inquiries came from Berlin concerning various strategic areas in England, but most striking was that we received an express request to engage the same agent who had brought the previous reports. And so, I sent Simon—who, naturally, was known in Berlin exclusively by his cover number—on his second journey in May.

This time, his trip lasted six weeks and was equally as successful as his first. My previous impression, that I would have a good man in Simon, had not deceived me. I had no one else of his caliber, and the temptation to send him on the road again so soon was great, but also dangerous. How often could a man like Simon go back and forth to England by the same route within one year without notice?

With a heavy heart, I put him on ice for a while until the flood of assignments, for which only he qualified, became overwhelming. We were especially swamped with repeated requests to send the same man, if possible, who had brought the previous excellent reports.

In the autumn of 1938, I finally decided to send Simon out for the third time. He wanted to take the old route again. I tried to dissuade him because I could not imagine he would not arouse suspicion, but he was adamant. Finally, I gave in.

This time Simon brought with him a friend's manuscript, which his friend had already corresponded about with two publishers in England. I looked at it closely. It described the friend's experience on a small Australian island and was illustrated with a series of rather primitive drawings intended to depict the somewhat unusual lifestyle of the natives. It was a book anyone might find of interest; it was about someone who wanted to live a Robinson Crusoe lifestyle on some deserted island. However, it would hardly be profitable for a publisher. This much was clear to Simon and me.

We also agreed that most of the border control officers were not literary critics. But the book was written in English, and we had no doubt they would let Simon pass with it.

When he arrived in Harwich with his manuscript, the customs officer did not hide his astonishment at seeing him once again, something I had been afraid of. The manuscript, of course, was actually our "Open Sesame." Simon sensed that the customs officer put a mark after his name.

Simon was on guard. He rented a room in a seaman's home in Whitechapel and made it his headquarters. With the help of the manuscript, and with his nautical jargon, we had put a code together, and we used his author friend as cover address.

In the meantime, Simon became acquainted with two British nationalists, who were ready to engage in sabotage against Britain. For such purposes, he arranged a cover address in Rotterdam, where his report would be passed on to Captain Lothar Witzke at the Hamburg Intelligence Station, Group II, Sabotage.

We received regular reports from Simon, until the connection suddenly broke off in February 1939. I was somewhat worried about his silence, but since I counted on his cleverness, I hoped this was merely a temporary obstacle. But that was false hope. There was no possible way to find out anything more precise. The only man I had in England was *Johnny,* and both *Johnny* and Simon were entirely too valuable to me to create any danger by establishing contact between the two. Both had to remain loners.

In the meantime, however, I could not let my actual work go. During one of my first trips after my return from the United States, I went to Stockholm, where I finally had to keep my belated appointment with *Lady May.* When I phoned her, she invited me for a cup of tea, on which occasion I also met her children. We chatted about Hamburg, and she emphasized again and again how much she still clung to Germany and that she would prefer working in Germany rather than England.

That gave me the opening to ask whether she might not want to assist Germany. She was not particularly surprised and said, "Just tell me what, and I'd love to help!" I told her she could serve as a relay station and that she would certainly do us a big service if, at the same time, she could report to us something about the activity of her employer in Grimsby and about the Royal Navy.

After that, I met her several times, twice in Hamburg and once in Sweden. In addition to naval service regulations, she also brought along some other interesting information.

During our last meeting, she had alerted me to her friend Maude, the Duchess of Château-Thierry. She thought the little lady might be useful to us. She had married a French duke; after his death she had moved to England, but still traveled a great deal on the continent. Besides, she owned some land in the neighborhood of Munich, which she had been trying to sell for a long time. Perhaps I could help her with that.

I wrote to the duchess, passed myself off as a business friend of Mrs. May Erickson, and suggested we might meet the next time she was in Munich. We could also talk about her real estate.

After some time, we met in Munich in the Bayerischer Hof. The duchess was a jolly little old lady, about 60, a small, lively, charming person, full of humor and joy. She was well dressed and had a cultivated manner of speech, and very evidently came from a refined background. She enjoyed having a small drink and sometimes even a bit more. After a couple of whiskeys, she asked me outright whether I might be able to help her sell her property. She said she had a large apartment in London, and, she added hesitantly, she needed money and also had good connections. I needed connections in London—above all, good contacts to the RAF—but first I had to have her checked out. We made a new date for a couple of weeks later in The Hague.

The next meeting was with a Swiss in Brussels who had offered his services to one of our investigators. I only had a personal description of him.

With foreigners who volunteer their services, you must be particularly careful. If you are lucky, these fellows are mostly just adventurers, but they might also be double agents, agents of a hostile intelligence agency who use this approach to gain access to their opponents.

It is not always easy to determine to which category foreign volunteers belong. Apart from that, these encounters are not without danger, above all in a foreign country. Then you can never know whether the intelligence service of that country has a hand in the game. Particular care was needed in Belgium, since the Francophile Walloons, contrary to the pro-German Flemings, were openly anti-German; and besides, Walloons and Flemings were hostile toward each other.

I had selected the lobby of a small hotel for our meeting. I sat down in a corner from which I could observe the entrance as I read a newspaper and smoked my cigar. The man turned up at the appointed time. A number of other guests sat in the lobby. He looked around, gave me a brief glance, and then stood as if he did not know where to go next. In other words, he did not have a personal description of me. But I had his, and I recognized him at first sight.

I headed toward him and introduced myself. His slovenly elegance, his sweetish smile, and his mushy handshake triggered a feeling of aversion in me from the very first moment. I invited him to a whiskey and asked him directly, "What made you offer your services to us?"

"I need money," he promptly replied.

You could not argue with that, but I wanted to know more. "Don't you have any other opportunity to make money?" I asked him.

"I don't really like to work," he answered rather cheekily.

The fellow was as shameless as he was slimy. I felt like dropping him, but I could not allow myself to be influenced by my personal feelings. "And what kind of work do you think you would be doing? What can you offer us?" I asked him.

"Well, you know there are a number of homosexuals in the Royal Air Force," he said with tantalizing frankness. "And that is why you can use me. I find it easier to get to those fellows than you 'normal' people, and once I have become intimate with one of them, I can very easily obtain valuable material for you."

I gave him the impression that I would accept his offer. Then he suddenly became talkative. He wanted to know where he could go in London and where he could drop his material off. Perhaps we might also have an address for him in Norway or Sweden through which he could send his reports?

For such questions, there was but a single source and a single interested party: the British Security Service [MI5]. But what amused me most was the fact that, in his eagerness, he had completely forgotten to ask about his pay, something that allegedly was the most important consideration for him. The case was quite clear to me now, but I could not let him suspect I had seen through him. I continued to give the impression I was seriously interested.

When I took my leave, I gave him a couple of nonsensical assignments with a fictitious London address, and we scheduled a second meeting in a couple of weeks. Of course, it never occurred to me to keep the appointment, but perhaps the matter might be of interest to III f. The mission of III f was to observe enemy intelligence officers and agents and to establish connections.

From Brussels, I drove to Antwerp, where my chances looked a little better. There I stayed again with my friend Helmut Thimm. He had become an "investigator" for me and informed me I should meet someone. After the usual cordial greeting, Helmut Thimm could not resist the temptation to keep me in suspense. When I finally asked him, "Whom do you have for me now?" he looked mischievously at me through his eyeglasses and said secretively, "A secretary who works in the consulate general of an overseas country!"

He placed whiskey and soda on the table, and we made ourselves comfortable in his beautiful library. "She will certainly interest you," he promised. "She's my girlfriend *Jenny.*"

"What," I said, "a girl?" Helmut was a widower. He had a steady girlfriend whom I knew well. I had never heard him speak of any other woman, and I was really astonished.

"No," he laughed, "not what you think! This is purely a business contact. She's a Fleming, and she works," at this point he paused meaningfully, "she works in the American Consulate General!"

"Damn!" I shouted. "That sounds really interesting."

"And it is, too," he promised. "She sits in the Passport and Overseas Department, and she always helps me whenever I need documents and permits. She's particularly pro-German, and she's a member of a Flemish fascist organization. She's done quite a few favors for me. I've been meaning to tell you about her for a long time."

"You certainly should have," I said. "I need to meet her." Simultaneously, many ways to establish a connection shot through my head. "How can I best meet her?" I asked Helmut.

"This is just why I wanted to talk to you."

"Let's think about this," I said. "In other words, you know her very well, and you have many business dealings with her. Do you also have private contact with her?"

"No," he replied, "that's what I've been avoiding so that no one could possibly get the idea that I'm bribing her to make it easier to get my travel permits."

"That's true." I nodded. "Stick with that, but that makes it somewhat more difficult for me to meet her. I can't just walk up to her."

We leaned back, drank our whiskey, and thought for a moment. Then Helmut said, "I've got it! We'll get *Joe* to arrange something so we can meet her. *Joe* knows her well privately."

Joe was a mutual friend and manager of a big international moving company in Antwerp. He was also a Fleming, and, like most Flemings, he was pro-German. He spoke fluent German and French. Originally, I had met him through a Hamburg connection, and *Joe* had brought us quite a few meaningful reports on international freight shipping. Being a Flemish nationalist, he knew *Jenny*, and he had known Helmut for a long time through his own moving company.

"Excellent," I said. "Let's have dinner together with *Joe*, and then we can make some proposals."

It was quite harmless that the three of us should meet in a restaurant. We selected a little Flemish place where both of them were known and where they frequently brought foreign guests. *Joe* was there when Helmut and I arrived. He sat in a corner and sipped a cup of coffee, something that he always did before every meal. Helmut and I had a martini cocktail, which I had gotten to know at the University Club in New York during Prohibition. After we placed our order, Helmut said, "*Joe*, I told the *Doktor* that he must meet *Jenny*."

"Why sure!" *Joe* agreed. "I should have thought of that myself. How do you want to handle that?"

"Why don't you invite her to dinner in some larger restaurant, perhaps where there is dancing," I suggested. "Then Helmut and I could meet her there quite by accident."

"Good idea," Helmut agreed. "I can suddenly spot *Joe* and *Jenny* and wave to them. Then I can go to their table and ask them to join us."

"In such cases," I added, "busiest places are always the safest!"

We set a date for the next evening. Helmut and I arrived somewhat early to get a table for four. Then we waited and hoped that the restaurant would not become overly crowded so we might have to share the other two seats before *Joe* and *Jenny* showed up. But we were lucky.

When they arrived, they sat down at a table on the opposite side, but in such a way that we could see them. We drank our glasses of wine and chatted as best we could, considering the loud music. Suddenly, Helmut nudged me, raised his arm, and waved. "Hello," he said, "*Joe* and his girlfriend are sitting over there!" *Joe* had also spotted us and waved back.

"Why don't you ask him to come to our table?" I proposed.

"As you wish."

Helmut stood up and walked over to them. *Joe* and *Jenny* seemed to hesitate a moment, but then they stood up and returned with Helmut. I was introduced to *Jenny*, and we put her between Helmut and me. She was very reserved and did not take any particular note of me. She made an intelligent impression. She was no great beauty, but she was quite sympathetic, a little wallflower, about thirty, unmarried, without particular sex appeal but obviously also still looking for a man. Short, blonde, neat. Inconspicuous.

We spoke in French, although my three partners knew German better than I knew French. We ordered our meal, and then I asked *Jenny* to dance. After a couple of dances, I asked her, "Do you work in an office?"

"Don't be so nosy." She smiled. "But I will tell you. I work in the American Consulate General."

"How interesting," I said. "What do you do there?"

I stopped dancing a waltz and now moved slowly, following the rhythm of the music. I did not want to miss a single word. "Passports and shipping documents," she replied.

"Passports?" I asked happily. "Could you get me a passport so that I can get out of Germany? I don't particularly like it there anymore."

She looked me square in the face and chuckled, but her eyes did not match her expression. "You can get what you want," she said.

Then we spoke about something else, and after another two dances, I took my leave of her and agreed to meet her the next evening at *Joe's*. *Jenny* was a clear case as far as I was concerned. She was clever and intelligent, and she was ready to collaborate.

When we met at *Joe's*, *Jenny* laughed and quipped that the four of us certainly put on a good show last night. "You know, I like Germans better than Walloons and French," she said. "And," she added, turning directly to me, "I knew that you were just kidding when you told me that you wanted a passport for yourself. But I wasn't kidding when I replied. I meant it. I can get you all kinds of passports that you might want, and perhaps other things, too."

Jenny told me that occasionally she could take blank passports with the required stamps. Moreover, she was also able to procure classified regulations on passport control and shipments. On top of that, she had access to a type of situation report that was published weekly and was intended strictly for official use. Similarly, she had access to investigation sheets and could also procure facsimiles of signatures of various officials.

That was far more than I had anticipated. Of course, I could hardly expect her to provide downright secret reports, apart, perhaps, from information that might indicate a rupture of United States and German relations. But she could supply material that would be of inestimable value for the passport center of Intelligence in Berlin.

But the most important matters concerned actual passports. For "Barbarossa," the red-haired doctor of chemistry and student adviser, who was a genius at manufacturing forged papers, this was a welcome bonus. It was especially difficult for him to get his hands on original passports that only needed a change of number or a signature. And he and his coworkers could sleep considerably better, knowing they were carefully briefed on the latest passport regulations of other countries so that the passports they had to keep manufacturing for various agents would meet all requirements down to the smallest detail and would withstand the severest scrutiny. I left Antwerp with the satisfying perception that I had made a good catch. That same night I returned to Germany, and by noon the next day, I was again sitting at my desk in Hamburg.

As political tensions escalated, such trips to Holland and Belgium became increasingly unpleasant. In both countries, not just their own intelligence services, but also the French Deuxième Bureau were extremely active. With the exception of the Flemings, the population was not exactly friendly toward Germans. In Switzerland, the Deuxième Bureau was a forceful presence in all French-speaking parts of the country. German influence prevailed in the Balkans. Italy was allied with Germany.

Spain and Portugal were pro-German, although the English influence in Portugal was very prominent due to strong, active economic ties. I always felt reassured whenever I was able to travel in one of the friendly countries.

That same night, I dictated necessary notes vis-à-vis *Jenny* and was happy to have this bothersome job behind me.

My next trip was to take me again to Holland, and from there once again to Antwerp and then on to Budapest and Athens. *Jenny* worked for us with great success until 1941, when the United States entered the war against Germany and the consulate general was closed.

14

Lily Stein

For my various meetings in Belgium and Holland, I needed some sort of private quarters. When I talked to Dierks about this, he said, "Please don't do that at the moment. That might arouse attention, because the authorities there are becoming increasingly suspicious of the Germans. I have a suitable address I can make available to you."

Two years earlier, when Dierks had had frequent business trips to The Hague, he had met a girl in Scheveningen. He had been struck by her athletic freshness and her long blonde hair, and he had sat down on the beach next to her. He was quite taken by her friendly and straightforward manner, but above all, he was pleased she did not try to flirt with him.

When he addressed her in Dutch, she unhesitatingly replied in perfect German. His accent had betrayed him. Being an old Intelligence type, his ears perked up. Might this accidental meeting have been arranged by some foreign intelligence service? But he became quickly aware that the pretty blonde was quite harmless. Her parents had emigrated from Germany to Holland when she was still an infant. She was salaried in some office; she was single and worked in The Hague. Her name was Hertha.

Dierks was romantically interested in Hertha; she was tall, good-looking, with a good shape, oval face, hazelnut eyes—almost beautiful. At the same time, however, he also considered the possibility of getting her to work for him on an official basis. In the evening, they went dancing, and he acted like a charming cavalier. He found it difficult not to take her back to his room, but if he wanted her to work for him, he could not risk any intimacies.

On this score, everyone surely has his own problems. Many women with whom we associated were attractive. Many were also eager to establish very close contacts. I tried to shield myself against that. That meant forbearance when it came to drinking, but often forced rejection as well. It was always the safest to be polite, friendly, and gallant, and stop at the right moment.

Dierks stuck to that rule in dealing with Hertha—to his own and, I believe, also the girl's regret, because I had the feeling she really liked him very much.

Hertha began to work for Dierks in the autumn. After some interval, he had found a suitable apartment in The Hague, which he rented for her. It was a three-room apartment on the ground floor so he would not have to run into too many tenants. It was somewhat removed from the main traffic artery, so that an agent who was led there alone in darkness could not easily find it again. It was located in an area that was not too poor and not too rich, but was, rather, an international center where a foreigner would not arouse particular attention.

No agent was ever given that address.

When I visited her for the first time, *Blonde Hertha*, as we called her, welcomed me like an old acquaintance. A room in the apartment was reserved for us. Dierks used it for meetings with agents with whom he did not want to be seen in public. I did exactly the same.

I also stayed with the girl several times. It was always a relief after the many hotels. She was an accomplished housewife and an excellent cook. She never asked any questions. Since she was obviously in love with Dierks, he always made certain he was accompanied by someone else, to prevent succumbing to temptation. That dangerous emotion did not apply to me. *Blonde Hertha* and I became good friends.

One evening, I had taken Witzke along to *Blonde Hertha*'s. For the first time, she seemed to be nervous as she looked at me, but after Witzke left, she calmed down. She was afraid of speaking openly in front of him. She said she had a date with a young Dutch friend who had invited her to dance, and she did not want to disappoint him.

I smiled understandingly and said, "You know, if it won't embarrass him when he sees me here, you can tell him that I'm your uncle. I'm old enough for that. Or is the circumstance not worth it?"

"I don't want to disappoint him," she said earnestly. "He's a sergeant in the Dutch Luchtvaartafdeling [aviation department], and this is the only evening he's free this month."

"Bingo," I thought and stopped smoking. "Just how well do you know this fellow?" I asked earnestly. "What do you know about him, and above all, what does he know about you? Don't forget that Dierks trusts you blindly, and so do I."

"That's the trouble," she complained. "I'm sure he's sincere with me. I believe he really loves me."

"And do you also love him?" I asked cautiously. I would certainly understand if she were to drop Dierks. He had let her know clearly that he did not want a love affair.

"I don't really know," she said hesitantly, and looked at me with questioning eyes. "He's nice and decent, but I believe he's too young for me."

"Does he know you were born in Germany?"

"Yes, of course. I told him that on the first day, but that doesn't bother him."

"Well," I encouraged her and stood up, "let him come. Sooner or later, he's bound to meet one of us. I am twenty years older than you, so he will not be jealous. Jealousy is always dangerous, and he could certainly believe that I'm your uncle from Germany. So get yourself all prettied up, and then we'll take a close look at him."

Blonde Hertha was visibly relieved. She ran into her room to change, and I sat down in my chair and poured myself an Oude Klare. My motto in such cases was one I had first learned from General Nolan in America, "Don't cross the bridge before you get to it." There was no need for unnecessary nervousness. But a "sergeant in the Dutch aviation department" had aroused my curiosity and had awakened my hunting fever.

Punctually, at 2000 hours, a tall, blond, young fellow about twenty years old turned up. He had a fresh, open face, and he had trouble concealing his disappointment when he saw a strange man in his girlfriend's apartment. I introduced myself as Hertha's uncle, *Dr. Weber,* and shook hands with him. "Now, get your coat," I told Hertha. "Don't mind me. I will accompany you for a short way, and then I'll go to my hotel!"

We chatted along the way about all sorts of things, and in passing, I remarked I had also been in the Luftwaffe during World War I. That, of course, was not quite true, but at any rate, I had been on some reconnaissance flights as an infantryman, so I was able to participate in the conversation. The young man was enthusiastic and, without being asked, told us everything he knew and possibly even more than he should have. I limited my remarks. As we arrived at the Korte Vorhout, where I had to turn off to get to the Hotel des Indes, I took my leave and admonished the young fellow not to bore the girl with too many official subjects.

The next day, *Blonde Hertha* awaited me with mixed feelings. When I assured her that her friend had made a good impression on me, she felt greatly relieved. I found myself in a rather tricky situation. On the one hand, I could trust the girl would not put us at risk, yet on the other hand I needed her to win the trust of the young man. This offered some suitable opportunities. I had to talk to her openly.

"I'd like to get to know your friend better," I said. "You know we're not particularly interested in Dutch aviation, but your friend will certainly hear all sorts of things about the Royal Air Force, and that interests us very much. What is his attitude toward Germany?"

"Because he loves me, he's naturally not anti," she said. "Of course, he doesn't like Hitler, but he sympathizes with Hitler's fight against Bolshevism. As far as England goes, he has neither friendly nor hostile feelings."

"Then you pay close attention," I told her, "to what he says about his British comrades, and the next time we all have a cup of coffee together, we'll talk about communism. After that everything else will fall into place."

During the next several months we were often together. The young fellow was a real patriot, and I carefully avoided asking him direct questions about Dutch aviation. He told me some details about airfields, but I merely made a mental note without asking any further questions, and later I related what I had heard.

I was primarily interested in the possibility of his collaboration against Britain. On that score, I asked open questions. One day, he told me about a relative in the RAF who had told him everything about the airfields in Wales, including the number and types of aircraft, and the armament of two bomber groups that were stationed there. Those were the kind of reports I needed.

During one of the next visits, I asked the young sergeant point-blank whether he would fight against the British as well as Germany if one day airborne units were to attack his airfield. I added that in Germany, under certain circumstances, one could absolutely count on it. If this should happen, then he should in any case inform Hertha in a timely manner. The young fellow thought that this was quite natural.

Blonde Hertha was given the order to pass such a report directly to Dierks's friend in Hilversum and to inform him she was "expecting a visit from *Willy.*" That meant an anticipated approach by the RAF! *Blonde Hertha* did not know that a secret transmitter was located in Hilversum. Basically, that's all I wanted. In this way, we would get advance notice of English flights into Holland before the public learned about it. At least this was an additional alert.

After my return to Hamburg, I received a call from one of our staff members who asked me to meet a young Jewess who wanted to immigrate to the United States. He wanted to know if I could use her. That was, under prevailing conditions, a rather uncomfortable situation for me. But I agreed and met Lily Stein in a café. She made a good impression on me. She was tall, pretty, and an absolute lady. She had worked as a model. Born in Austria, she wanted to leave Austria and Germany. I could well understand that. Because she realized this would not be simple, she believed it would be easier for me to assist her if she offered to work for us in America.

I did not really know whether and how I should do that. Finally, however, I thought I could still use a good cover address, and when I offered her that opportunity, she was ready to accept. On that basis, we were in a position to get her an exit visa for the United States. Lily first worked in New York as a fashion model and became the girlfriend of a Washington diplomat. She moved into an elegant apartment on 79th Street East and traveled often back and forth between New York City and Washington. In New York, she established a type of salon in her apartment and actually became a relay station, very much like *Blonde Hertha* in The Hague.

At that time, I met yet another young lady through *Johnny*. She was an employee in the Hotel Moltke, where he had met her. He thought perhaps we could use her as an informant. She spoke fluent English and had the type of personality that would encourage hotel guests to voluntarily divulge their life stories.

When I told *Johnny* I would like to take Miss *Busch* along to the meeting, he became somewhat embarrassed. Perhaps he thought the girl would be jealous. We met in a pub where we left Miss *Busch* at the bar. She was to chat with the barmaid, whom we knew, in order to learn something about the other girl. *Johnny* had fun telling the barmaid that Miss *Busch* was an American actress who did not understand German.

Meanwhile, *Johnny* took me to meet the girl from the Hotel Moltke. She made a respectable impression, and I was astonished the Gestapo had not yet engaged her. I could not use her for our purpose, but the Immigration Control Police picked her up. For a moment, I had the idea that *Johnny* perhaps knew her more intimately, but he never saw her again, and neither did I.

In the meantime, Miss *Busch* and I had become closer. At Christmas in 1938, we became engaged, and were married in March of the following year. When I told Dierks the news, he looked at me reproachfully and said, "You mustn't do that to her. Don't you know her father was killed in action during the last war? You shouldn't get married now that a new war is imminent."

15

Ein Glas Bier

The tensions in Europe increased, and anyone who did not wander through the world with his eyes closed knew for certain a war was in the offing. Naturally, we would be the first to notice. Our assignments from Berlin were increasingly focused on the exploration of purely military secrets. Apprehensively, we realized more clearly day by day how difficult it would become to maintain contact with our agents.

After the war broke out, our path would be restricted to travel via neutral countries. Direct contact would be limited to secret transmitters. I had asked *Johnny* quite some time ago whether he might be able to handle a secret transmitter, which, of course, should be used only in case of extreme necessity, that is to say, in wartime. Being an electrical engineer, he did not hesitate long and agreed. I immediately established the appropriate connection with Berlin.

At that time, we did not yet have a secret radio station in Hamburg. The nearest was in Stettin and was under the leadership of Lieutenant Colonel Werner Trautmann. I went to Stettin and talked to him about the possibility of training *Johnny*, and I asked him whether he personally could do the job.

Trautmann arrived in Hamburg in the autumn of 1938. Together with *Johnny*, initial preparations were made in the residence of Miss *Busch*'s grandmother. *Johnny* had used this cover address previously for meetings that required written documentation.

Johnny's actual training was to take place in Hamburg during the spring and summer of 1939. By then, Trautmann would be settled in and ready to create and direct a new radio station. In time, it would become the largest and most successful classified radio transmitter station of the entire Abwehr, next to Berlin's. It was established on an old baronial estate in Wohldorf near Hamburg. The procurement of secret transmitters lightened the load for everyone.

I had formally reported my engagement to Miss von Klitzing, alias Miss *Busch*, and after my marriage was approved, I had submitted a request for a vacation for a honeymoon in April. In February, I was told I could not get a vacation in April. I suggested it be moved up to early March. That was the first time political events interfered in my private life.

Conditions in Czechoslovakia continued to escalate, and we were faced with the fateful question of whether England and France would stand aside if Ger-

Herbert Wichmann and Nikolaus Ritter (right), 1972, in front of the World War II radio transmission center. Originally published in *Hamburger Abendblatt,* December 1972, pages 9 and 10.

many were to act, as was anticipated. I had given up any hope for a honeymoon any time soon. But contrary to expectations, once again everything went well. On March 15, the German troops marched into Prague, and we knew Britain and France would do nothing.

On March 18, we would be able to begin our trip. We had a delayed stay in Berlin. Then suddenly I heard my name being called at the platform. It was Major Friedrich Brasser (aka Friedrich Busch), who at that time was the department head of I Air in Berlin. He greeted me with a smile. "I wanted to personally wish you every happiness," he said cordially, "and bon voyage and a trouble-free vacation." With that, he handed my wife a big box of chocolates. As we boarded the train, I finally began to realize there would be no further obstacles to our trip.

In the interim, my wife had resigned from her job, but she frequently still accompanied me to particular meetings, and on occasion traveled with me. A married couple attracted less attention than a gentleman traveling alone.

When *Johnny* came to Hamburg in the summer for training with the secret transmitter, he brought along his new girlfriend, Lily. My wife accompanied her during that time. Lily was blonde, like *Johnny*'s wife, but that ended the resemblance. While his wife was short, calm, and neat, Lily was tall and robust, a whole head taller and quite a few years younger than *Johnny*. She was light-hearted, intelligent, with a good deal of natural sex appeal. *Johnny* was visibly in love with her.

Trautmann and his assistant Wein had undertaken *Johnny*'s training, which consisted primarily of sending radio messages, learning the comprehensive skills to construct a radio device independently, and being able to identify secure hiding places. His training was completed in July, and he received the radio in August 1939. It was brought to Southampton on a fishing boat, and it was placed in the baggage check room at the railroad station. They sent *Johnny* the baggage claim check.

In the meantime, *Johnny* had been assigned his own special code, which Berlin had developed for his apparatus. He based it on a book code. Every important agent had his own book, usually a well-known novel that would fit into any home library, that he could easily take along on his travels without arousing attention. The code reflected the broadcast day and, therefore, changed daily. *Johnny*'s book was the bestseller of that time, *Oil for the Lamps of China* by Alice Hobart.

The transmitter was strictly for use under very special circumstances. It was not to be used for general reports. I continued to receive *Johnny*'s reports exclusively through personal meetings in Holland or Belgium.

After *Johnny* had assembled his unit, we scheduled the first test on a designated day. At the appointed hour, Trautmann and his men sat pensively around the receiver in Wohldorf. Trautmann's assistant, Wein, operated the unit himself. On the precise second, Wein excitedly raised his hand and called out, "Here it comes!" Wein answered with the agreed-upon call signal and entered the transmission in a log. Trautmann and the others eagerly bent over him as he decoded the message. Suddenly, there was a wave of Homeric laughter. *Johnny*'s first message read as follows: "*Ein Glas Bier*"!

"A glass of beer" were the only German words *Johnny* had learned. Trautmann, Wein, and I had emptied many a glass with *Johnny* on the Reeperbahn and in the Hofbräuhaus; we had heard those words often and were amused.

We took precautions against any emergencies, and the connection was successful. We anticipated only too well that the emergency would soon occur. Just as we intensified our work on the outside, our counterpart did exactly the same in England. In July, while *Johnny* was still training, quite unexpectedly my old friend Captain Simon turned up, calm and self-assured, as if the nine months that had passed in the meantime never happened. My wife and I invited him to dinner and listened eagerly as he briefed us on the past nine months of his life, including his report pertaining to the "hospitality" of the English.

Simon had discovered details about a large airfield under construction during his trip through Kent. He had taken a room in a small boardinghouse, but both the owner and he forgot to fill out the necessary registration form. When he returned home on the evening of the third day, the police were waiting for him. They charged him with failure to fill out the police registration form and arrested him because he was a foreigner.

That was hardly a good reason for his arrest, and Simon wondered what might be behind this. He had the feeling that this time he had been under observation from the very moment he returned to England and had not been let out of their sight. On the day prior to his arrest, he had met a Welshman who, like many of his compatriots, was at war with the British government. The Welshman had stated he was a fascist. Simon had listened to him carefully, and after he made sure the man was genuine, he had wondered whether he should not try to get him to work for him. But Simon had not hinted anything to him to that effect during their first meeting. Instead, he had scheduled a meeting with him for the next day.

In his cell, he thought at length and initially suspected the Welshman had betrayed him to the police, but he had to discard that idea because he was absolutely sure he had not told that fellow anything that could arouse suspicion.

Simon assumed he would be released with a fine, but when he faced the judge two days later, he was sentenced to three months in prison for violation of the registration regulations since he was a foreigner. When he heard this unusually harsh sentence, he knew the Welshman could not have had anything to do with his arrest.

One of the officers who interrogated Simon was Lieutenant Colonel William Edward Hinchley-Cooke of British MI5. When Simon related how unpleasant that fellow Hinchley-Cooke was, the name somehow triggered my memory, although at that time I had no clue that one day I would face this same man during an interrogation.

Lieutenant Colonel Hinchley-Cooke had Simon's notebook and asked him about the undecipherable entries therein. But Simon was too smart for him, and he was finally able to convince Hinchley-Cooke the entries were completely harmless.

The British Security Service had not been able to implicate Simon. Nevertheless, he had to serve his three months in prison because his registration in the boardinghouse had not been reported. In prison, Simon told us with a smirk, he became an expert at making straw mattresses, and he became particularly friendly with one of the guards. He was a model prisoner, and when he was discharged, he was astonished to receive his civilian clothing back in excellent condition, along with all of his money and the notebook with the mysterious entries.

Indeed, the entries contained the answers that he had been ordered to provide. In spite of the long interval, quite a bit of the data was still very important for us.

After this failed excursion, England was taboo for Simon, but I kept him on the waiting list with pay. When in April 1940 we had not yet heard anything new from him, the Navy asked me to "loan" Simon to them.

Simon was not particularly happy about that, and neither was I, but we needed a good man for Ireland. So, one day Simon embarked on a German submarine that took him from Wilhelmshaven, all around Scotland, all the way into Dingle Bay in southern Ireland. Sometime later, we heard that he had been nabbed in a little town called Tralee shortly after landing. He had been taken to court in Dublin and sentenced to prison. That time, he could not wiggle out again.

That was the end of his work for us; and for me, it meant the loss of an ideal agent. Simon had accomplished all of his assignments with prudence, élan, and courage. For me, he was the perfect, classic secret agent, the deliberate, intelligent, and reliable spy, the kind every intelligence officer dreams about.

In the same summer that Simon returned from England, the history of one of our most remarkable and beautiful lady agents, who called herself Vera von Schalburg, began for all of us, both personally and officially. It was no accident she belonged to Dierks.

One morning, Dierks entered my office and stuck a $100 bill under my nose. "Do you think this is genuine?" he asked.

I took a close look at it and said, "As far as I can tell, yes! But you don't run into many $100 bills in the United States. Even $50 bills are often difficult to change."

"Hm . . .," Dierks said and rubbed the note back and forth between thumb and index finger. "Then they will not be much use for us if they are used so rarely in everyday transactions. Well, I'll have to determine first of all whether they can make smaller bills!"

"Who is 'they'?"

"A gang of forgers," Dierks replied. "It is said that they are in touch with the Italian Mafia. I don't know; I got this one from my friend Theodore Drüke in Brussels."

Drüke and Dierks had been friends for many years. Dierks met him during one of his longer stays in Belgium. Ever since Dierks had joined the Abwehr,

Drüke had worked for him. He had become a successful investigator and had established contacts with good agents for Dierks. He often provided important information.

Drüke himself was a somewhat unusual personality. He was a tall, good-looking, stately man in his middle thirties, energetic, open, and self-assured. He had a penchant for rather dubious places and shady characters, although that literally did not fit with his personality. He had all sorts of possible connections with the underworld, something that could be of critical importance to Dierks. If, in a certain case, an informant could not get his hands on particular secret service regulations, then Drüke found a professional thief who did the job.

I was not surprised the forged bill came from Drüke. I took it to the bank, and after a very careful examination, they were ready to change it for me. Instead, however, I gave it to one of the bank managers I happened to know and told him the whole story. He was astonished by the quality of the forgery. From there, we sent the bill to the Reichsbank in Berlin, where the forgery was finally confirmed. It was so outstandingly brilliant that the people at Central in the Abwehr began to wonder whether forged money might not be useful in the Abwehr. We bought a couple of notes from the forgers and asked whether they could also print smaller bills for us; but that turned out to be so expensive that we dropped the idea. At any rate, the contact was maintained, and from there we moved to procure notes for our agents in other countries.

During the negotiations with the forgers in Brussels, Drüke introduced Vera to Dierks. There was hardly a man who was not swept off his feet upon meeting Vera von Schalburg. When I later worked directly together with her, I never met her alone, and I urged my fellow workers to use the same precaution.

The daughter of a White Russian aristocrat, Vera had been born in Riga. Her father, a rear admiral in the Tsarist Navy, had been murdered during the Russian Revolution of 1917.

After an adventurous escape, her mother managed to get to Denmark with Vera and her brother. The children were raised under a simple and strict regimen and received an outstanding education in school. They were fluent in Russian, German, and French. During her time in boarding school, Vera fell in love with an older Frenchman, and when her mother didn't want to tolerate their relationship anymore, Vera left home immediately and went with him to Paris. As her mother had anticipated, Vera's lover soon left her in the lurch. She became a dancer in a nightclub and fell for a French colleague, who exploited her shamelessly. When she wanted to leave him, he slashed her with his knife, inflicting a serious wound. That is when Drüke met her and promptly fell in love with her.

But for Vera, Drüke was just a caring guardian. They became good friends, and Vera simply let him protect her. In the long run, he could not care for her indefinitely, but he conceived the idea that Vera might be useful to Dierks. He put her up in a boardinghouse in Brussels and maintained her there until Dierks was able to meet her.

Despite her dubious love affairs, beautiful Vera was an aristocrat from head to toe. She was medium-tall, had dark hair, blue eyes, and a strikingly soft, olive-colored skin. She had a perfect shape and pretty legs, and she usually wore a sports jacket with a wide belt and a cap. When Dierks met Vera, he lost all his inborn self-control. Here was a woman whom he simply had to conquer in spite of all official considerations. Obviously, the mutual attraction between the two was great, but perhaps even somewhat greater on Vera's side. While Dierks was in love with her, he became her great love.

Due to his personal affection for her, Dierks initially hesitated to use her for active duty in the Abwehr, but her beauty, her intellect, her manners, and her linguistic skills made her the center of any social group. Such rare talents must not be left unused. He briefed her well on all contingencies, including which questions she should ask, and saw to it that she appeared in Brussels, Paris, and London and was able to circulate incognito as a communist in underworld social circles. In this way, he obtained a great deal of interesting information from all nations about amorous relationships of dignitaries and the military.

But the more imminent the war, the more such sources ran dry, and Dierks decided to take Vera with him to Hamburg. He moved her into a boarding-house in Papenhuderstrasse and saw her as often as his duty permitted. Vera was happy and satisfied so long as Dierks was nearby. But his work took up most of his time, and he was not able to take care of her as much as she might have wished. Several times, he tried to persuade her to return to her mother and her brother, who was the commander of a Danish SS volunteer unit.

Dierks had established contact with her brother without Vera knowing any-thing about it, and one day, the brother also contacted me and fervently asked us to get Vera to return to her family. Although her brother personally was an active supporter of Germany's fight against Bolshevism, he decidedly objected to the idea of Vera working for the Abwehr and urged us to drop her; but Vera would have none of it. She refused to leave Hamburg, or Dierks, and categor-ically rejected the opportunity of working in the Brussels Intelligence Station, which Dierks had advocated.

Dierks loved Vera in his own way, but she was not the right woman for him—if there is such a woman at all. He decided to separate from her. But in spite of all his vast experience, he did not take into account the inscrutably sen-sitive emotions of a woman who is truly in love.

He told her a nice, elaborate story, saying that he was going to be transferred to Poland and would not be able to see her for a long time, so she had to make plans now to leave Hamburg. Vera listened to him silently until he had finished with his fairy tale and let him go with a seemingly understanding smile. She wanted to think about it.

Immediately afterward, Dierks dropped in on me and told me the whole story. He felt terribly guilty. He described to me how disappointed Vera looked when they said good-bye to each other; then, he stopped in midsentence, jumped up, took his hat off the hook, and, without any further ado, rushed out of the place where we were meeting.

When he rang the doorbell at Vera's boardinghouse, the hostess opened the door. Without saying a word, he pushed her aside and tore open the door to Vera's room. He had a premonition, and he was not wrong. Vera was lying on the sofa, her eyes closed, unconscious. He failed to resuscitate her. She had taken an overdose of sleeping tablets. The doctor ordered her to be taken to a hospital, but Dierks would not have any of that. The doctor had to approve his request for outpatient treatment, on the condition Vera would not be left alone for a single moment.

For days on end, Vera lay unconscious. When she awoke, her first call was for Dierks. It was many weeks before she was somewhat back to normal. When she returned from a brief stay at a rest home, she seemed outwardly healthy, but there had been a big change in her. She had obviously renounced her love. Without further explanations, she asked Dierks to place her as an agent in some enemy country.

Dierks used all his art of persuasion to get her to drop the idea, but Vera stuck with it. When he realized his pleading was in vain, he came to me and asked me to send her to England.

At first, I advised him against the idea. At that particular moment, I did not see any opportunity for Vera over there. But when I realized that my attempt was useless, I began to look seriously into the matter. I recalled the lively little Duchess of Château-Thierry. So far, my contacts with her had not produced any results. She was living in London at the time. She was not merely a socialite, but also an adventuress. It would be easy for her to open a salon in some house in London where officers and government officials would drop in. A woman with Vera's beauty and attractiveness would be an ideal hostess for those circles.

Previously, the duchess and I had discussed the possibility of establishing a salon in her home as a way to receive messages. I had rejected that idea for various reasons. Something made me feel uncertain, but I was never able to figure out what the issue really was. I could not imagine her as a British female agent. After all, she was always short of money, but on the other hand, she was a confidante of *Lady May's*. Nevertheless, I had so far always hesitated.

Now, everything came back into focus. Perhaps, Vera might be suitable for organizing a salon. That undertaking should actually be successful, considering the social connections the duchess had and the irresistible force of attraction Vera radiated.

In the summer of 1939, I invited the duchess to come to Hamburg. I told her I had thought about the possibility of establishing a salon once again, and I told her all about Vera.

"That is a grandiose idea," she replied, her eyes flashing. "To be successful, a salon has to have a beautiful woman. I have to see her first."

"I'll take care of that," I promised her. "You can then have a look before you make your decision."

I arranged with Dierks that my wife and I would invite the duchess for coffee in the Alsterpavillon, and Dierks was supposed to join us there with Vera. That was ideal scenery for a meeting between two genteel lady spies. The Alsterpavillon had been built by the city of Hamburg on the occasion of the first visit of Kaiser Wilhelm II. There was a large café along the Binnenalster, with a large cupola, plush furniture, heavy carpets, and gold decorations. The Alsterpavillon, which was destroyed by bombs during the war, was the most luxurious café in Hamburg. A wonderful orchestra always performed there, and you could enjoy a magnificent view of the Alster. It was a preferred gathering place for lunch or dinner or tea.

We were drinking our coffee with the duchess when we spotted Dierks and Vera approaching. I alerted the duchess to the two, and as they passed our table, she was able to take a close look at Vera. She seemed enthusiastic. "That's exactly the kind of girl I could use," she said.

Then we began plotting how we could employ Vera in England.

16

Count László Almásy

The growing conviction that America would not fight in a war against Bolshevism, but rather against Germany, required reorganizing the American sector of the Abwehr. In 1939, it was finally decided to carry out the reorganization without the consent of the Foreign Office. The Foreign Office avoided anything that might annoy the United States. Ribbentrop was of the personal opinion that under no circumstances should it become public knowledge that the Abwehr was reinforcing its activities in the United States.

Indeed, it was too late anyway, since building up a larger organization is very time-consuming. In case of war, all German citizens would have to be deleted from our agent lists, because they would automatically come under rigorous scrutiny. As for the neutrals, their observations would be focused on monitoring the degree of their country's neutrality. All that would be left for the Abwehr were members of diplomatic services or other foreign missions. The time for recruiting them was too short. A so-called fifth column would have been a big help, but nothing like that existed.

While we were contemplating how we could strengthen our presence in the United States, I was summoned to Berlin and asked if I would be willing to return to the United States and, in the event of war, direct the organization. I was not entirely comfortable with the idea, but when I discussed it with my wife, and she offered to come with me, I decided to commit. Together, we learned how to use radio sets and everything connected with secret transmitters; we informed ourselves about the latest achievements in microphotography and secret codes. A sum of $100,000 was made available to us. Then I was informed I would have to resign from my official duties the moment I left Germany. I had a long, serious talk about this with Lieutenant Colonel Seber, the distinguished gentleman with the monocle who, at the start of my career in the Abwehr, had thought I should go through regular training before I began duty in Hamburg. He urgently advised me against resigning my current assignment, and I decided to reject the appointment. The mission was withdrawn.

When I gave up the idea of returning to the United States, I began scouting around for anyone who could be trained as an agent with a secret transmitter. This was communicated to all intelligence stations, and one day I received a note from a comrade in Münster saying he had someone who was a citizen of the United States and who was willing to take a secret transmitter back with him.

I went to Münster to take a personal look at the fellow. Since I had been assured this man had been checked out, I did not do my own review. He did not particularly impress me. He looked quite ordinary, was of average intelligence, and obviously came from modest means. He said he worked in America as a mechanic. He had been born in Germany; he had fought for Germany during World War I and had migrated to the United States in 1922, where he became an American citizen in 1936. He was a convicted felon and had changed his name. His mother, whom he was visiting at the time, was living in Cologne. The Gestapo had run across his criminal record and passed him on to the Abwehr.

The decisive point in this matter for me was the fact he was German born and had fought as a German soldier during the First World War. Since I had his personal data, I did not waste any time with any other questions but went straight to the point, "We are afraid that the United States might enter the war against us," I said. "We need information from there, and we can't get that except from someone who lives there and who is an American citizen. How long can you stay in Germany?"

"I really just wanted to stay here for two weeks," the man said. "If I'm to stay longer, I'd like to have my wife join me, but for that I lack the money and the visa."

"Money is the least of it," I said. "We can take care of that."

"But the authorities know how much foreign currency I have on me," he said thoughtfully. "In other words, they would notice it if I could suddenly pay $300 for my wife's round trip."

"We can take care of that," I promised him. "You need not worry about it."

But the man still did not seem satisfied. "I believe it would be best if I go to the American Consul in Cologne and tell them that I have an opportunity to receive more money for a longer stay in Germany, and in connection with that, I would ask them for a travel permit for my wife."

I did not see what business the consul had with money matters, but I let him proceed. I gave Sebold the order to report to me in Hamburg the moment his personal affairs had been settled. To him, I was *Dr. Renken*. Sebold turned up in Hamburg eight days later. I set him up in the Klopstock boardinghouse near the Alster, where we often billeted agents during their training. His cover name was *Tramp*, and his number was *3559*.

I personally oversaw *Tramp*'s training during the summer of 1939. Besides radio messaging, his education also extended to self-constructing a transmitter-receiver unit. He learned everything necessary about general espionage work to be able to serve as informant and contact man with our agents in the

United States. In case of war, *Tramp* would be their main link for the transmission of reports to us.

I had always refused to link several agents together because each individual is more secure on his own. In this case, however, we might be forced to hitch Tramp to other agents since it was quite unlikely that there would be enough time to place more than one unit in America. Nevertheless, in the beginning, I simply gave him Duquesne's address. We were not yet at war, and the others could wait until an emergency arose. After *Tramp*'s training was finished, we sent him and his equipment back into the United States via Genoa.

On September 1, 1939, we realized it was just a matter of a couple of days before Britain would declare war. We needed firsthand situation reports, and I asked my friend Röder whether he might be able to arrange some round-trip flights. Although he knew as well as I did how dangerous such trips were, Röder agreed without hesitation. We decided on a specific code that was adapted to the language of his line of business. He was to call me from London, and I would expect his call at a certain hour at his private home. I would answer like his authorization officer, ready to accept business orders.

That evening, I arrived early at Röder's home, nervous and expectant. It was a long, anxious wait. I was unable to sit still, and I walked up and down on the heavy carpet in the living room, unable to think of anything other than jumping to the telephone.

The phone rang twice. I snatched the receiver up, only to find that some private acquaintance had called. "No, Mr. Röder is not at home. He is outside of Hamburg." I responded quite mechanically, hoping the caller would hang up quickly. Röder's call from London might come through at any moment.

At 2030 hours, the scheduled time, nothing. At 2045 hours, nothing. The quiet was unbearable. The phone finally rang at 2100 hours. I picked up the receiver. He was half an hour late. "I'm sorry," said Röder. "I could not get through. All lines to Europe were blocked."

"Well, how do things look, Mr. Röder?" I asked.

"The business does not look so good," he answered. "The last order had to be canceled. You should get confirmation tomorrow or the day after. I spoke with many people, and everyone is nervous. Other than that, I have nothing at this moment."

"Thank you very much," I said. "When will you be back? Do you have any kind of instructions for me in the meantime?"

"No," he replied. "I hope to return tomorrow evening on the last flight. Please pick me up at the airport."

"Good," I said, but Röder had already hung up. Perhaps somebody cut our conversation off.

"Orders were canceled, and confirmation would follow tomorrow or the day after tomorrow"—that meant that a war declaration was expected within the next couple of days. I immediately passed the message on to Berlin. Most likely, they had already heard the news from other sources, but this was further, and reliable, confirmation.

When Röder returned the next evening, we immediately sat down together, and he reported. It was eerie to listen to accounts from the capital of a country that was just about to declare war. Röder said London was like a powder keg. Various ocean liners his business associates were supposed to sail on had already received the order not to leave their ports. Ships on the high seas heading for England were redirected to other ports. The airport at Northolt, which Röder knew well from his explorations, was full of military aircraft and was teeming with soldiers.

Röder was still dazed. What now? Of course, we knew of the desperate attempts that had been made in recent days by France, England, and Germany to prevent the worst. We had learned of the Swede, Dalerus, becoming involved as middleman. Röder had heard of a secret meeting among Sir Nevile Henderson, the British ambassador in Berlin, Neville Chamberlain, Great Britain's prime minister, and Lord Halifax, Britain's foreign secretary, and it sounded as if Henderson would this very night fly to meet the Führer with a message. We also knew from our own sources how serious the situation with Poland was. The Führer had risked much, and much had gone well. If England were now to go to war with us, with its entire worldwide empire, would that also end well? Röder was a farsighted man, and I had to share his fears. I could not now afford to think of America and of everything I had already conveyed to Captain Burghardt in 1937.

We looked at each other anxiously, and for the first time, we were beginning to have some quiet doubts, but we could not allow it to affect us. Our job was to make our arrangements in keeping with the facts.

When Britain declared war on Germany on September 3, my section was the only one in all of Intelligence I Air that had a secret transmitter in Britain. Because of the interruption of all normal communications facilities, *Johnny* was our single direct contact with England until we were able to slip other agents in by boat or airplane. After the outbreak of the war, *Johnny*'s transmitter was cleared for sending coded messages. His regular messages began in September 1939. Undoubtedly, his messages from 1937 to 1939 had been reliable and valuable, but they were not overwhelmingly significant. But now, after the outbreak of the war, *Johnny* brought information of inestimable value.

He reported the first classified information to Germany about radar stations and the exact locations of the four major radar stations on the Dover coast [see

Chain Home in Glossary]. *Johnny* detailed ship movements, concentrations of RAF aircraft in England and France, delivery of war material from the United States, the strengthening of coastal defenses, the use of balloon barriers, the assembly of merchant vessels, the location and camouflage of oil depots (recognition characteristics for air reconnaissance), and he sent us daily weather reports, frequently twice, in the morning and in the evening. *Johnny*'s reports were distinguished by their accuracy and detail, as well as their relevant confidential importance. He provided outstanding reference points for bombing targets. He assembled his messages himself and never trusted anyone else.

In February 1940, *Tramp* began to send his reports from the United States. They were nothing to get excited about, but they did, at any rate, contain enough information that the Luftwaffe General Staff and the Navy High Command graded the work of this agent as good.

At that time, Budapest was one of my most important rendezvous points for conferences with agents. Early in 1938, through a researcher in Budapest, I had met the dentist Schmidt-Gyula, a prosperous and influential man whom I could trust and whom I often visited. He, in turn, introduced me to a furniture manufacturer.

Since I needed an innocuous meeting place for agents outside of Germany, we came up with the idea to establish a company for the export of Hungarian furniture to Germany and other countries. Together with the Hamburg importer-exporter Relling, we organized a firm that engaged in regular business transactions. It was to become the center for our agents in the Balkans and in the Near East. Although the agents did not make any furniture, they were disguised as salesmen and representatives and, in this way, were able to move about freely. The firm soon became the center for all our work in the Balkans. Here we were able to receive mail from everywhere, and the "furniture" agents were able to come and go without arousing any suspicions. It became an efficient business—for furniture as well as for classified information.

There were not many such centers because my principle remained consistent—that agents should work alone. A secret is a secret only as long as just one man knows about it. I was always very worried whenever it became unavoidable to hitch agents together.

Throughout 1939, I was regularly in Budapest, almost once a month. It was a carefree city, where the fear of war never hung in the air, as it did in the cities of Holland and Belgium. The atmosphere was relaxed, and you could still find everything in Budapest that was nowhere else to be found in Europe. After war broke out, I was able to buy clothing for my wife in Budapest and a tailor-made suit and shirts for myself. The only problem was that, in Hungary, I traveled under the name of *Dr. Jansen,* and the tailor insisted on providing all shirts with my stitched monogram. When I came home, my wife had to tediously cut the threads out again.

During my stay in Budapest, I met Count László Almásy. He was of old Hungarian nobility and was a well-known expert on the desert. He had served in the Austrian Luftwaffe during the first war and continued as an aviator after the war. Along with many other members of his class, his family had lost their property after the war, and he now lived in an old city mansion that had formerly been owned by his family. He had become a land surveyor and, by invitation of the Egyptian government, had gone to Egypt to conduct land surveys in the desert. He had to leave Cairo when war broke out. When I met him, he lived on his memories and collections, so to speak.

I visited the count often when I was in Budapest, and we spent quite a few pleasant hours in his library, which was full of pictures, mementos, and weapons from Africa and Arabia. The count was a tall, slim, good-looking man with a finely chiseled aristocratic face and the nonchalant erect posture of a former cavalry officer, and besides, he was an amusing conversationalist. I enjoyed his company. One evening, he gave me a detailed account about some of his influential acquaintances in Cairo and about the great uncertainty of the British in their dealings with the Egyptians, particularly among the upper strata and among the officers.

The count was particularly fond of his friend, General El Masri Pasha [Aziz Ali al-Misri], who had been chief of staff of the Egyptian army and who recently had been maneuvered out of his position as a result of intrigues. He was in close contact with a group of revolutionary officers who had gathered around a young lieutenant-colonel by the name of Abdel Nasser. The general and his nationalist Egyptian friends were fervently hoping for a German victory because, as Almásy related to me, they were sure a German victory would signify liberation for Egypt from the British yoke.

While Almásy was pontificating about Egyptian circumstances in every minute detail, I conceived a fantastic idea. It was crazy, but it was possible. My heart began to beat faster. It was the most ambitious plan I'd had so far. I was thinking of what Almásy had often told me, "If you ever need to know anything about Africa that I can help you with, let me know. I know the land and the people like my vest pocket."

After Almásy had persuaded his friend, the former chief of the general staff, to stand firmly behind Germany, I could work with his confidants. The boldness of such an idea took my breath away. That could influence the war in Egypt in our favor. "Could this man, this general, perhaps be influenced to work with us against the British?" I asked Almásy.

Nikolaus Ritter making plans with Laszlo Almásy to airlift El Masri Pasha out of Cairo. From the editor's private collection.

He did not seem in the least astonished by my crazy proposal. "Of course, he could do it," he said. "I'm even sure that he would do it. I have often thought along the same lines." He smiled indulgently. "If you had not beaten me to it, you would have gotten the same proposal from me. Before I met you, I didn't have the right connection to present this idea to anyone."

And so, our carefully crafted plan began to take on shape. We had to smuggle the general—or the Pasha, as we called him from then on—out of Egypt right under the noses of the British. We had to move him to Berlin, where he could negotiate with our general staff and afterward try to persuade Egyptian revolutionaries to switch to the German side.

The execution of such a plan called for much detailed work, but it was useless to think about that before we had cleared the basic plan with Canaris. When I met with my group leader in Berlin regarding this issue, Canaris looked at me pityingly as if he wanted to say, "My dear Ritter, are you normal?"

"That's a crazy idea," he finally said. "Just forget it!"

There was no use in pressing the matter, especially since I was not quite sure about it either, although, on the other hand, I was totally infatuated by the idea. So, I had to file the plan *ad acta* for a while, but Canaris would not have been Canaris if he had allowed such an enticing project to die. Four weeks later, I received a message from Berlin that Canaris was again looking into the matter. He had given orders to pursue it further and to provide exact details within one month.

The next day, I was back in Budapest and spoke with Almásy. He was absolutely sure of himself—although I was certain his personal wish to return to Egypt contributed to his confidence. He had already begun to outline the technical details of this adventurous undertaking. It would hardly have been proper to announce our arrival in Cairo on the radio and to inform the Pasha we were waiting for him at the Heliopolis Airport. After all, it was war in Africa, and there were no direct connections. Besides, it was a fact that the Pasha was monitored under strict British control. We needed a middleman. Again, it was Almásy who knew the right fellow, but it would be my task to persuade him to go along with our undertaking.

The new Hungarian ambassador to Egypt happened to be in Budapest to receive instructions from his government, and Almásy arranged a meeting with him for me. We met in his luxurious Budapest apartment. The ambassador was a diplomat of the old school, well-bred, a scientist and researcher, with a good portion of adventurism. Like all educated Hungarians, he spoke fluent German. It soon became evident he was a fervent admirer of Germany, and that made my task considerably easier. I quickly gained his confidence, and before my visit was over, he promised to take one of our secret transmitters with him to Egypt. That was more than I had dared to hope. I immediately asked my associate, Trautmann, to come to Budapest right away in order to discuss the necessary details with the ambassador and his radio operator.

With a transmitter in Cairo and transmitters to come in Derna and Taormina, and then the other two intelligence stations in Athens and Ankara, our ring around the Mediterranean would be closed. Along with general intelligence information, the daily weather reports, which had ceased after the war started and which were currently being radioed by our secret transmitters, were of utmost importance for the mission of our Luftwaffe in the Mediterranean. Now, we had an uninterrupted chain of weather reports that could guide the planning staff in its operations. So far, the inability to receive regular radio reports had presented us with many headaches.

If that transmitter in Cairo would work reliably, then our African enterprise could already be termed a success and was well worth the trouble. When I was able to report this accomplishment to Canaris, he ordered me to launch the entire project.

I asked Almásy to come to Hamburg to meet all relevant authorities in order to procure the necessary charts, compasses, and whatever else was needed in terms of desert gear and, under his direction, to build specially designed handcarts that would be suitable for transport in the desert. We had to have the right radio operators, and we insisted they be volunteers. It was not difficult to find them among our splendid young men whom Trautmann had lined up in Wohldorf.

While we rapidly progressed with our plans, the Hungarian ambassador in Cairo had assumed his post and moved into his quarters. Soon thereafter, he let us know everything was ready. He had established contact with the Pasha, and he now awaited our further instructions.

17

Sabotage across Borders

At the same time as the plans for Africa were being drafted, temporarily postponed, and finally picked up again, I had to make other trips to other less friendly cities than Budapest. During one particularly frustrating trip, I had to relinquish one of my agents to Captain Witzke of Abwehr II for sabotage.

Originally, I had met the agent through Röder, one of my friends. The man, whom we gave the number *3115,* was an American of Boer origin. He'd had some nasty experiences as a prisoner in a British concentration camp in Africa before relatives were able to get him back to America and then to England. There, he was a department head in a British factory and had a good income.

As was his custom, my friend had had some lively discussions with various employees on the occasion of one of his business visits to the factory, and the history of this man awakened his research hunting fever. Upon his next visit, he arranged it so he could invite the Boer to lunch, and with the passage of time, the two became friends. Over sandwiches and a couple of glasses of ale, Röder soon learned the entire life history of the Boer, including his experiences in the British concentration camp during his youth, and he was convinced of his abysmal hatred of Britain.

That was the opportunity for Röder to bait the hook. Now he knew the miseries and joys, the pride, and the hobbies of the Boer, and as a skilled interrogator, he knew where his weaknesses were. The Boer was obsessed with an enormous desire to travel. He used his vacation, all his free time, and all of his savings on this obsession. When Röder noticed this, he remembered, conveniently, that he had a relative in Holland, and he suggested they could meet there during his next vacation. He even went so far as to invite the Boer to the house of his conveniently bogus relative. That relative was a *Dr. Weber,* who bore a conspicuous resemblance to me. The Boer went enthusiastically along, and they agreed to meet in The Hague, where, at the same time, *Dr. Weber* would also be visiting with *Blonde Hertha.*

Fortunately, the Boer turned down Röder's offer to stay with his relative. He preferred to spend his time with his own friends. That relieved us of the need to fabricate a relative and a home environment.

On a marvelous, clear July day, the first joint excursion to Scheveningen took place. They enjoyed promenading, bathing, and many good meals in the evening. They drank a little wine, had animated discussions, and quite naturally, Röder brought the Boer War into the conversation. *Dr. Weber,* quite in passing, made a derogatory remark about the concentration camps, just to display his sympathy to the Boer, and then he pretended to lose interest in the topic. But the Boer was worked up, continued to talk excitedly, and did not hold back when it came to expressing his feelings against the British. *Dr. Weber* ostentatiously avoided the subject.

The cabaret performance had begun and seemed to capture *Dr. Weber's* complete attention. He did, of course, note that his apparent lack of interest disappointed the Boer. But first I, as *Dr. Weber,* had to gain his trust and his friendship. The whiskey did the trick, and the evening continued without end. I found it difficult to suppress my fatigue, but I had to give the impression that I liked nothing better than spending a night surrounded by boisterous cheerfulness and a good drink.

As we took our leave, we agreed we would meet again soon, but that was to be done without Röder. He must not be compromised by my overtures with the Boer. So, Röder returned to Germany.

At our next meeting, I was able to urge the Boer to collaborate with us without danger. Since he had no scruples in dealing with the British, he was ready to report everything he considered worth reporting. Once, without being prompted, he supplied us with details about the planned construction of a new airfield in Bristol, where his company was supposed to deliver steel frames for the hangars. That was a valuable report. Otherwise, he did not bring much that was useful, and I finally decided to cut the connection with him.

But then I recalled that, in the heat of the moment, he had once exclaimed in English, "One day I'm going to blow up the whole joint!" and then he repeated it in German, "Someday I'm going to blow up the whole joint, and you'll help me get the dynamite." Perhaps he might be of use to our sabotage department Intelligence II. So, I told him that whenever he felt the urge to assist us with some sabotage work, he should notify us specifically via the Dutch "relative." That, of course, would be *Blonde Hertha,* whom we used as our relay station.

One day, *Blonde Hertha* received a letter that read as follows: "I very much look forward to us getting together again during these weeks as we had agreed upon last year. *Now we will probably have to wait a long time!*" When this letter reached us, *The Skipper* leafed through *Blonde Hertha's* file and found that the agreed-upon code really meant "sabotage possible."

I took it immediately to Captain Witzke of Intelligence II. "If you want to use this opportunity, I'll get *Blonde Hertha* to communicate via the 'relative' that she was also very sorry that they could not meet." Thereupon, *3115* would wait for a middleman who would bring him legitimate orders disguised as greetings from *Pete*.

Naturally, Witzke was interested. He had such a middleman and said, "Because the factory apparently is making steel structures for aircraft hangars, it would be worth the trouble to send those folks a couple of explosive gifts for their engine room."

"That's what I also thought," I agreed. "I'll write the good girl accordingly, and then, I'm afraid both of us will once again have to get under way in order to bring your charming gift to the man."

"That is what we must do," Witzke said in his quiet manner.

The following weekend, the merchant, *Dr. Bremer,* and the shipping company employee, *Wintig,* stepped into a second-class compartment on the train to Holland. There were two other travelers in their compartment, a Berlin business representative and a courier of the Foreign Office; Witzke, alias *Wintig,* and I gave each other a knowing look when we saw the green official identity paper. We agreed that we should shake the two gentlemen off as soon as possible. We did not want to be suddenly welcomed in Holland by some official German government employees.

In Osnabrück, we left our compartment and moved up a couple of cars into another compartment. On the German side of the border, we had to open our suitcases and show our foreign currency. In spite of utmost care, I, alias *Dr. Bremer,* had failed to stash my foreign currency away before leaving. When the official counted it, he found that it amounted to more than noted on the passport. That was not exactly pleasant. If I could not persuade the controller to deposit the excess until my return, then I would have to ask an appropriate Intelligence contact to help. But that was precisely what I wanted to avoid at all costs. I was still trying to figure out how I could best get out of this affair when I heard Witzke, next to me, tell the controlling officer quite calmly that he had no currency and that he did not need any. That was my cue.

"Well," I exclaimed, "don't embarrass me. I happen to have your currency here with me. It was subsequently seized from me because it hadn't been noted on my passport."

Witzke was Witzke. He did not even need the proverbial moment of shock before he instantly got the picture. Greatly relieved, he said, "Well, then I don't have to try to deceive you, Mr. Inspector. I was afraid *Dr. Bremer* here forgot to bring it along for me, so just hand it to me, Bremerboy!"

I had just laid it on the table. The amount, of course, did not exactly check with the entries in Witzke's passport, but since it was less, nobody bothered any further. When we put our passports back and returned to our train, Witzke could not help saying with quite a sneer, "Once again, we were damn lucky." I said nothing but was greatly relieved and lit my cigar.

On the Dutch side, everything went without a glitch. In Hengelo, Witzke opened the window and leaned far out to buy a newspaper. There were a few travelers on the platform. Witzke closed the window and, with feigned relaxation, sat in his corner again. With pretended interest, I was reading *Nieuwe Rotterdamse Courant!* Outwardly, we did not let on how uneasy we were, but a certain tension still hung over us.

Then a little, unassuming man entered our compartment and, with a grouchy greeting, put a brown cardboard suitcase into the baggage net above Witzke's seat. He sat opposite me in the corner, lit a cigarette, and then began to doze. We paid no attention to each other. In Lochem, he disembarked again. He left his suitcase in the net. The only other traveler in our compartment had been sleeping since Oldenzaal and had not heard or seen anything. When we disembarked at Amersfoort, Witzke took the suitcase left by the little man from Hengelo from the overhead net, acting quite naturally, as though it had always belonged to him. In the waiting room, he said, "You can always rely on that young fellow. Without this standard suitcase, we would be in a real fix."

Mr. Hering had done a good job. He was a member of the mysterious group Witzke had developed into a well-functioning border crossing organization.

We ordered a good Dutch lunch and waited for our train to Rotterdam.

And this was not merely desk work! Many a night he went searching for smugglers with the customs officer until he found what he needed. He had made astounding deals with these people. He would assure them of impunity if they would continue to pursue their trade and occasionally take one of his people secretly across the border. They would not have any difficulty on the German side. On the other side, they had to continue to be unidentified smugglers. In that way, Witzke's suitcase had gotten to Hengelo, just the way all important letters avoided censorship.

We arrived in Rotterdam late in the afternoon and stopped at a little hotel, where we checked into a double room. Two big iron "eggs" lay below his underwear. I knew little about sabotage work, but I did not feel quite comfortable as I looked at those things. Not that I should be afraid of pineapple hand grenades; as an infantryman during the First World War, I had had plenty of exposure to those products of "progressive" human intelligence all too frequently. But for a frontline soldier, the situation was quite different. He had his weapon and could use it to defend himself according to international law. If something went wrong, there was a comrade who would come to assist you. But here, who could help us if we were nabbed for violating local regulations? I did not believe my eyes when I saw Witzke openly put the iron eggs in the closet and push them against the back wall.

"Are you going to let those things stay there like that?" I asked.

"Relax, Doctor Boy," Witzke replied with total calmness. "This is an old trick. Come on! Let's go downstairs!"

We went out to wait in the lobby for a "representative" of Witzke's shipping company. Later on, we wanted to eat in an old harbor tavern. The business "representative" was late. I went back upstairs. I had forgotten my cigarette case. When I pushed down the handle to our door, I noticed the door was barely touching. I was sure I had closed it. At first, I thought the chambermaid might have left it open, but then I clearly heard somebody fiddling with my suitcase. Would he discover the bombs? I took a deep breath, pushed the door open, and suddenly stood opposite a startled, strange gentleman, whom at first sight I figured to be the house detective. I had to focus hard not to glance at the closet. "Well," I said in German with a cheerful smile, "it's a good thing that we didn't lock our suitcases. It would have been a bit embarrassing if you had to break into them, wouldn't it?"

The man understood my German very well, and I was sure he also spoke German, but he stuttered in Dutch, "Oh, I beg your pardon, Mijnheer. Mijnheer van Straaten asked me to get his cigars from his suitcase." I could tell the guy had not found anything incriminating and that, obviously, he had not yet looked into the closet.

"That's just fine," I said. "I also came to fetch mine. May I offer you one?"

I knew my business papers had been rifled through, but that was fine with me. They were all in order. It was no secret that almost all hotels all over the world have their personal private detectives, as happened in this case, and any secret service would always have one of their agents among these personnel. Involuntarily, I had to smile at the disappointment of that man.

When I told Witzke about the incident, he simply smirked. "Right! I'm familiar with it. If you want to hide something really well, then it's best to leave it exposed and just stick it in some corner. Then nobody will stumble on it."

The "representative" from the shipping company had turned up in the meantime. He had a thick briefcase under his arm. Witzke went upstairs with him. When they turned up in the lobby again, the briefcase was still as thick as before, but it seemed to be much heavier. Then the three of us went out to eat. After supper, the business "representative" took his leave. The iron eggs had started on their way to *3115*. The next evening, they were to sail across the channel on a smuggler boat.

Fourteen days later, *3115* wrote to his relatives that he had been sick for three days, but now he was feeling very well again. That meant the bombs had been received, and they had been placed successfully. We could believe him because we knew him well, but it was rarely possible to provide evidence in such cases because British censorship assured that bombings or sabotage damage would never become public.

Much later, there would be a short note in some neutral country's newspaper about an explosion in the hometowns of our agents. That was the beginning of secret acts of sabotage, but then the German invasion of the Netherlands stopped the resupply for *3115*.

The fellow had done his utmost, but the Empire was just too big a chunk to blow up. That was also the end of the Witzke case for me, and I could focus on my work again.

18

Border Closings

On May 3, 1940, I received the "top secret" order to explore airborne landing possibilities in Luxembourg, to investigate previously reported airborne landing obstacles in Holland and Belgium, and to examine and report on the overall status. This order was unique in the sense that it had to be carried out by May 8. It was clear what that meant!

My knowledge and experience were sufficient to enable me to draw certain conclusions. But it was not my job to engage in politics or political intelligence; although Canaris, in connection with important diplomatic events, always violated his own order to keep our fingers out of political intelligence, and he always called upon his own Intelligence I. Basically, the political reports from the SD always seemed entirely too austere and inaccurate to him.

At the time of the invasion of Czechoslovakia, everything had gone well once again, and the Munich Agreement had prevented the worst. But before the war with Poland, everyone who had access to more insight into the situation, even if only rumors from the anterooms of the Supreme Command, already had serious doubts about the consequences. Of course, the big success during the Polish war had enabled us to take a deep breath once more. It had again boosted our confidence in the leadership. But now, we were confronted by a new frightening uncertainty since we, based on our actions, could no longer doubt there would be an invasion of Holland and Belgium, although the general public was not yet aware. After September 1939 it would no longer be possible to stop a world war. [On September 1, 1939, Nazi Germany invaded Poland; this was the beginning of World War II.] Now, we just needed to carry out our mission. I would personally handle Belgium and Holland, and for Luxembourg, only Röder came into consideration.

It was no mystery that secret talks had taken place among the general staffs of France, Britain, and Belgium even before the outbreak of the war. In November 1939, informants had brought messages regarding the buildup of fortifications in Gembloux in Namur, Belgium, as well as the buildup of tank barriers.

At the end of November, we received reports on terrain reconnaissance by French officers in Belgium. Our reconnaissance activities were stepped up. On November 4, Captain Thoran in Berlin had been given orders to explore the area around Ghent for suitable airborne landing sites.

By then, everything had been prepared down to the least detail, but the marching orders never arrived. Now, the prevailing circumstances were such that there could be no doubt about our invasion. Ongoing agent reports clearly indicated that all defense measures were concentrated almost exclusively on the eastern border of Belgium and Holland, in other words, confined to Germany.

In recent weeks, we had received new reports regarding the increased incidences of French officers seen in Belgian territory, and fourteen days before, a more reliable informant from Abwehr I had reported to our duty station that French tanks were positioned in the area around Bertrix. We did not look forward to crossing the border once again. The animosity toward the Germans kept growing week after week. Earlier, it had been unpleasant enough when we received a secret order to go to Belgium and Holland; but now it would be a matter of mere luck whether we would be able to return in one piece.

The Belgian Intelligence Service was not asleep. It cooperated quite openly with the French Deuxième Bureau and the British Secret Intelligence Service and was as well informed about our preparations as we were about theirs.

I had no illusions whatsoever that my identity was still secret, but the fact that we had to rush left me unable to create a new alias. While I was discussing the last details with Tornow and *The Skipper,* the secretary reported the arrival of our London friend Röder. Röder came in right on her heels and greeted me in his somewhat brash manner, "Well, *Doktor,* where are you going to send me now?"

"It's just like you to ask such a question," I laughed, "but you're correct."

"Well, sure," said Röder, and unceremoniously sat down on the corner of my desk. "When you take time to make a personal call to me and are exceptionally polite, it's for certain that in a couple of days there's going to be a war someplace. But, joking aside, do I still have to go away today?"

"No," I laughed, "but tomorrow! Tomorrow you go to Luxembourg. Have you any kind of business there?"

"Yes, *sir,*" he replied, "but what's going on in Luxembourg? Are we going to declare war on those poor little harmless people?"

"You can figure that out for yourself." I smiled and opened a map. "Within three days, we have to know whether this area," and I pointed to an area on the map north of Luxembourg, "has any landing possibilities for cargo gliders. But being a pilot yourself, you know that this is not enough. Above all, we have to know if there might be some major obstacles."

Röder bent over the map and took a few notes in his pocket calendar. These were special notes relating to his line of business that we had often used earlier as code in our conversations across the border. In that connection, we merely mentioned offers and orders so everybody could listen in.

"Do you know, *Doktor*, I feel kind of uncomfortable with this trip," Röder said.

"So do I," I admitted.

Röder pulled a copy of the *Daily Telegraph* out of his coat pocket, dated April 20, and pointed at the headline: "AUSTRALIA'S WATCH OF DUTCH INDIES, in other words, Australia is observing Dutch India—Australia is carefully examining the effect of a German invasion of the Netherlands upon the Dutch East Indies."

"Let me see." I took the paper out of his hand. "That is the first official indication regarding a possible German invasion. I have gone through all Belgian, Dutch, and British newspapers, and I was astonished not to find a single hint referencing any forthcoming German attack."

"Well," Röder remarked, "further on, it says that the state of siege has been extended in Holland."

"I read that," I said, "but at the same time, it says that Holland will forcefully defend its neutrality and, they add, 'toward both sides.'"

"Do you really believe," Röder interrupted me, "that Belgium and Holland would resist any invasion from France or England? That seems highly unlikely."

"You may be right," I replied, "but that is not our worry. The newspapers may officially declare their neutrality, but our reports indicate the opposite." Then from the rack, I took a couple of copies of the Brussels *Soir* and read: "May 2, 1940—IN FRANCE AVEC LES ANGLAIS—in France with the British—glorification of the English troops and their confidence in victory."

"Well, and so it continues. First thing this morning, Helmut Thimm told me on the phone from Antwerp that as he happened to look out of the window while shaving, an antiaircraft battery in the park opposite his house had been moved into position."

I had been shocked by this bold frankness in the middle of what was usually a guarded conversation, because I had to assume that Thimm's phone was being tapped, but this kind of firsthand report only confirmed our suspicion. "As far as we're concerned," I again turned to Röder, "we are now interested in the public's attitude toward Germany, and that undoubtedly is hostile. We have to be on guard. If one of us, and it just so happens that I'm the one who has to go to Holland and Belgium tomorrow, would run into some trouble on this 'excursion,' then no one will be able to help us."

In the meantime, I had cleared my desk. Once again, I pulled on the door of the safe to make sure it was secured, and then I left the office building with Röder. The next morning, I sat on the usual train heading for Antwerp. In order not to attract attention, even at the German border control, I had this time, by teletype, announced my arrival to the appropriate intelligence agent, who would process me personally. On the Belgian side, the officials were strikingly unfriendly, and the processing took forever.

The questions that were asked and the detail with which my business papers were examined pointed to their own nervousness. My invitations (which I had written to myself on original official stationery belonging to my friends in Belgium and Holland and of which I always kept several in my safe) were flawless. Only the signatures were forged, but that could not be determined before I was back in Germany again.

While I was waiting, the Belgian official leafed through a particular list. I forced myself to ask rather nonchalantly, "The list of criminals?" The official did not answer and finally put a stamp on my passport.

In Antwerp, I went directly to Helmut Thimm. "Mensch," he said, "it's getting increasingly more troubled here from day to day."

"I noticed that already at the border," I replied. "I'm not surprised after everything that has happened over the past several weeks."

Helmut asked, "When are you all coming? Every child knows that the Germans will march in sooner or later. All this uncertainty gradually gets on your nerves."

"Certainly not today or tomorrow." I laughed. "Otherwise, I wouldn't be here. But the moment I know something, I will call you," I joked, but I did not feel comfortable. I would have preferred to give him some kind of hint, but that would be unwise. It might have caused him to take precautionary measures, and that certainly would have been noticed.

I tried to distract him. "Let's hang all this business on a nail for the moment and take a train through the city," I proposed.

"That's no fun either any longer. The local businesses are full of soldiers, and in the bars the officers have the last word."

"Let them," I encouraged him. "We will get our money's worth sooner or later anyway."

In reality, I wanted to see what it looked like in a country that war would befall in a few days. An oppressive atmosphere hovered heavily over the population. Some were hoping against all odds, while others seemed to have come to terms with the inevitable. Many had openly taken sides, but everyone knew they were sitting on a powder keg and tried simply to anesthetize themselves, as it were. I didn't feel comfortable in my own skin. We quickly left the first two locations. Previously, Helmut had always been received there with a gracious hello. Today, the greeting was courteous but unpleasantly cool. Even a girl who for years had been madly in love with him tried to avoid him behind the bar.

Only when the officer who had been sitting on the barstool next to us left did she whisper, "Don't be mad at me, chéri, but you know people don't like it when I am overly affectionate toward a German."

Helmut smiled bitterly, "*Pas de quoi*, it does not matter!" and paid the bill. He wanted to go home, but I pulled him on. I had to see how the general public would behave in a larger establishment. We entered a large tavern. The people were crowded on the dance floor. We found two seats at a larger table in a corner. We spoke only English, in other words, American. In the other establishments, hardly anyone would enter into a casual chat with a German. Now I wanted to try conversing and acting like an American. As such, I would be completely neutral, and I could express my opinions unhindered. I had no reason to fear my speech would betray me.

In America, no one ever asked me, "What country do you come from?" Instead, they would say, "What part of the country are you from?"

In the beginning, the chat with my neighbor at the table did not extend beyond the usual pleasantries. But then the musicians played the British soldier song, "We're Gonna Hang Out the Washing on the Siegfried Line." I listened carefully. As a German, I did not particularly like it, but as an American, I could laugh about it. Here I saw an opportunity to get into a more intimate conversation with the Belgians.

"Well, now," I laughed, "you people are funny. I thought you were neutral, and now here you dance and play music, and you sing an English war song!" The Belgian laughed, but I would not let it go, "I would like to know whether the band will play a German song. Do you know the song that goes something like this, 'We are Sailing against England'?"

The Belgian hesitated a moment. Then he said, "Naturally," and grinned, "we are neutral, after all." And then he went to the band leader. I was able to see clearly that the musician was making a shocked face, but the Belgian seemed to have persuaded him. The band leader made a courteous bow and whispered something to the other players. Suddenly, Helmut and I began to get worried. If the band leader would now announce that the England song suggested was requested by the Americans, and then point at me, things could go wrong for both of us. All it would take was for some secret agent to demand our identification. But then the band leader raised his baton, and the band started. And then all neutral Belgians danced across the dance floor against England! I was speechless. "Dammit," I said to Helmut, "that is something."

"Yes," said the Belgian proudly. "We are neutral after all, or are we not?"

"Well," I said, "sometimes you don't really give the impression that you are."

"You are not entirely wrong," he agreed, "and I confess to you quite openly that we Walloons are on the side of the Allies."

"Oh," I said. "So, what are you doing to stop the Nazis?"

"Well," said the Belgian, "don't you see that we have mobilized ourselves, and that we are firmly determined to fight? Let them not think that they are going to overrun us as easily as in 1914. Things were not easy for them in Norway, and things are going to be a lot rougher around here."

"Well and good," I teased him, "but all that would be necessary is to drop a couple of paratroopers behind your back on your beautiful streets, and they'll soon be all over you."

"You will be astonished," he countered. "We have taken all precautions to make it impossible for them to land there. Just look at the camouflaged machine-gun nests and the road obstacles. No, my good man, this time it will not be so easy."

In the meantime, my friend Thimm had become restless, and I could not blame him. We paid, and then we said "so long" to our Belgian friend. "Dammit! If you can't keep your mouth shut," Helmut said angrily, "then at least leave me out of your game."

I linked his arm and said calmly, "From your point of view, you are quite right, but you're forgetting that we in Germany fight a tough war. If through my messages I can prevent our young fellows from jumping into a trap, then unfortunately I cannot be worried about you. You have to understand that."

Helmut mumbled something incomprehensible, but it did not bother me any further. I was satisfied with the evening's results. Now all I needed was to confirm the locations. It was not my assignment to explore the new positions and obstacles. Also, I needed to verify the available agents' reports again.

The next morning, one of Helmut's drivers took me to Brussels and Namur. Jacques, the driver, knew nothing except that *Monsieur le Docteur* was a friend of his boss. He found it absolutely normal when, as we passed an airfield, I ordered him to drive more slowly. Once, earlier, I had told him I had been a pilot in World War I. As for the rest, Jacques, born in Brussels, was a reservist with the Belgian antiaircraft artillery. His identity card and his Belgian manners helped me. Twice we were stopped, and each time Jacques was asked for the identity card. Twice, as if neglectful, I greeted the guard with a friendly "how do you do," and then I excused myself as well as I could in French with an American accent. Both times we were told to drive on. I saw what I wanted, and what I had not seen Jacques pointed out to me without being asked.

Once I said to him, "I would rather you were somewhat more cautious and not show all these military things to a foreigner."

He grinned and said, "But, *Herr Doktor*, everybody already knows it." I made a few notes in my little booklet. These were kilometer markings, which later would aid me in writing my report. My assignment in Antwerp was completed that evening, but, as is always the case with me, as long as I'm busy, I'm calm. After everything is over, I'm nervous.

I could only allow myself a brief respite because that same evening I had to continue on to Holland. It was merely a short distance from Antwerp to the Dutch border. I had the Dutch papers right on top in my briefcase. I had barely glanced at my passport before the Dutch border officials came in. I sat alone in my compartment. An officer asked for my passport and disappeared with it. I thought that was rather odd. Normally, the passengers get out and take their passport to the window. Only the suitcases were controlled on the train. That made me suspicious. Because I was sitting alone in my compartment, I was not able to tell whether the other travelers also had to surrender their passports. Suddenly, I felt unsure. I sensed something was not quite right. Then the door to my compartment was pushed open again. I thought they were bringing my passport back, but then I looked into the dark face of a different uniformed person who, without any further explanation, asked for my business papers and my notes. I had been in intelligence too long not to know what that meant. I tried to hide my fright behind a friendly smile, reached for my briefcase, and opened it. I started to dig around in my briefcase. I pulled out first one and then the other paper, gave them to the official and acted as if I would try to look further, and then I said, "This is stupid. Why don't you take the whole briefcase with you? What is going on today anyway?"

The uniformed officer did not move a muscle. Without saying a word, he put the briefcase under his arm and disappeared with it, just like the first time with the passport. Now I knew that there was danger around the corner, and as always happened in such cases, I was completely calm. I was thinking hard. The briefcase contained business letters from Belgian and Dutch firms. However, it was too late this evening to call any of the companies. My business friend in Dordrecht, 50 kilometers away, had long known me by my name of *Reinhardt*. If necessary, I would suggest that they call him early tomorrow morning in order to verify the accuracy of the invitation.

But the whole thing was not really all that dangerous. The danger was that they wanted my notebook. My briefcase did not contain any notes, but everybody knows that a businessman carries a notebook with him. In other words, they would come once again and ask for the notebook. Of course, I could have thrown it out of the window. It was dark outside, and it was hardly likely that anyone would find it before daybreak. But I still wouldn't be across the border by that time. And they wouldn't believe me if I told them that I didn't carry a notebook. I had no other choice! I could simply hope. I pulled my notebook out and convinced myself once again that there was nothing incriminating in my numbers. Let them come.

And they came! This time they came in twos!

"You can have your briefcase back," one of them said, "but where are your notes?"

I acted surprised, but immediately reached into my back pocket and handed him my notebook. The official appeared to be somewhat disappointed. He had probably expected some kind of excuse. He took my little booklet and spoke rather brashly, "Take your suitcase, and come with me!"

I wanted to protest. I could not afford to lose so much time. "Why don't you tell me what this is all about!"

But the official said, "Once everything has been cleared up, you can take the next train."

Now my focus was to stay in complete control. The briefcase certainly did not contain anything. They had not yet looked through the notebook, but they had some suspicion and were looking for evidence.

In the office, I was first questioned about my personal information. The official was not really that stupid. Twice he misspoke when he repeated the birthdates and the house number of *Reinhardt*'s apartment, but I was wide awake. I knew the personal data of *Dr. Reinhardt*. The official had quoted the personal data of *Dr. Weber*. They suspected something, but they had not yet figured out that these were the same persons. Suddenly I noticed a passport picture of me as *Dr. Weber*, which had slipped out of my notebook as the official held it. Almost automatically, I put my hat over it and angrily raised my hands.

"Gentlemen, I have the impression that this is an error. I propose that you take me to Dordrecht, and that you hand me over to an official. He can personally request any desired information from my business associates."

The inquisitors were somewhat unsure. I quickly followed up, "As far as I'm concerned, you can find a place for me to sleep here, and early tomorrow, you can call Dordrecht." The officials agreed.

I knew too well that it's usually the innocent party in this sort of inquisition who is more nervous than the guilty party, because they don't know where this is leading. The guilty party is frequently calmer because he or she knows what is involved. I looked at the leading agent with feigned excitement, and said, "Please, gentlemen, do not make any trouble for me. You are certainly doing me an injustice."

Then something unexpected happened. The second official, who had remained quiet all along, suddenly asked, "Why do you always say that we should call Dordrecht? Why not Amsterdam?"

"How come?" I asked, astonished. "I do not want to extend this unnecessary stay any longer. Dordrecht is nearby, and I thought things would go faster than in Amsterdam. But," I was now completely calm, "if you prefer Amsterdam that is up to you." I acted insulted. I knew that the next couple of seconds would be critical.

The two officials whispered a couple of words to each other. Then the man who had my papers laid them on the table. I knew I had won. "I am sorry, *Herr Doktor,*" said one of the fellows, "but we must do our duty. You can continue on the next train early tomorrow morning."

"Thanks," I said. "I can understand it during these uncertain times, but my involuntary stay here now costs me an entire day. I wanted to get back to Germany by tomorrow evening."

While I was talking, I took my hat with the picture under it off the table and made it disappear. I did not want to tempt these fellows to check my passport picture again with this one. I put my notebook back, took my suitcase, and headed for the waiting room. I suddenly felt very hungry, but I had forgotten it was one o'clock in the morning, so the snack shop was closed.

My next train was scheduled after seven o'clock in the morning. Disappointed, I sat down in a dark corner. I was totally exhausted with all of this tension. The official, of course, had not found anything for the moment, but I was sure their report would go immediately to their headquarters. Around ten o'clock the next morning, I arrived at the office of my business friend Keer, in Dordrecht. He had been born in Hamburg, and both of us had served in the same regiment in World War I; but during the interim, he had become a Dutch citizen.

Before Keer had recovered from his surprise at my unexpected visit, I stood next to him, and I thanked him ostentatiously for his invitation, which I put on the table before him at the same time. His secretary, meanwhile, had stepped out of the office again, and my friend laughed when he read the letter.

"You are a sassy dog," he said. "What brings you here once again?" He handed me a box of cigars and poured me a glass of Oude Klare.

But I turned them both down and said in a loud and clear voice, "I absolutely need two crates of Philips tubes from you," and then I whispered, "later on in the car, I'll explain everything to you."

Keer immediately got the picture. He called one of his assistants and asked him about the stack of tubes. After we had talked business for some time, Keer told his secretary we were leaving. Then we got into his car, and we slowly drove into the city.

"It is absolutely certain that I'm being watched," I explained to him. "Actually, I did not want to go to Amsterdam, but under these circumstances, it's absolutely necessary. You should really be driving me along the superhighways via Rotterdam, The Hague, Utrecht, Arnhem, and back. I wanted to take a look at the airborne landing obstacles. That is now impossible; so, you need to help me. Just drive me to the train station now. There we will conspicuously take leave of each other, and then I'll ride on to Amsterdam. You do the tour vice versa via Arnhem, and then come via The Hague to Amsterdam. There we will meet as usual."

Keer had listened to me attentively. Now he interrupted me, "I'll drive via Arnhem and Utrecht. I can tell you what goes on between here, Rotterdam, and The Hague. I drive that way almost every day." Then he described for me the known obstacles and the camouflaged gun positions. I repeated everything precisely and was confident I would be able to retain the most important things in my head.

Late in the afternoon, we met in a small restaurant in the inner city of Amsterdam. Keer had parked his car with a business friend, walked a couple of blocks to a taxi stand on a street parallel to the restaurant, and after a short ride, completed the last leg on foot in the event someone might have followed him.

He told me that in the morning when he returned to his office from the train station, his secretary had reported to him that somebody had called and had asked for *Dr. Reinhardt.* She replied that *Dr. Reinhardt* had just been taken to the train station by her boss so that he could continue on to Amsterdam. The caller did not give his name. He said he was a friend of *Dr. Reinhardt,* and he had heard quite by accident he was in Dordrecht. He said he would try to reach *Dr. Reinhardt* in Amsterdam. Since the unknown friend did not inquire about the address in Amsterdam, he would certainly have been an official of the political police. Probably the information supplied by Keer's secretary was sufficient, but, of course, nobody called Amsterdam.

As I sat on the night train to Cologne, I suddenly became aware of how shamelessly lucky I had been once again. My mission had been accomplished. The important issue now was to forward my reports on to Berlin on time.

The border control on the Dutch side came off without any difficulties, but the unexpected happened on the German side. The German official, who was even more nervous and excited than his counterpart on the Dutch side, insisted on fumbling through all my papers and notes. I waited with growing impatience. But instead of giving me my papers back, I was asked to step into a small cell.

"What does this mean?" I asked, astonished.

"Body search," the official said curtly. "Please undress."

I was furious. I would have loved to yell at him, but I had to be cautious because of the other travelers. In the cell, however, I could not restrain myself any longer. Angrily, I identified myself and demanded to be put in touch immediately with the local intelligence agent. "And if I miss my train," I snarled at him, "then you will be in deep trouble." He seemed to understand at last. He hastened to fetch the agent. I asked him to immediately arrange an urgent official call to Hamburg in order to check with the duty officer.

I arrived at my train in the nick of time. My report reached Berlin on schedule. On May 6, Röder returned to Germany with the precise sketches, including clarifications needed by the Luftwaffe Operations Staff. I returned on May 8. On May 10, German troops crossed the borders. The Blitzkrieg had begun. Our surreptitious trips to Holland and Belgium were over.

19

Sea Rendezvous

In the spring of 1940, in addition to all my other work, I was also charged with training a group of specially selected officers for the Abwehr. My class consisted of men who, earlier in private life, had held independent positions in commerce and industry. They all had a command of various foreign languages—English, French, Spanish, Italian, or Portuguese. Some had lived abroad for many years. Their ranks and ages differed. They appeared to have good common sense, and they could also act independently. Instead of imparting merely theoretical instructions and discussing closed cases with them, I also allowed them to participate, hands-on, in current work projects

To my great relief, in June 1940, I was assigned a particularly capable coworker, Captain Jules Böckel. He was tall, stately, dark blond and blue-eyed, and looked particularly handsome; an acquaintance once said about him, "He looks like a model for a ski poster." Böckel was quite a fellow from head to toe. He had been a pilot during World War I, and subsequently, using his own recreational aircraft, he had flown over the Andes. Reliable, diligent, well-balanced, he was a steadfast comrade. It was a pleasure to work with him. He had been transferred to me from the aide to Commanding General [Corps Commander] von Friedensburg. In every respect, he was the best representative I could imagine. This gave me an opportunity to once again turn my attention to *Johnny* with deeper intensity.

Now that all possibilities for meetings in Belgium and Holland were suppressed, it became more difficult each day for me to process agents. *Johnny* and I, therefore, had quite often discussed meeting at sea in case of war. Now we drafted a plan to meet on the North Sea and set the date of May 24, 1940.

After thoroughly checking with the local navy experts, we selected a point at sea in the vicinity of Dogger Bank for this meeting. *Johnny* lined up a friend, Sam McCarthy, code name Biscuit to MI5, who owned a fishing boat. Fishermen also went to sea to fish during the war, so such a boat in the vicinity of Dogger Bank would not arouse undue attention.

In the course of a conference with the Commander of Submarines, Admiral Otto Cyliax, who also had naval reconnaissance aircraft available, I arranged for a flying boat to be made available for my mission. I obtained the instruments and the specific navigation point, and the calls went back and forth between

Johnny in England and our radio station in Wohldorf. Dates and times were compared twice to eliminate any misunderstandings.

I was to take off from List on Sylt. We were flying in a civilian aircraft, and, for camouflage, I had pulled my civilian coat over my uniform. The aircraft was a Do 18. All armor plate had been removed to allow for maximum fuel load, because our carefully plotted course was long. It would not be simple to find a tiny fishing trawler in the vastness of the sea. The day was clear, and vision was good. A few low-hanging clouds enabled us to disappear should we encounter approaching enemy aircraft.

Naturally, I was in flight uniform in the event we should wind up in enemy territory. On the one hand, we had to anticipate a surprise attack by enemy aircraft; on the other hand, the entire mission could also have been betrayed. I wasn't concerned about whether the British SIS [Secret Intelligence Service] had gotten in on this. *Johnny*'s code could not be deciphered because it changed automatically from day to day; but we only had *Johnny*'s word for the reliability of his friend.

We took off at the specified hour. Since we had to avoid any encounter with enemy aircraft, we flew as much as possible in the low-hanging clouds. Above the rendezvous spot, we dove down until we had a good view of the open sea. Not a single boat was to be seen. We made measurements. The position was accurate. Because we had enough fuel, I requested a search course. It was no good: no fishing boat, but no enemy aircraft either. We had to break off and start flying home. It was already getting dark as we tied up in port. Our tanks were almost empty.

The undertaking had been a failure! I was disappointed, and I reviewed, once again, the individual phases of the plan. I had just arrived at the conclusion that it could not have been our error when an orderly gave me a teletype from Hamburg; in the meantime, *Johnny* had already radioed. "I had to stay under cover. Captain under observation. Report follows."

Now, at least a sign of life! I ordered that *Johnny* was to skip two periods of transmissions. Then I flew back to Hamburg.

As I left the airport in Hamburg-Fuhlsbüttel, I was just barely able to jump on the rear platform of the streetcar that went to the inner city. I flung my suit-case ahead of me. A middle-aged woman dodged to avoid the suitcase and scowled. I took my hat off politely and was just about to excuse myself when she snarled at me with fury. "Again, one of those who belongs in a uniform and should be at the front! It's a shame that the fine gentlemen can travel all over the world while others are taken away from their homes and have to get their bones shot to pieces."

My first instinct was to remonstrate, but I quickly gained control of myself and said in a calm voice, "Perhaps you're right, but each of us must carry out the job assigned to him."

No scene ensued and the other passengers did not interfere, but the woman was deprived of a confrontation. She turned around and, accidently on purpose, rammed her elbow into my stomach. Again, I found it difficult to restrain myself, but I had to smile ironically as I thought how presumptuous human nature is. But how could she have known.

When I returned to the office, one of the younger men jumped up and took off my civilian coat. Everybody eagerly awaited my report.

"Well," I said, "that was the first enemy mission over the North Sea."

After this failed mission at sea, Portugal was the only remaining possibility for a personal meeting with *Johnny*. Perhaps he would have luck getting a visa. We made the corresponding plans for Lisbon.

On June 5, I received a radio message from *Johnny* informing me that he had made the necessary preparations and would arrive in Lisbon by ship between June 12 and 17. The instant I heard the news, I was genuinely happy and proud the little man had accomplished so much in the middle of a war, but calm consideration poured cold water on my joy. No matter how hard I struggled against the idea, I was now sure *Johnny* was no longer a free agent.

To get out of England, he surely must have offered his services to the British Security Service. In Germany, a man in his position would never have been allowed to leave the country without the approval of the Secret Service, certainly not in time of war. It was bound to be the same in England; I had previously suggested to him he should offer his services to the Security Service in order to ensure his freedom of movement. In that case, we could supply him with "play material" so he could continue accepting messages in order to reassure his employers he was actually working for them, whereas at the same time, he would be able to travel around freely for us with their approval. I knew he had connections to the Security Service, but so far, he had not made any use of my offer. Now, I believed that, in the meantime, he had done it anyway without informing me.

In that regard, I made my preparations for the trip with particular care. I had no time left to build a bulletproof alibi for myself; without that, a businessman could not get a visa for Portugal. I decided to fly as courier for the Foreign Ministry with false identity papers. Besides, I had gotten some bogus material for *Johnny* from Berlin, which, if necessary, he could take with him to England. This type of material that was slipped into the hands of the enemy intelligence service required special clearance and had to be genuine enough not to be immediately recognized as a deception.

At that time, it was difficult even for us to take such trips without arousing suspicion. Portugal, of course, was not involved on any side of the war, but it was closely tied to Britain by virtue of commercial treaties. My British counterpart, by whom *Johnny* was now perhaps being advised, was bound to be interested in maintaining contact with *Johnny* and, consequently, would not allow his agents in Lisbon to interfere with me. My primary concern was how to get from Hamburg to Lisbon.

Since fighting was still going on in France, the most expeditious way to get there was by air via Italy and Spain. I was not particularly fond of the idea of having to take a civilian Italian airliner. Our concern that the Italian Intelligence Service might be cooperating with the British Secret Intelligence Service was not entirely unfounded. We had several indications supporting that. That would mean my flight plans would already be known in Madrid and London even before I arrived in Lisbon.

I didn't want to make it quite that easy for the British, so I searched for other possibilities. Then, through an informant with Lufthansa, I learned that German aircraft, as part of a confidential commercial agreement, had for some time been transporting precious metals to Spain. These flights were kept classified as much as possible. They were launched at irregular times and always from a different airfield. With the help of I Air Berlin, I managed permission to access one of these aircraft. The flight was scheduled for June 11, but Lufthansa was not able to announce the departure field and schedule until the very last moment.

While I was organizing my papers, my wife came in with some items of clothing over her arm and asked, "Can you pack these things?"

I stared at the soft bundle and asked, "What in heaven's name is that?"

"These are baby things for *Lily,*" she explained to me. "I know it would be difficult for her to get such things in England now." I was not particularly taken with the idea, but I did pack the bundle under my shirts, and I tried to figure out how I might explain the contents to the customs officers in Spain and Portugal.

I flew to Berlin on June 9, and from there, immediately after takeoff time and place were announced, I was taken by a special aircraft to the departing airfield. At noon on June 10, I was informed I would have to be in Stuttgart on the morning of June 11. There, I checked in as *Dr. Renken* with the pilot, who, sitting in his Ju 90, was waiting for the announcement of his stopover field. At noon on June 11, the order was received to fly to Viterbo, north of Rome, and from there to continue on at night to Barcelona.

"Shit," bellowed the pilot. Turning toward me, he said, "I don't like Viterbo. It looks too small for my bird. Hopefully, at least our visibility is clear."

I was his only passenger. Only one double seat had been left for me in the massive, cavernous fuselage of the aircraft. Everything else had been removed.

The pilot noticed my astonishment and laughingly pointed at the floor. A uniformly distributed row of little crates filled the deck.

"Is that all?" I asked.

"Just try to lift one of them," the captain invited me. I tried to lift it, but it was so heavy that the little box stuck solid to the floor.

"Precious metals," the captain said. Then he disappeared into the cockpit with his copilot, and I sat alone in the dark, empty fuselage. The flight over the Alps was calm, and we landed in Viterbo around noon. In an ordinary tiny hut at the end of the runway, I ate my spaghetti with lots of Parmesan cheese, and I was pleased I was able to chat astonishingly well with the serving girl, using my self-taught Italian.

We were able to take off for the next leg of our journey late in the evening because we had to fly over Corsica, that is to say, over hostile territory, and darkness was our shield. Time seemed endless to me. Again, I sat alone in the black, hollow aircraft. Finally, around midnight, the captain came in and asked me to fasten up. We were to land in Barcelona in a few minutes.

I looked outside as the engines were being turned off. I could see nothing that resembled an airfield. There was no landing strip, nor were there any other lights. The captain had to land with the help of his own searchlight. When we stepped off, just one representative from Lufthansa and three assistants were waiting for us in the darkness. A Spanish official stood behind them. No one concerned himself about the courier, *Dr. Renken*.

The three assistants began to unload. The flight captain and the Spaniard exchanged papers. Then it occurred to them I was still there, and together, we drove to the Hotel Ritz. The Spaniard took my passport and promised to bring it back to me the next morning, with the necessary visa stamps. Collaboration with the Spanish Intelligence Service seemed to work.

My last stopover was Madrid. There I was received by an old buddy from the Intelligence Service, who was employed as assistant attaché in the embassy for security purposes. He asked me to take along a heavy suitcase for his colleagues at the legation in Lisbon.

"Are the bombs secured?" I asked, joking.

"Yikes, be quiet," my friend whispered, rather shaken. "What gave you the idea?"

"I really didn't know," I said, "but for Pete's sake, couldn't you find anybody more stupid than me, of all things? I don't know anything about sabotage. Next time, you carry those things yourself."

"Nothing can really happen," he promised. "The suitcase is in the category of 'courier baggage.' Besides, you're traveling with an official service passport and with courier papers. My people in Lisbon are stuck there. They keep screaming for explosive materials."

"If you say so," I finally said, "but if somebody should notice something, it is your responsibility. I believe that my work at this time is more valuable than one or two sunken tubs."

When I noticed the other fellow was insulted, I added, "Sorry, old boy, but I am indeed supposed to meet a valuable contact from England who brings me important information. Information that could save lives, time, and money is more important than a sunken freighter."

On the same evening, I took a regular airliner to Lisbon. My informant there was *Don Carlos* (Calixto Rodriguez Duarte, who used the aliases H. Duarte and Herbert Dobler among others), whom I had not yet met. He had been born in Brazil, of German extraction, and had worked for the Hamburg Intelligence Station even before the war.

Don Carlos was one of their best and most reliable informants. From Lisbon, he had direct contact with Hamburg via a transmitter at the German legation. All technical details for the meeting with *Johnny* were arranged via *Don Carlos*. So that *Johnny* would not have access to his address, a specific café had been selected as a rendezvous point. *Don Carlos* had also reserved a room for me in the Hotel Duas Nações, where he would brief me prior to *Johnny*'s arrival.

The owner of the hotel was a friend of *Don Carlos*'s. He, too, was of German extraction and always had Northern European cuisine waiting for his guests. They cooked with butter instead of oil—something for which I was particularly grateful, because I didn't have time for any stomach trouble.

We had left all of the details to *Don Carlos*. He knew Lisbon better than any of us. Lisbon was full of refugees from all countries; there were numerous embassies, legations, and consulates of regular and exiled governments, and naturally, there were also very many intelligence agents. Nowhere were there as many cars with the well-known "CD," and nowhere had this "CD" acquired a more significant interpretation in the vernacular: *contrabandistas distinguidos*—distinguished contrabandists.

I arrived in Lisbon on June 14, the same day as the surrender of Paris. Everything was normal during the processing at the airport until, ahead of me, a Japanese traveler erupted into an animated dispute with the customs agent about his baggage.

Suddenly, I flushed boiling hot. It occurred to me that the Madrid suitcase had not been listed in my courier papers. It shot through my head that when the customs agent opens it, I'm done for. My friend in Madrid is a goner; I'm a goner. The ambassador in Madrid will be demoted, and the foreign press has new headlines about the misuse of courier baggage. The customs agent came while I was still trying to figure out what to do. I put my personal suitcase in front of him on the counter and opened it. Everything was in order, and not even the baby clothing made any trouble. I pulled out my courier identity papers, and I quickly saw a way out. I showed the customs officer the two items from Berlin that were clearly listed, and then I put the "dynamite suitcase" from Madrid in front of him, but very cautiously, and acted as if I were looking for accompanying papers. "I cannot find the papers," I said. "I purchased an extra suitcase in Madrid. What do we do now?"

"I'm probably not allowed to open it?" the officer asked, and looked at me rather oddly. "Or do you want to leave it here and get a second identity slip?"

"I would not like to have it opened here. It is not from my duty station, you know."

His reference to a second identity slip gave me an idea. The fellow who was to pick me up had not yet arrived. I asked to be allowed to call the legation. I asked the legation to connect me with our informant. All I had to say to them was that *Rodrigo* had given me a suitcase without accompanying papers, and he knew what the situation was. He asked me to wait for him. In less than an hour, he had arrived with the necessary papers, and I was then able to take my suitcase along. I was certain the customs officer knew precisely what was going on, but officially he was unable to do anything about it.

As I arrived at the hotel, the porter handed me a letter. It was an invitation to tea with *Signora Juanita* for five o'clock in the afternoon on June 15. I did not know any *Signora Juanita*, but I knew the invitation came from *Don Carlos*.

The next afternoon, I entered a house in Lisbon that had been furnished in Portuguese style. A southern beauty overwhelmed me with greetings and a flood of Portuguese words, of which I did not understand a single one. I kissed her hand and tried to stammer some Portuguese greeting, but the *Signora* laughed and said in pure *Berlinerisch*, "Don't trip over your tongue, young man!" And before I could express my astonishment, she took my arm and continued in perfect German, "Come, *Don Carlos* has an interesting story for you."

Carlos was alone in the salon. He was quite a bit taller than I, good-looking, slim, with dark hair, gray at the temples. And without great fanfare, he reported, "He is here! Since yesterday."

"Well," I said, and wondered why I had not been told about that earlier.

"Yes, that is correct," *Carlos* interrupted me. "We could have met earlier. And we would have, if your *Johnny* had done a better job in telling the difference between lemons and oranges."

It had been agreed that between June 12 and June 17 every morning between 1100 hours and 1200 hours, *Carlos* would sit in a certain café and wait for *Johnny*. *Johnny* had orders immediately after arriving in Lisbon to go to this café around 1100 hours, to order a big glass of lemon juice, and to read the *Times* (London).

"So, I sit there as ordered around eleven o'clock," *Carlos* told me. "The café is pretty empty. *Johnny* turns up punctually at eleven o'clock. I recognized him at first sight, and I could have headed toward him and greeted him right away, but I always remember what my father used to say, 'Don't trip over your feet.' So, I just observed him. He acted quite naturally, looked around, and sat down at my table. I acted as if I were angry, and I thought, let him first order his lemon juice. Then I will send him greetings from Jack."

"So," *Carlos* continued, "the waiter comes, and *Johnny* orders orange juice, not lemon juice! Perhaps he just sent me a substitute. I waited until twelve o'clock. *Johnny* did not say a word. I clapped my hands. The waiter comes. I pay. *Johnny* looks at me questioningly. I look at his orange juice, which he had not touched, and I leave. Something is wrong, I think. But tomorrow we will try once again.

"So, at the same time, I went back there, and I sat at the same table. Again, around 11:15, your *Johnny* turned up. Again, as yesterday, he heads directly for my table. The difference is that this time, he said, 'Good morning.' I nodded, and I thought that I ought to let him place his order and read his paper. Again, as yesterday, he ordered orange juice and looked at me challengingly. I turned hot under the collar.

"The waiter brings the orange juice, and *Johnny* looks at me again. That was too much for me. My Brazilian mother outdid my Prussian father, and I said, 'Excuse me. It is not really my business. But why do you always order orange juice, and why do you not drink it then?'

"He stared at me without understanding. His eyes became quite big. He slapped his forehead, and in a booming voice called loud enough for everyone to hear, 'I'll be a monkey's uncle! Damned! This seasickness apparently rattled my brain.' He called the waiter, 'Take this thing away, and bring me lemon juice!' And again he looks at me and said, 'That is better; isn't it?' If he were not such a nice fellow, I would have let him have it. But I almost hugged him around the neck. In other words, he will be here around 2100 hours. He takes two different taxis, enters a certain side street, and there, Juan, my driver, picks him up in my car."

Although I really wasn't in the mood, I had to laugh. "And I, too, have had quite an experience," I said, but then *Juanita* appeared and I immediately stopped.

"You can keep talking. *Juanita* knows what this is all about. She's my secretary." But I hesitated until she had served the tea and then left again.

"You know that fellow, *Rodrigo* in Madrid? Next time, he had better not turn up again at my place!" I continued, and told *Don Carlos* my own story.

Johnny turned up shortly after 2100 hours. He looked miserable and made a nervous impression, something that was quite unusual for him. "*Doktor,* I am so glad to see you again, and that I escaped not simply the hell of the storm but also the hell in England. Believe you me, it was not so easy."

"I expect you're right," I said. As I shook hands with him, I noted the little man had a fever. With a heavy heart, I decided to let him have another night of rest and to postpone our talk for the next day.

As we met the next morning, I did not read him the riot act. I knew *Johnny* could not have gotten to Lisbon without the help of the Secret Intelligence Service. "How did you clear things up with the SIS?" I asked.

"There was no other way," he said. "In the beginning, I thought I might be able to come along as a blind passenger with a captain friend, but that was impossible. They did not let me approach the train station without a special identity paper, even though the captain was with me. Then I finally followed your advice, and I offered my services to the IS [SIS]. The captain with the SIS was extremely distrustful, for which I cannot blame him. He wanted to know precisely why I suddenly decided to offer my services. First, I tried the patriotic route. I told him I could not serve with weapons in the army, and I believed that I might have a better opportunity to operate in the IS. Since I was a Welshman, the officer did not believe my patriotic approach, but wanted me to tell him what I would propose. Quite modestly, I noted that he ought to know that better than I.

"Now he ran me through the wringer and told me point-blank that I worked for the Nazis. My God, *Doktor,* I can assure you I did not feel at all well when he said that. It might have been that they had really observed me already in the past. But then he said, 'Okay! If you are completely frank, then I will help you. Otherwise, you're finished.' Now what could I do? You yourself had told me that I should offer my services. I told him that I had met you shortly before the war in Brussels, and that you had given me a couple of assignments, and that I met you once in Hamburg where I had some business. 'And what did you give your fine *Herr Doktor* in Hamburg?' he asked me. 'Details about the airfield at Bristol and about the depot in Wolverhampton,' I told him. 'Well, see here,' said the captain, 'and I am supposed to believe you?'

"'Captain,' I said, 'I swear, as I live and breathe.' And then I drew a precise picture for him of the location of both airfields on a piece of paper. I figured that if I could do that, he would have to believe me. Suddenly, he began to laugh, and I realized that I had fallen for his bluff. But perhaps it was all right that way. He asked me about you."

I had observed the little fellow sharply. "And what name did you give him?"

"'I do not know any name,'" *Johnny* replied. "'I just know the *Doktor.*' But I gave him some address in Norway, because I thought he wouldn't be able to get there anyway. Then he suddenly suggested, quite on his own, that I should meet you someplace. At first, I thought Casablanca, but he said you would not find it easy to get there. He suggested Madrid or Lisbon."

I had listened attentively, and I was thinking, Could I still believe Johnny or not? For two years, I had gotten used to trusting him completely. I liked him personally, also. But now, everything suddenly took on an unpleasant aftertaste. Putting myself in the shoes of my British counterpart, I really could not quite imagine that he had allowed Johnny to go to Lisbon alone. At any rate, we would soon find out whether the little one was now deceiving me or my British colleague. I smiled somewhat ironically and said, "That is a tall tale!"

The little one sat up straight but immediately shrank again when I continued, "I mean, that story the two of you have figured out!"

"*Doktor,*" he implored me. "Don't you believe me? Did I deserve that?"

"Okay," I calmed him. "We will see, but how is this all going to play out now?"

Johnny looked up, astonished. "How? What do you mean? Just as before. Perhaps even better." He looked at me triumphantly and continued, "I will tell you precisely what is genuine and what material is just bogus."

I was defeated. Either *Johnny* was smarter than I thought, or he was really honest. There is one thing I could not understand. How would he be able to procure material now without being observed? But I did not let on what I was thinking.

Johnny produced some notes. First, the bogus material: the construction of a new airfield and a report on a search radar for night fighters. The report about the airfield was bound to be true, because our reconnaissance aircraft could easily check that out. That meant my counterpart in England was concerned with boosting my confidence in the little fellow. He could not know that the latter would reveal to me where the report had originated. As for the search radar, I was not able to evaluate it myself. I had to leave that to the technicians in Berlin.

Johnny's own material consisted of a new alloy for shell casings, a sample of which he brought and which a friend of his had taken along on board, plus a fountain pen that was filled with explosives and was to be dropped over German cities. I looked at the thing and shook my head. As an old frontline soldier, I did not understand that sort of warfare.

Then *Johnny* said, "So, *Doktor* . . ." and I noticed he had saved something special for last. "That sort of stuff is just small fry, but you'll never guess what I have now. Next time, I will bring you a genuine former RAF man."

He leaned back in his chair and waited for my reaction, which came quite promptly. "Now, that's quite a bit," I said. "What you could not do in peacetime you now must do in wartime? No, my little magician. That is even too much for me. Keep your flyer in the Royal Luftwaffe, and go home again with special greetings to your Captain!"

I knew I had struck pay dirt. I really felt sorry for him. The little fellow became pale as chalk in the face. He could hardly speak, but I forced myself to remain tough. His behavior told me the man was fighting for his life and had to implement the orders from his new boss out of mere self-preservation. He had no obligations toward me or Germany.

Johnny had gotten control of himself and stammered, "Dear *Doktor,* I understand you. I do not blame you for your distrust, but don't be suspicious. You know my hatred of the British, and you know what minority group I belong to and what that means. Of course, you might not be touched at all by that. It means nothing to you that I trusted you far enough to bring *Lily* along. Don't you remember that immediately prior to the war I asked you to be able to bring my wife and baby along and to let me move to Germany? I told you that I wanted to stay in Germany. You cannot simply ignore that!"

I did not interrupt him. It was the first time that he spoke so emphatically for himself and that I had seen him so excited. I felt sorry for *Johnny,* but I could no longer trust him as I had in the past. He looked at me questioningly.

Finally, I said, "Well, and good! Tell me more."

"You didn't ask me before how I met that RAF man," *Johnny* continued. "Earlier I had told you quite often about my favorite tavern. Since Easter, a stranger kept returning every now and then. He never said a word. He drank his glass alone, and it was hinted that he had done something inappropriate. It took a long time before we greeted each other and finally exchanged a few words. One day, he told me that he had been a pilot with the Royal Luftwaffe. Something went wrong. He was demoted and then discharged. When the war broke out, he volunteered."

"But they would not take him back," I interrupted him.

Johnny noticed the sarcastic undertone. He continued, "That is true! Of course, I immediately thought that this would be the right man for the *Doktor.* Then he told me that he had been offered a job as an employee with the British counterintelligence of the Security Service, MI5. I was shaken, and I was sure that they had sent him to snoop on me."

I am just as sure, I thought to myself. I became impatient. I do not like to be made a fool of, but I merely replied, "I can well imagine."

"A couple of days later," *Johnny* continued, "we were discussing his work. Above all, he found it unpleasant because he never had any money. I treated him a couple of times. I was still thinking of Lisbon. One day, when I realized that I was not getting anywhere, I asked him whether he could not tell me something about his duty station. I would love to work there myself. He replied, 'You'll go to the dogs there.'

"'Maybe I know some other possibilities for both of us to earn some money,' I proposed. The next evening, he asked me, 'What were you talking about yesterday when you mentioned another possibility?' Then I told him that I knew someone in Lisbon who could help him earn some money. If he would help me get there, I could also do something for him, and we soon agreed to move ahead."

And we all live happily ever after, I finished the story mentally. My comrades from Group III could not have come up with a better plan.

"Okay," I said. "When will he come?"

"If all goes well, in October. Do you believe that the Germans will be in London by then?"

Now he really began to question me. I said quickly, "Hopefully. But then he need no longer take the trouble, and I will personally get to meet your clever Captain."

I discussed all possibilities with him and gave him 50 pounds. *Johnny* had always been modest, and I believed him when he said he could not get along on that until October, especially not now when he had to give something to his new partner. So, I gave him another 50 pounds, and we took our leave of each other.

The reports that *Johnny* had given to me received a good evaluation and triggered a series of further questions that were passed on to *Johnny* in order to continue the new "game."

With a heavy heart, I drafted my report. I was not quite sure what kind of game *Johnny* would play, but I would have to drop the little man from my roster after he had worked so long and successfully for me. Nevertheless, I wanted to meet him in Lisbon again to take a good look at the RAF man.

20

Operation Sea Lion

Six weeks after the German troops had occupied Belgium, Holland, and finally France, Marshal Pétain asked for an armistice. The victory over France was huge, but not decisive. As long as Britain was still in the fight and rejected the earnest offers made by Hitler, an end to the war was unthinkable.

The submarine war caused great disruption for the British, but it did not suffice to bring Britain to its knees. The German Navy and Luftwaffe could not break Britain's supremacy, but that supremacy was not powerful enough to decide the war in Britain's favor. Although France had fallen in the meantime, there was still no doubt that America, under Roosevelt, would, in this case, once again fight on the side of Germany's enemies.

Churchill was unquestionably ahead of Germany in recognizing that priority expansion of the British Royal Air Force was the only option that could save England. The German General Staff also recognized this and, therefore, suggested to Hitler a landing in England; victory over Britain would not be possible except by defeat on land.

For the German population, war with the British had become routine. With naïve habit, every couple of days we expected a special announcement concerning the sinking of British shipping tonnage. The air raid alarms became practically a daily occurrence. The initial worry or fear that had been felt during the first air raid alarms gradually decreased to a minimum, and we began to think of the wail of the sirens during those weeks as merely annoying interruptions of our sleep or work.

The ostentatiously displayed calm was purely external among the operations staffs and the Abwehr. A new event was being prepared before any of the uninitiated could guess what it might be. Operation Sea Lion, the cover name for the planned invasion of England, was born.

Precise orders for the exploration of certain sections of terrain in southern England definitely pointed to preparations for a German landing operation. And, as all operational preparations are connected with advanced reconnaissance of enemy positions, here again, the Abwehr was increasingly called upon to step up to the plate before the troops had any inkling about such plans.

The agents in England were ordered, in addition to their daily weather reports, to sideline all ongoing tasks and, based on precise guidelines, focus exclusively on terrain reconnaissance. Naturally, direct questions about landing possibilities or paratroops and cargo gliders had to be avoided, as well as questions concerning the fortifications and defensive positions along certain coastal strips for sea landings.

The agents on the other side inhaled the morning breeze and, with redoubled zeal, went to work. Their work was accordingly good and prompt. Their reports, as well as the air and sea reconnaissance missions, constituted the basis for training the German troops who were earmarked for the invasion. Enemy strongpoints and other defensive measures were replicated in suitable exercise areas, based on reports, and the overcoming of obstacles was practiced.

After all, the northern coasts of mainland Europe were in German hands. Direct civilian traffic between the continent and England had finally stopped. Such contact existed now with Sweden, Spain, and Portugal, but the information we gleaned via those detours was rather worthless for the operational command due to considerable delays.

The few secret transmitters we were still able to use in England prior to the start of the war (*Johnny*'s transmitter was the most important) did not suffice to close this information gap. As a result, we immediately had to take other measures. All intelligence stations received orders to look for volunteers who were ready to parachute into England or were ready to cross via fishing boats from Belgium.

Training and deployment of parachute agents were delegated to me. The operation was given the cover name "Lena." [Lena was the Abwehr's information-gathering operation to aid Operation Sea Lion.] I was to follow them to England later with the second invasion wave, as part of Sea Lion.

There were no models we could use for guidance. Everything had to be created from scratch, and no time was to be lost. The volunteers for Operation Lena were governed by special parameters. Far more was required of them than of an average agent. Not only did they have to be ready to parachute under the most difficult of circumstances, they also were expected to be in top physical condition. They could not be younger than twenty or older than thirty.

They had to be intelligent enough to understand the broader range of their tasks, and so technically talented that they could learn to build and operate a secret transmitter in a short period of time. Their curriculum was to include comprehensive training regarding aircraft, airfields, and industrial facilities, as well as basic instructions for drafting weather reports.

The first two volunteers were sent to me a few days after the order was issued. One was *Hansen* (Wulf Dietrich Christian Schmidt [Tate to MI5], later known as Harry Williamson), a Dane. The other, Gösta Caroli (Summer to MI5), whom we named *Nilberg*, was a Finn. Both were of German extraction, were fluent in

German, and spoke English rather well. *Hansen* was a mechanical engineer, and *Nilberg* was a mechanic. Both had worked in Germany.

I viewed them with mixed feelings as they reported to me. They were good-looking young men. *Hansen* was about twenty-four years old, a little taller than average, slim, with dark blond hair and fine but energetic facial features. *Nilberg* was somewhat older and taller than *Hansen*. His face was rather irregular and long; but, over a narrow, slightly hooked nose, a pair of clear blue eyes sparkled at me, inspiring confidence. I liked them both. I needed such men, but it weighed heavily on my soul when I thought of the dangers ahead that were far beyond routine military duty. I alone carried responsibility for them. While all of this went through my mind, I noted I also was being keenly observed, as if they knew how much their fate depended on me.

Then I broke the silence and said, "I believe you know what you have volunteered for. We won't beat around the bush. You know that you will have to put your life on the line and that, after you have parachuted, you are entirely on your own. I want you to consider me your colleague. I'm responsible for your training, but I expect conscientious cooperation. The special training course, which we have arranged for you, demands your full commitment. Time is urgent. We must, at the latest, be ready in six weeks. We will start tomorrow morning."

"You can also rely on us, as we must rely on you," *Hansen* said, simply, and *Nilberg* nodded in agreement.

I shook hands with them, but before they took their leave, I reminded them once again of their duty to maintain absolute silence. "You will be billeted in a small boardinghouse with which we have no official connection. I must caution you urgently against making the slightest hint as to your membership in our outfit. Your work, of course, will keep you busy most of the day and frequently also at night; but you have to be particularly careful, especially during your off-duty times."

"Miss Friede," I then said, "these are Mr. *Hansen* and Mr. *Nilberg*. Please give them additional food ration stamps and the necessary pocket money."

The next morning, both men were already seated with their transmitter device.

"Not only your work, but under certain circumstances, also your life, will depend on this little machine," they were told by their instructor, Wein, Major Trautmann's assistant. "The more you become one with it, the greater your success will be and, above all, your survival."

After lengthy experimentation, the equipment had been specifically adapted for this purpose. It had to be small and light. It had to be sturdy so it could withstand any impact upon parachuting. It had to operate in such a basic manner that the routine could be mastered quickly, and, with the smallest possible antenna, it had to work perfectly at the greatest possible distance.

In addition to operating the radio, everyone had to learn how to build a properly working unit with standard commercially available parts, and they had to practice how to stash the unit in hiding places: under floors, in window frames, between walls, in trees, in the earth, and so forth. They had to be ready at any moment to instantaneously change their position, but that was not all.

A parachute agent must be an "all-around man." Participants received detailed briefings on various airfields, how to observe flight paths, and how to sketch different types of installations on maps for later comparisons. They practiced identifying various aircraft and visited antiaircraft armament factories, where they learned about specific flak calibers and distinguishing features of guns. Instruction in weather service was particularly intensive. Weather reports were of utmost importance for the Luftwaffe, since all official weather reports had been suspended. The two young men worked so diligently and conscientiously that they were ready shortly before the end of the six-week term.

Berlin sent us British identity cards, ration cards, and large quantities of British pounds. Identity cards and ration cards had been delivered earlier by *Johnny* and had been filled out according to *Barbarossa*'s specifications.

Both men could explain their presence in England with comparative ease: they were Scandinavian refugees who had come to England on a fishing boat. They had met in Oslo. With help from the intelligence station there, we had obtained all necessary details and the required papers that indicated the men had worked in England before.

On a hot July day, we started our trip together in an open car into the unknown. Whoever might see us on the way and grumble about the "cruddy civilians" could not possibly know that the two were heading for one of the most serious missions soldiers could tackle. Shortly before Cologne, we took our last break near the autobahn so they could test their equipment at a greater distance from Hamburg, for the first time acting entirely on their own. Their excitement prior to this first test was understandable. Everything came off automatically. They gave their call sign. Eagerly, they waited for the reply.

Hansen thought he had heard it. Then his face became somber. Once again, he checked everything. Finally, he tore the earphones off, cursed, and exclaimed, "This miserable thing fails on the first attempt!"

Nilberg was quite calm. He listened attentively and then observed the passing cars. He nodded his head and said, "I have contact, but whenever a car passes, the background noise is so great that everything else is blotted out. We have to get further away from the autobahn."

We switched locations and immediately made connection. The unit had passed its acid test. Relieved, we packed up and enjoyed our breakfast with greater appetite. The drive to Brussels proceeded without notable incidents.

The sun burned from a cloudless heaven. The heat and the monotonous sound of the car's engine made us drowsy. *Hansen* and *Nilberg* dozed, half-asleep. I puffed on my cigar and, from time to time, forced myself to say a few words to the driver to prevent him and myself from falling asleep.

But there was another reason why I could not fall asleep under any circumstances. For once in my life, I wanted to cross a border where no one could stop me. Nevertheless, as we came to the barrier at the old autobahn, we had to get out. The customs station had been reinforced by several members of the military police, and the officer on duty scrutinized us civilians with suspicious glances. Our papers were checked even more thoroughly than usual. I thus was deprived of my anticipated pleasure. But the identity papers issued by the Wehrmacht High Command did their job, and the barrier was raised so we could go on.

The streets in Belgium were comparatively empty. Here and there, you could see a house that had been shot to pieces or a burned-out tank that had been pushed aside. There was hardly anything to remind us that the war had swept over the country two months earlier. Of German troops, we saw few. Only once did we meet a long supply convoy. It was not until evening, as we neared Brussels, that the streets filled with life.

In Brussels, we parked near the intelligence station in a row of other civilian cars, where our field-gray paint would not arouse any attention. I went to the duty station alone. I wanted to avoid, at all costs, having my companions exposed to unauthorized representatives of the Intelligence Service. All necessary preparations had been made from here. *Hansen* and *Nilberg* were housed in a hotel that was inhabited by military personnel and civilians. They were instructed to meet me the next morning at a designated house. Then they returned to their hotel alone. That same night, a captain and a first lieutenant of the Luftwaffe reported to me.

The captain was the best reconnaissance pilot in the Luftwaffe squadron assigned to intelligence. He had been given the mission of dropping the parachute agents, and he was responsible for the technical implementation of the operation. The first lieutenant was his observer; in civilian life, he was a meteorologist. During his student years, he had spent some time in England, and from his own experience he was familiar with weather and ground conditions in southern England and Wales.

We spread the maps out on a large table in my spacious room. The drop areas had to be different for each mission and had to be defined with utmost circumspection. Unfortunately, there was no organization on the ground that could provide secret messages. The time between the jump and hitting the ground is the most dangerous. The greatest obstacle is overcome after the jumper releases himself from the parachute without detection.

Besides the regular area map, there was another one that showed in detail the ground organizations of the Royal Air Force, sham airfields, and antiaircraft artillery positions. As we spread the maps out before us, the captain said, "The RAF's original map can't be any better than this. When I previously photographed these fields from an altitude of 10,000 meters using our newest instruments, I did not suspect that one fine day I would stand in front of this map and contemplate how I could possibly fly between them unscathed."

"And when I received information regarding the construction of this field," I pointed to a big red triangle in Wales, a field that Simon had explored, "Berlin would not believe the report. Some wise guy in the Fifth Department asserted that this could not be an appropriate place for an airfield."

The various maps were checked out most carefully, and when we thought we had found the right drop zone, the meteorologist came with another map and alerted us to the fact that the area happened to be moor bogs. After we also consulted the population density map, we finally agreed on a spot near Salisbury, where the Royal Artillery gunnery training range was located.

Now, it was my job to familiarize my two informants with the surrounding area. I ordered the intelligence station to prepare exact sketches on an enlarged scale, showing the trails and roads as well as the nearest settlements so *Hansen* and *Nilberg* could memorize everything accurately. The captain and the first lieutenant plotted their course, and now all that was needed was to wait for a dark night. The meteorologist had done his best, but the following few nights were too bright for a mission.

Hansen and *Nilberg* went sightseeing in Brussels. Once, I let them drive to Antwerp. After two days, I became concerned. I thought it entirely too dangerous to leave those two young fellows alone for too long. Indeed, on the fourth day, *Hansen* turned up in my room, although he had been strictly forbidden to do so. I was barely able to control myself.

"*Herr Doktor*, I'm dropping out," he gasped. "*Nilberg* got involved with a Belgian woman. Last night he brought her along without telling me. Now, all of our elaborate cover story is in vain."

So, I had been right to worry. I should have put them on a regular duty schedule. I sat *Hansen* down in a chair and gave him a cigarette. Then I said, seemingly going along with him, "Well, that is something! I always thought *Nilberg* was a rational chap. Naturally, we must do something right away." And, for emphasis, I added, "Under these circumstances, you must jump alone."

That seemed to settle the matter. *Hansen*'s fury immediately turned to worry. I knew how close the two were. I did not really want to send them out individually, but the most important thing right now was to calm *Hansen* down. *Nilberg* and the girl could not stay together, regardless. So, I asked, "Did *Nilberg* give the girl his right name?"

"No," *Hansen* replied, considerably calmer. "That would not be so bad because our identity cards gave another name anyway, but who knows what else he might have told her."

"Well," I said, "not every little girl is an agent, and besides, we don't really know ourselves exactly when and where the jump is going to take place."

Then I put my hand on his shoulder and continued, "Now, today, you act as if nothing has happened. *Nilberg* will see the girl once more, but he won't know that beforehand. You let me know as soon as possible when and where they will meet, and then you join them. Act quite normal, and do not reproach him. People in love must be taken seriously; otherwise, they get very defensive. On the contrary, tell him that the girl has made a good impression on you. Everything else you leave to me; tomorrow everything will look different."

Actually, I wasn't so sure of that myself. Briefly, I considered the idea that *Hansen* might have been looking for a pretext to chicken out at the last minute. However, in the final analysis, I was convinced I was doing him an injustice. I was no longer anxious about *Nilberg*. I would straighten him out again, and he might not even notice it. I went to the intelligence station and had a long talk there with the head of Group III, Counterespionage.

In the afternoon as *Hansen*, *Nilberg*, and the girl were drinking a glass of bad, but at any rate cold, beer on the terrace of a little café opposite the Gare du Nord, a stocky, dark gentleman wearing a light-gray business suit sat at the next table. He smoked a Dutch cigar and, acting bored, looked at the colorful street scene. The still-unaccustomed German uniforms seemed to make him feel uncomfortable. Several times when a uniformed man passed the tiny open terrace, he buried his face in his newspaper; but the world around them did not exist for *Nilberg* and the girl. *Hansen* participated in the conversation, which was occasionally in German. The girl spoke with a heavy French accent. The gentleman at the next table was just lighting a second cigar when the three stood up. He paid, followed them at a respectful distance, and acted as if he was window shopping. They wandered along Boulevard du Nord for a while and then turned off onto a side street. *Hansen* took his leave in front of a small, unobtrusive tavern.

Nilberg followed the girl through the side door and up a staircase. After about an hour, he emerged again. He was alone and, without looking around further, headed toward the train station.

The gentleman in the light suit, who was still standing in front of a store window, turned around and observed the entrance to the tavern. After a short time, the girl appeared in the door, looked down the boulevard, and quickly ran off in the opposite direction. The man in the light-gray suit threw his cigar away and followed her. He caught up with her at the next corner. He hardly raised his hat as he addressed her, and when the girl apparently became fresh, he showed her his identification. Resigned, she shrugged her shoulders, and the two disappeared around the next corner.

The next evening, *Hansen* phoned me and asked me to get together and talk. He seemed greatly relieved when he entered my room shortly thereafter. *Nilberg* had again made a date with the girl, he told me. When she did not show up, he went to the obscure little tavern. There he learned she had not been seen since the day before. He was disappointed and angry, but by the time he got back to *Hansen*, his anger had dissipated, and he only laughed, somewhat embarrassed.

Then both of them had a good laugh and decided to go out together in the evening. I had already gotten the picture, but I didn't let on and wished them both a nice evening.

The situation with the girl did not seem to have become dangerous yet. She was a "girl for money," and that made it comparatively easy to put her in custody for a couple of days. It was not possible to prove that she had any contact with the enemy intelligence service. At any rate, I thought it better *Nilberg* should not meet her again.

To prevent any further trouble, I scheduled a side trip to Paris with *Nilberg* and *Hansen*. They had already expressed a desire to go there. In Paris, I could not avoid taking them along with me to the intelligence station in the Hotel Lutetia on Boulevard Raspail. I had no doubt that everybody who came and went there would be watched, and I let the two of them wear hats and dark glasses, contrary to their usual habit.

Several tests using transmitters were conducted from the rooftop of the hotel. Reception was perfect on both sides. *Hansen* and *Nilberg* were doubly satisfied, because the distance from Paris to Hamburg was greater than the distance from London to Hamburg. Moreover, they had been able to visit Paris.

On the morning of the second day, we returned to Brussels. As we slowly drove along the Champs Élysées heading toward Compiègne, I felt the irresistible urge to revisit the old battlefield at Lécluse from World War I. Just once I wanted to walk across the fields, upright and in the bright light of day. On our first night at Lécluse, our trench had received its baptism by fire with ten hours of artillery barrage, and at the foot of the termite hill at Boiry-Notre-Dame, I had run for my life as company runner when the gas alarm had suddenly sounded. I had forgotten my gas mask. Now, the area lay peacefully before me in bright sunshine. It seemed the war had swept over so quickly that there was nothing left here to remind us.

After being wounded in 1918, I had been billeted with a French farmer not far from here. At that time, I was not quite twenty, and I remembered again how my NCO had shown me an inscription on the framework of a French shelter we had captured: *"En vingt ans on pense plus à la loine amie quà la destinée de la patrie"* (At twenty, one thinks more about their distant beloved than the destiny of their fatherland).

Walking along there now, I was again overcome by a melancholy feeling as my thoughts drifted to that time twenty years earlier. I recalled a particular evening when I had returned late from the Officer's Club. The street had been lit with bright moonlight, and the air had been filled with the aroma of freshly cut grass. In the distance, I had been able to hear the dull rumbling of the artillery. My thoughts had been far away from all military actions.

I had not thought of danger or death. An inexplicable yearning had arisen in me. I inhaled deeply, and my heart was filled with that indescribable longing one only feels when they are twenty. As if in a dream, I had walked under the poplar trees lining this quiet village street and hoped it would never end. I approached the farmhouse, but the door was locked. The old farmer was not there to greet me with his friendly *"Bonsoir"* and to chat with his young "enemy" and tactfully help him with the rough spots of his schoolboy French.

Cautiously, I had opened the door with the big iron key so as not to disturb anybody, and on tiptoe, I crossed the clay floor of the small, dark hut. Suddenly, I noticed light under the threshold. Could the old man still be waiting for me in the kitchen? I heard a softly suppressed sobbing. Cautiously, I opened the kitchen door. The room was lit up. Baffled, I just stood there. The floor was covered with crates, boxes, and suitcases, and then in the opposite corner, in the shadows, on one of the larger suitcases, I spotted the dainty shape of a young girl. She took her hands away from her face and looked at me in despair with tear-filled dark eyes.

I thought I was dreaming. "Pardon," I stammered.

But as I tried to withdraw, feeling distraught, I heard a clear, delicate little voice, *"Bonsoir."* She timidly motioned me to come in. I was mesmerized and stared at her, and since I did not know what to say, I sat down on a crate opposite her.

She wiped the tears off with one finger and said, "I am the niece of Mr. Foucault here. My father is a doctor in Lécluse. When the Germans marched through our city, all civilians were evacuated behind the lines. My father had to stay in the field hospital and help them. I was brought here to my uncle's place in an ambulance."

I still felt that secret yearning that had overcome me on the moonlit way back, and she appeared to me like a being from another world. I had the urge to stroke her hair, but how could I, a German officer with my puritanical education, touch this deserted French girl? And how could she allow an enemy to come closer? We simply sat there and looked at each other and tried to speak a few foolish words of excuse and war and duty and the senselessness of having to fight each other.

After a long, embarrassed silence, I forced myself to stand up; I bowed briefly, and said goodnight. She looked at me, smiling with a glance that betrayed both fear and yearning, disappointment and relief. "*Merci, monsieur le lieutenant,*" she said gently.

How often had I thought of this evening, but never as vividly as today. I had to smile about these two platonic children of twenty years ago. In those days, our paths were charted for us in advance by our ancestors, our parents, our superiors, and our governments. We had been educated to become obedient citizens, but above all, we had been taught what was right and to perform our duty. We were happy in our own individual ways, and what about now? We had to start all over. We had worked; we had starved; we had studied; we had toiled; and we had built up a new life with new experiences and new ideals. Now here we were again in the midst of a cruel war. It was not the war that was so horrible. The horrible thing was that it had come to us again despite the lessons we had learned, despite our new ideas and ideals. Or perhaps precisely because of them?

Again, on both sides of the border, we had to bear the burden conscientiously, diligently, dutifully, equally good and equally bad. The average citizen, just like me, my little platonic French love, and her uncle. What should we do? We did our duty, and we fought for our lives, each in his own way. I had done my duty then, and I was doing it now, although not with the same illusions.

With a sudden jolt, I returned to reality as my driver brought me breakfast from our marching rations.

We returned to Brussels late on the evening of the same day. I found a series of dispatches and inquiries from my duty station in Hamburg. Several other volunteers had arrived during my absence, and they were already being trained.

The weather reports for our mission were favorable, and *Hansen* and *Nilberg* were once again "put through the wringer."

The next morning, I drove with them to the forward staging base; they would take off from historical Rennes, Brittany. The last time I had been here, I had come to visit the well-known Palais de Justice, built in the seventeenth century, the famous Fine Arts Museum, and the magnificent library of the old university, which housed 350,000 volumes.

The captain and his observer were ready to take off in their specially equipped He 111. For the last time, I shook hands with *Hansen* and *Nilberg* before they disappeared into the fuselage of the aircraft. The black bird had already vanished into the darkness before it reached the end of the runway; and I, again in deep thought, climbed into my car and returned to Brussels.

Now came the big test of nerves until the first radio contact was made and the endless wait was finally over, at which time I could at last tell myself that the two fellows, who had become my comrades, had not sacrificed themselves for nothing. If everything went smoothly, then the captain and the first lieutenant were bound to return by early morning. I could not sleep, so I worked on my correspondence through the rest of the night.

The captain reported back from the operation at 0430 hours. They had flown over the English Channel so low that they almost touched the crests of the waves so that British radar could not pick them up. Shortly before they reached the coast, the newly installed high-altitude engine had quickly taken them up to 7,000 meters. The night was ideal for this kind of mission. In a foam of thin cirrus clouds, high above the thick lower cloud layer, they flew without trouble through the dark night. After half an hour of straight-ahead flying, they almost dove down to 1,000 meters, and continued to slide with their engines choked down at a height of 150 meters to the jump zone. They had luck. In front of a low, black mountain of clouds, the aircraft, which had been covered with fresh soot paint that would swallow even the last beam of light, became completely invisible, and the strong wind drowned out the sharp whistling of the contoured metal.

Hansen and *Nilberg* had been sitting quietly in the dark fuselage and had waited for the moment when the captain would give them the signal to jump. Mechanically, they had once again checked the fit of their belts. In an instant the captain was next to them and had opened the little door in the fuselage. *Hansen* had been the first to jump into the unknown darkness. Now *Nilberg* had suddenly hesitated, but the captain hadn't left him much time. Before *Nilberg* knew it, he was out of the plane. The captain had waited to close the hatch until after he had made sure the two parachutes had opened and had cleared the aircraft.

Now there was no other choice but to wait. The captain was firmly convinced that all had gone well.

"Thank, God," I said, relieved, "but the waiting that comes now is the worst of all."

At the Hamburg radio station, both radios had been on permanent reception since the jump. Hardly anything was to be expected on the first day, but on the second day, I called the radio station several times only to be told, "Nothing yet, Major." Now I knew the radio operators were just as tense as I was.

Finally, around midnight of the third day, the phone rang next to my bed. I was wide awake immediately. "*3725* is here, Major." I jumped out of the bed.

"The connection is perfect. Wein himself is operating the unit. There is no doubt that *Hansen* has been transmitting."

"What does he have to say?" I asked.

"First of all, he just wanted to check in so that we would know that he's still alive. He'll come back on again soon."

"Well," I said, very happy, "please call me the moment you hear from him. Good night."

I was no longer able to sleep. This was undoubtedly our first success, but now some new worries cropped up. On the next day, we waited in vain. Not until the third day, between three and four o'clock, did we get the next message, along with an explanation for the long silence.

Nilberg's chute had been caught in a tree, and he had been badly bounced around and injured. *Hansen* didn't know what to do. They were hiding at a little farmstead. Desperately, he called for help. That was a new burden for me. They both knew I had *Johnny* in England, but I had warned them repeatedly that they would have to get through on their own.

Now I faced a grave decision. I would have to violate my strict principle, but I knew no other way out. While I was still hesitating, *Hansen*'s messages became increasingly desperate. Again and again, I had Wein, my instructor, confirm for me that he was absolutely certain that it was *Hansen*'s "fist," so that he finally convinced me. With great trepidation, I decided somehow to get *Johnny* involved in this.

After the next contact with *Johnny*, the radio messages flew back and forth between Hamburg and *Hansen* and Hamburg, back and forth. *Hansen* wanted to know details about *Johnny*, but I adamantly refused. After *Johnny* had reported the time and place for a meeting, we agreed upon a code word for each.

Later on, in Lisbon, *Johnny* told me, "Believe me, *Doktor*, that was a nail-biter for me. I let *Nilberg* wait for a long time, and I kept watching him. I had to make sure that he was alone. There were not many people in this little railroad station. Your man was standing in front of a train schedule, diligently making notes on trains. No one could have noticed anything unusual about him, but I was sure he was taking notes in order to hide his agitation. As I finally stood next to him and acted as if I was also looking for a train and gave him the code word, he asked briefly, 'Where can I go?' I gave him the address of a Welsh doctor to meet at a specific time. When I noted the poor physical condition *Nilberg* was in, I advised him to surrender voluntarily and to offer to work with the British Security Service. He accepted my proposal."

A fellow prisoner of *Nilberg*'s told me after the war that *Johnny* had turned up the next day accompanied by two men from the British Security Service. After *Johnny* left, they mistreated *Nilberg*. He had tried to flee but was caught again and placed in prison. Again, he had tried to escape, but without success. He had implored his fellow prisoners to inform me immediately of *Johnny*'s treason should they be discharged sooner.

As *Johnny* had told me in Lisbon, he now had a "big number" with the British Security Service. I did not know this had happened at *Nilberg*'s expense. *Johnny* believed he could justify his actions because *Nilberg* could not have done us any good due to his injury, whereas *Johnny*'s old position was greatly strengthened, so he could now do much more for me. Very brutal, but very realistic.

Hansen never saw *Nilberg* again. He continued to work diligently. He brought us important daily weather reports, and after a short time, he sent us valuable reports about airfields, aircraft, and other information. We also were the first to learn from *Hansen* that Eisenhower had visited England. Six weeks later, I nominated him for the award of the Iron Cross, 1st Class, and soon thereafter, I was able to report to him the award of this medal via radio. *Hansen* and *Nilberg* were both captured by the British. Schmidt cooperated with the British to avoid execution.

In the meantime, Sea Lion, in which we had placed all our assurance, never jumped as we had hoped but instead went to sleep.

21

Suspending Sea Lion

We received a flood of messages concerning the expansion of British defensive measures. Exact figures gave a clear picture of an almost unimaginable increase in mass production of weapons, especially fighters. Also, the course of the United States heading for war against Germany became ever clearer. We in the Abwehr, and also those within the corporate office, were becoming increasingly uneasy.

With air raids on the rise and the growing certainty of an impending invasion, the British population seemed to grasp for the first time that the war was right at their front door. The response was typically British. Even the most phlegmatic citizen was ready to assist wherever they could.

On the one hand, the German goes into battle with natural discipline and sweeping courage, and his enthusiasm grows along with the initial successes but suffers after every setback. The Englishman, on the other hand, goes into battle with less courage and enthusiasm. His discipline and determination are strengthened, however, with every loss, by the stubborn conviction that he will emerge the victor.

The average German, with his superficial national pride, is soon inclined to give up in a difficult situation, falling victim to disgruntlement and carping, and easily falling victim to even the clumsiest foreign propaganda. The Englishman, however, rejects the enemy's propaganda with even greater haughtiness. Where the German believes everything the foreign radio commentator says with avaricious schadenfreude, the Englishman freely listens to the enemy broadcasts and does not believe a single word they say. And William Joyce is rendered ridiculous and almost harmless as they simply dub him "Lord Haw-Haw." ["William Joyce, aka Lord Haw-Haw, was a notorious broadcaster of Nazi propaganda to the UK during World War II. His announcement 'Germany calling, Germany calling' was a familiar sound across the airwaves, introducing threats and misinformation that he broadcast from his Hamburg base," http://www.bbc.co.uk/archive/hawhaw/. He was hanged in London in 1946.]

Reports from our agents overseas presented a clear picture of increased resistance among the population in the street. The greater the danger, the tougher, the more disciplined, and the more resolute they became, and the more frequently the informants had to listen to the grim "We'll win the war."

But such news seemed unwelcome in Berlin. Even internal reports that related to specific statistics regarding increasing enemy aircraft production were thought to be genuine. In addition, the training directives of the various Wehrmacht forces for Operation Sea Lion obviously lacked a common plan for mutual collaboration.

We dared to hope that our informants could hold on at least until Sea Lion perhaps dared to jump. Their funds had been calculated to last for three to four months, and the secret decryption code that the parachute agents had been given could withstand deciphering a little longer. Everyone had been geared toward an invasion to come soon.

But the Sea Lion was still hesitating. The air battle over Great Britain ended in a definite failure. An invasion was impossible without the necessary air supremacy. On occasion, Sea Lion again tried to raise its sleepy-eyed head, until it finally went into hibernation in September 1940. On November 12, 1940, in his directive No. 18 (Seizure of Gibraltar), the Führer and Supreme Commander of the Wehrmacht added, "Due to changes in the overall situation there might still be a possibility or necessity of returning to Operation 'Sea Lion' in the spring of 1941. In every respect, the three services of the Wehrmacht must make a serious commitment to improve the rudiments for such an undertaking."

By the end of August, we already knew for certain that Operation Lena was doomed to fail. We had already abolished the special mission for our parachute agents, but we still had ways to continue their employment. In February 1942, Sea Lion was permanently canceled.

We had heard nothing further from *Nilberg*. *Hansen* continued to work reliably, but now he began to have difficulties. He had no more money, and we did not come through. He felt deserted and didn't know where to turn.

We had no doubt that *Hansen*'s code could not remain secret for long, provided it had not already been deciphered. Accordingly, our radio messages were drafted cautiously so the British could at least be easily misled. I advised *Hansen* to change positions as often as possible and to transmit only every three days and at different times. Putting him once again in touch with *Johnny* would have been a betrayal of both. As our prospects for helping *Hansen* kept deteriorating, I solemnly decided to advise him to volunteer for war service. Perhaps in that way he might be able to save his life and his freedom. His papers were in best order. I saw no other way out.

Then I suddenly recalled that Dr. Thoran, one of my earlier "pupils" who was now in Central Headquarters in Berlin, had at one time talked to *Hansen* about the Japanese. *Hansen* had used an expression that was typical of him. He had said, "A yellow snail with the face of a white man." This was an expression known only to him and us.

"That is the code word," said Thoran, very excited, when I called him on the direct line to Berlin. "We will use that, and the British can go ahead and take their time to decipher it without solving the riddle."

"Do you think that the Japanese would go along?" I asked.

"Yes," Thoran said. "We are in close contact here with the Japanese Secret Service. They are ready to collaborate with us. I'm sure that we could help *Hansen* via one of their people in London."

Dr. Thoran came to Hamburg, and together we worked out a plan to bring *Hansen* and the Japanese together. With this plan, Thoran went back to Berlin to make the necessary arrangements with the Japanese, while we did everything possible to keep *Hansen* at his perch.

Hansen was like hounded game. He lived in barns and almost starved to death, but when we urgently begged him to hold out for a couple more days, his reply startled the radio operators in Wohldorf, "L.m.A. [*Leck mich am Arsch* (kiss my ass)]," he radioed in open text, "I sh . . . on the shitty German Intelligence Service." Now, I had no doubt whatsoever he was the real *Hansen*. It was so typical of him, and his message really calmed me down.

In the meantime, Dr. Thoran had also received permission from Canaris to establish direct contact with the Japanese Intelligence Service. The radio messages went back and forth between Berlin and Tokyo. All details were worked out after a short time.

My first response to *Hansen* read like this, "Thanks for the shit (unencrypted)"; whereas in code, I continued, "Help under way." At first, my assurance did not seem to make any big impression on him. He was desperate, and he was pissed off, even though his curses had toned down somewhat.

Dr. Thoran had done a good job. His thorough knowledge of London and his good memory regarding bus lines facilitated the unique solution to this convoluted problem. The instructions to the Japanese agents in London went from Berlin to Tokyo and from there via two secret transmitters to London. *Hansen* gradually realized that help was actually on the way, and his language became somewhat politer.

Of course, he did not like the idea of being placed in contact with the Japanese, but when he realized he would not have to interact with a Japanese agent face-to-face, he was calmed by the prospect of being liberated from his desperate situation. This was the plan: on the agreed-upon day, *Hansen* waited at a certain bus stop at a certain time. On the second bus that stopped before him, he saw a Japanese reading the *Times*. As the bus stopped, the Japanese put the newspaper on his knee, took off his spectacles and breathed on them, wiped them once with a handkerchief, and put them back on again. *Hansen* then knew he had seen the right man. He allowed the bus to continue and got on the next one. At the fifth stop, he again got off and waited for the fourth bus. On this one, again, sat the same Japanese who, previously, at one of the intermediate stops, had skipped two buses. *Hansen* stepped in and sat on the free seat next to the Japanese, who was still reading his newspaper.

After they had sat quietly next to each other for the next three stops, *Hansen* asked quite casually, "Anything special in the newspaper today?"

The Japanese looked up briefly. "Please," he said, "take it. I get off here."

Hansen picked up the paper. The Japanese disappeared. *Hansen* acted as if he were reading the paper and continued for another couple of stops until he, too, disembarked, folded the newspaper carefully, and stuck it in his coat pocket.

That same night, I sat in the reception room in Wohldorf, anticipating *Hansen*'s radio message with great excitement. He corresponded in typical style, "Tonight I get drunk. Back again tomorrow."

We, too, allowed ourselves a glass. Hidden in the paper that *Hansen* had received was the equivalent of 20,000 marks in English pound notes, some of which, of course, were forged, enough to supply *Hansen* for the rest of the war.

In the middle of the final preparations for my transfer to North Africa, a message arrived in September from *Johnny* that he would be in Lisbon with his new man between the twenty-sixth and thirtieth of the month.

I again flew as courier *Dr. Renken*, as I had in June. Of course, this trip was considerably more comfortable. Now, after the end of the campaign in France, I was able to fly directly via Lyon and Madrid to Lisbon, using a standard Lufthansa aircraft. And this time, I did not allow anyone to force a bomb-loaded suitcase on me. Again, *Don Carlos* reserved a room for me in the Duas Nações.

Johnny had not yet arrived by the twenty-sixth. On the twenty-seventh, an English ship came in, but without the little fellow. Nothing again on the twenty-eighth and twenty-ninth. I became worried, and *Carlos* kept cursing. Two English ships were to come in on September 30. *Don Carlos* himself was at the harbor, but the ships did not come. Either they were held up by the severe storm that raged for twenty-four hours off the Atlantic coast, or they had been sunk by German submarines. Time was short, but nevertheless, I decided to wait another couple of days.

The storm moved from the Atlantic over land and drenched the city so that I could not even manage a little sightseeing trip. Resigned, I was making ready for my overnight return flight on October 1, when, toward evening, I received a letter from *Don Carlos*. *Johnny* had arrived! But, as the result of a long bout with seasickness, he was in such miserable condition that *Carlos* proposed to let him rest until the next morning. I was happy *Johnny* had arrived at last. I would not have liked to go back without having seen him. But then I read *Carlos*'s lines once again, and I noticed there was no mention of the second man *Johnny* had wanted to bring along.

The next morning the storm had calmed down somewhat. *Johnny* beamed when he spotted me. "I would not do this again even for you, *Doktor*," he greeted me. "That was worse than purgatory. I was sure that you would keep your submarines away from us, but that apparently did not work. They chased us for the entire day the moment we came out of the English Channel. They sank half of the sixteen-ship convoy. That is the first time I cussed the Germans. After all, they should have known that I was working for them."

Carlos and I smiled. By the way, this gave us perfect confirmation of the sinkings without *Johnny* even being aware of it.

He continued to talk excitedly, "The storm was hell. I hope *Jack* comes through it safely."

"Why didn't he come with you?" I asked suspiciously.

"Our 'boss' didn't want that," he retorted, "but he'll be here tomorrow, assuming the submarines didn't sink him."

Another lost day. I was disgruntled. "Well," I said, "then let's at least use today for our own affairs. Did you bring something along?"

Johnny's face flushed. "Not much of my own stuff, *Doktor*," he said. "I can't move around as freely as before. They are constantly watching me. And whenever I radio my messages, everything is written out for me, and they look sharply at my fingers. I only do the weather reports alone, but they check them out, too."

I knew *Johnny* was always honest in this respect. He could have told me an entirely different story. "OK, come on," I said to *Carlos*. "Drive us around in your car. We'll be undisturbed in the car."

The wind had swept the clouds away. The sun was shining, and we turned away slightly from the shore, stopping between two hills on the open country road. *Johnny* made his report. It was true. He didn't have much personal data. Personal information could be of value.

I said, "That's not much. My time is too valuable for this sort of thing."

Johnny shrank visibly and crushed his cigarette in the ashtray between his dark yellow, nicotine-stained fingers. "Well, *Doktor*, that is true! But did I not bring you the new man? Is that not enough? I believe that is more than I have supplied you with over the past two years. *Jack* handles the big things. Why don't you take us with you to Germany, and you'll not be sorry."

"I will not buy a cat in a bag," I said curtly. "I'll make my decision once I see your man."

"Don't be angry with me," the little man said. "It's really not my fault. There is nothing now left except sabotage through my brother-in-law. He always helped me in the past. He's working in an ammunition factory, but for that, we need fuses. Everything else we can get for ourselves."

Carlos and I looked at each other. Why not, we thought. So, it has to be sabotage. Just one man can sometimes do more damage this way than an entire group of bombers.

"Let's go see *Rudolf*," I said. "He'll have something." *Rudolf* was our sabotage expert in Lisbon. *Carlos* released the break, pushed the stick into neutral, and let the car roll. He was pleased to let the car glide down the hill and save his old battery by popping the clutch up. Each of us was alone with his own thoughts.

Suddenly, a wind gust slammed hard against the car. Astonished, we looked outside. The sun was shining. In a split second it was dark. The sky was covered with heavy black clouds. The storm swept over the water in front of us with wild squalls. The palm trees bent to the ground. Again and again, the wind thrashed the car with such force that *Carlos* was barely able to hold on to the steering wheel.

"Tornado!" he shouted into the roar and stepped on the gas. We raced down the hill, but it was too late. The storm swept the foaming waters over the pier wall. The corrugated steel sheds in the fields flew through the air. One of the sections sliced the top off of our car. A second blow hit the car from the side like a huge steel hammer. A window shattered, and *Carlos* was injured on the left cheek. The car was flung to the other side and bounced against a tree.

Carlos bled heavily, and I used my necktie to wrap my handkerchief over his wound. All of us were soaked to the bone. The car would not move. The tornado swept over Lisbon as quickly as it had come. We stepped out and stood in water up to our knees.

Suddenly, *Johnny* called out "*Jack!*" and grabbed my arm. "If he was caught in this storm, we may never see him."

We had to have the car towed. In the evening, we met *Rudolf*. *Carlos* had a big bandage on his cheek. I introduced *Johnny* to *Rudolf* and said, in English so that *Johnny* would understand, "*Johnny* has been working for me for several years. His brother-in-law can propel munitions factories into the air. This is why we came to you. They can get their own explosives. From you, they need fuses."

Rudolf was excited. He'd had a long losing streak. Some of his laboriously prepared undertakings had failed. "I'll get you the fuses," he said, "and you'll also get something extra special besides." He opened a big closet and took out a small, long box, which he gave to *Johnny*. "Just open it up."

Johnny opened it, took out a fountain pen, unscrewed the cap, took the pen out, and held it under the lamp. *Rudolf* seemed to be disappointed that *Johnny* was not at all astonished, but he himself was astonished when he saw how expertly *Johnny* broke the pen apart into its individual components. "How did you know how this thing works? Have you ever seen one of those?" *Rudolf* asked.

"Nothing like that," *Johnny* smiled, "but basically, they are all the same. Some time ago, I had given the *Doktor* here something similar, but I must admit, this mechanism is better."

"Let me take a look," I interrupted and examined the casing of the pen. Then I shook my head.

"So, what's the matter?" *Rudolf* asked, somewhat irritated. My head shaking had annoyed him.

"That won't do, mister," I said and gave the thing back.

"And why not, if I may ask?" he asked me.

"Don't act so insulted. This is a Pelikan pen. I hardly think they would have them in England during the war. If you had used a Montblanc . . . but the correct thing would be a Parker!"

"Damned, yes, Doc," *Johnny* said. "You're right. I'd failed to notice."

Rudolf's face turned red, but then he pulled himself together and took a Parker model out of the closet. "My mistake," he apologized.

I was not quite sure whether it was just a mistake or negligence. Maybe it was just bad luck, but I said nothing more.

They began going over instructions for the insertion of the detonator and other technical details. We all had a whiskey and returned to the city.

The next morning, we waited eagerly for the ship reports: in the morning, two Portuguese and one Spanish; in the afternoon, one American. I was getting restless. Too many things were lying around in Hamburg, things that had to be taken care of. Finally, a British vessel came on the afternoon of the following day and brought *Jack*! After dark, we met in a room *Carlos* had rented for such purposes, one that a stranger would have difficulty locating. He had lodged *Johnny* and *Jack* in a hotel that belonged to a German whose daughter was working for *Carlos*. Another associate slept in the room next to them so they could not plan anything unobserved.

From the moment I entered, an unmistakable tension hovered over the room. *Jack* was a medium-sized man, about middle thirties, dark, with regular features. His eyes had a hint of Graves' disease. [According to his granddaughter, Carolinda Witt, author of *Double Agent Celery*, there is no evidence that Walter Dicketts had Graves' disease, or bulging eyes. "His eyes were large and brown and he was tall, with dark combed back hair, a round face, and a prominent dimple on his chin."] They were brownish-green and cold.

"This is *Mr. Brown*," [alias for Walter Dicketts (*Celery* to MI5)] the little one made the introduction proudly.

"I hope you had a better crossing than *Johnny*," I said. *Johnny* was beaming, but I was still suspicious.

"How do you do?" the stranger said. His voice was soft, and his facial expression was not unpleasant, but his eyes did not fit in. He talked slowly and cautiously, as if carefully weighing each word in his greeting.

"Well," I said. "*Johnny* has told us your story. Do you think you could bring us something?"

"I'm certain of it," he said.

"On what basis did you think you could work with us?" I asked him.

"*Johnny* told me that you are looking for an expert with aviation training. That's what I am, and with my contacts, I can certainly answer many of your questions."

"And your compensation?"

"I thought *Johnny* had told you," he said. "I have debts, and I need money."

I was disappointed. That was the usual ruse employed by the average counterpart. He would have sounded somewhat more credible if he had stuck to the story of his discharge, as *Johnny* had related it to me, and if he perhaps had added, "Of course, I have to live, and the risk is great."

"Good," I said. "How much?"

"200 pounds a month," he replied promptly.

"If you are worth it," I said. "You know that we could easily have you arrested in view of our connections here in Portugal."

"My God, *Doktor*!" *Johnny* shouted as he sprang up. "You would not do that! I told *Jack* that he can rely on you."

Even *Brown* livened up a bit. "You won't have occasion for that, Doctor," he said, and turned to *Johnny*. "So, out with it. Perhaps then everything will become self-explanatory."

Johnny squirmed. "Oh, yes, *Doktor*," he said. "I'm supposed to offer you $200,000 from my boss, in gold, if you come to England. But," he added timidly, "I told him right away that this would be useless. Isn't that right, *Jack*?"

"That is correct," *Brown* confirmed and looked at me questioningly.

I had to laugh. They were telling me a tall tale for beginners, and now they offered me a large sum of money to neutralize or eliminate me.

"Why did you tell your boss that it was useless? $200,000, in gold, that's a lot of money!" *Johnny* looked at me baffled, and *Brown* smiled a little bit mischievously. "You are funny people," I said to *Johnny*. "I'm afraid you gave your boss a poor description of me, and now I think we can get down to business."

Johnny was visibly relieved. *Brown* did not display any reaction. I had the feeling that he had deceived the little one and that *Johnny* was afraid of him.

And, as if to confirm my thoughts, he said, "You're not going to deceive me, *Jack*?"

"Naturally not," said *Brown*, completely detached.

Now the smokescreen had been lifted for me. Both of these fellows were genuine, but in a reverse sense. *Johnny* really tried to remain honest with me and had fallen into the trap laid for him by *Brown*. *Brown* was genuine, like an actor. Now I sadly knew I could not expect anything further from *Johnny*. I had to drop him. I was really sorry for the little man. I would have preferred to send them both back, but then I said to myself we could get something out of *Brown* if we took him with us to Germany. I said, "We need all sorts of time for our work, but I'm not technically inclined, and besides I do not have the time to stay in Lisbon any longer. Come with me to Germany, and I'll assure you a safe return."

Johnny was excited. "That's wonderful, *Doktor*! Let's go with him, Jack!"

"Sorry, *Johnny*," I waved him off, "but I cannot take both." *Johnny* looked at me without understanding. I had to force myself to remain tough, so I said to *Brown*, "So how about it, *Mr. Brown*?" I called him by his alleged name for the first time. I noted he was struggling with himself.

Things seemed to have taken a turn that had not been calculated. I knew I had given him a dangerous test. If he wanted to continue to play his role, he would have to accept my offer. If he were a real representative of the Security Service, this would be a chance for him like none other, to travel to enemy territory in the midst of a war. But that took courage.

Then *Johnny* came to my assistance. "Go along, *Jack*," he said. "When the *Doktor* promises something, he keeps his promise."

I was embarrassed because I had to leave *Johnny* sitting high and dry. By now, *Brown* had made his decision. "If you promise that I can get out of Germany safely, then I will come along." He extended his hand, and without really wanting to, I shook it.

Johnny hung his head. He tried once again, but my decision was firm. Sentiment could play no role here.

The next morning, I flew back to Germany. Three days later, *Brown* was brought to Hamburg under escort. He was billeted in the Hotel Vier Jahreszeiten and received a list of questions especially prepared for him in Berlin. He worked hard and filled sheet after sheet with his answers.

He was allowed to move around freely. A Gestapo agent followed him, unnoticed. His work was carefully checked. Various specialists came from Berlin in succession. It was found he was indeed a pilot and an expert, as he had maintained. Some of his information was new and good. That gave me some satisfaction. In other words, the mission had not been in vain. The Gestapo agent confirmed that *Brown* had not made any attempts to contact anyone. That proved he had never really planned to stay in Germany.

Once, *Brown* asked me if he could visit some bars and restaurants under escort. He wanted to get an impression of the general war conditions and of the behavior of the population after one year of war. I recalled my last trip to Holland and Belgium and found his request to be quite natural. One evening, we went out together. I took one of my section chiefs along, and to give the outing a harmless appearance, I asked my wife to come along.

Since I still wanted to discuss some issues with *Brown,* we first went to my office in the city on Gerhofstrasse. Like a number of older Hamburg office buildings, this one had a paternoster lift instead of an elevator. My wife took my briefcase while I was still giving instructions to the driver. She went ahead with *Brown.* When she wanted to get into the paternoster, *Brown* said to her politely, "May I carry the briefcase, Madam?" Spontaneously, she handed it to him and stepped into the next cabin, assuming *Brown* would get in with her. To her horror, however, he stayed behind. What could she do! So far, none of us had forgotten anything or left anything official lying around. The briefcase, however, contained some important papers. She knew I did not trust *Brown.* On the next floor, she stepped out, her heart beating, and she waited until, to her great relief, *Brown*'s head turned up over the threshold in the next cabin, so that she could enter it and, together with him, continue on to my office. Like so many visitors to Hamburg who are not familiar with the paternoster, he had simply waited a moment before entering this unfamiliar, and, for a stranger, eerie means of transportation.

We left the office and went to supper. When, after cocktails, we went to our reserved niche, my wife whispered to me, "Did you see his big ring? It's made for opening. Should I ask him?"

"Naturally," I whispered, and I was annoyed I had not noticed it myself.

The meal was good; the wine was also good. *Brown* enjoyed it. As he raised his glass, I heard my wife say, "My, what a beautiful ring you have there!"

That was the first time I saw the man baffled. Look out, I thought. *Brown* smiled and showed my wife the ring but did not take it off.

Then she remarked quite harmlessly, "It looks as if one could open it."

Brown was prepared. "You're a good observer, Madam," he said politely, and opened the ring.

"A pretty girl," my wife said and looked at the tiny photo. "Your wife?"

"Not yet." *Brown* smiled, and closed the ring again.

"Interesting," I said, and acted as if I was no longer interested in the ring. After a couple of minutes, I excused myself. From the phone booth in the restaurant, I called the duty officer at our duty station and gave him some instructions. The waiter brought the after-dinner drink. We urged *Brown* to keep drinking. After the meal, I had my wife driven home. We gentlemen left for a nearby bar.

Brown protested, "I'm not accustomed to drinking so much. I'd rather like to go back to the hotel."

"But you wanted to take a good look around," I said, and insisted he come along.

In the bar, the business manager greeted us with special politeness and took us to a table in a booth. Only one individual, a harmless-looking man, was sitting there. We greeted each other briefly and sat down. I ordered three big cognacs. The stranger stood up and asked the head waiter for the checkroom. A short while later, the three cognacs arrived. We toasted each other. In the meantime, the stranger had returned.

Suddenly, *Brown* stopped in the middle of a sentence. He had fallen asleep. The stranger said, "Everything is in order, *Herr Doktor.*"

"How long?" I asked.

"At least two hours."

He pulled the ring off *Brown*'s finger, took the picture out, and made sure that there was nothing else under it. Cautiously, he put it in an envelope and pushed the ring back on *Brown*'s finger.

My associate and I continued to chat. Everything had happened so imperceptibly that nobody could have noticed anything. A couple of people glanced at the sleeping man and smiled understandingly.

After an hour and a half, the same strange man came back. "Everything is in order," he said. He opened *Brown*'s ring and pushed the little picture in again unobtrusively.

"Should we wake him up?" I asked.

"That isn't necessary. He'll wake up by himself. Then there will be no aftereffects, and he won't notice anything."

Brown awakened after just about half an hour. He looked around, annoyed. Then he recognized us. "Did you sleep well?" I asked.

"I'm sorry," he apologized. "I'm not accustomed to so much alcohol."

"That's all right," I said. "Now we'll have a little snack, and then we go to sleep."

The next morning, the "strange" man stood in front of my desk and showed me some photographic enlargements. We could not understand the letters. "This has to be deciphered right away," I ordered.

"That's already being done," he replied.

"Now I'm really curious," I said. "At any rate, we have to be particularly careful. We cannot possibly let him go before we have an answer."

The answer came after a couple of days. We found several disconnected letters that did not indicate anything. We were able to recognize one Spanish name and a number. That could be a street in Madrid. The other letters obviously were memory aids.

The time was short for my preparations for my mission in Africa, and I could no longer personally bring *Brown* back to Lisbon. I insisted that he should under no circumstances be sent out alone, but always with a reliable escort.

When I reported to Canaris on Africa, he asked, "Why do you not keep this mysterious Englishman here as a prisoner of war?"

"Because I gave him my word, Admiral. Otherwise, he wouldn't have come along." "So," Canaris said calmly, "then there is no further need for any discussion."

I noticed the old man did not quite understand. I knew him well enough to realize that after this remark, any further explanation would be misplaced. Canaris respected the fact that I had given my word. That was the end of the *Brown* affair.

A couple of days later, *Brown* and his escort flew to Lisbon. In Madrid, where they had to transfer to another plane, they had a long stopover. The escort allowed *Brown* to step out without going along. *Brown* did not return, so he did fool us in the end.

Subsequent documents showed that he had actually been an RAF man in the past. He was a communist and used this opportunity to get to Russia with the help of the Spanish communist underground. The street with the number from his ring did not exist in Madrid.

22

Africa Mission

As I returned to Budapest from my last trip in December 1940, Captain Böckel greeted me with the shocking news, "Dierks is dead!"

The training for Drüke and Vera prior to their England mission had been completed, and a farewell dinner had been planned with Dierks and others. Dierks had asked Captain Böckel to take Vera home and to try one last time to persuade her to drop out of her mission with Drüke.

The others had gone to Jacob, one of the first-class restaurants in Hamburg, located on Elbchaussee with a magnificent view of the Elbe. On the way over, they had picked up a Swiss friend of Drüke's by the name of Werner Heinrich Wälti (alias for Robert Petter), who had been earmarked as a substitute for Vera.

It was an exciting evening. They ate and dined well, and Dierks drank more than usual. When they left, they had difficulty persuading him not to drive. Finally, he gave in, climbed into the car, and fell onto the rear seat. Drüke was driving because he had had less to drink than his companions. On the dark, foggy Elbchaussee, he was blinded by a car coming at him, which despite the blackout law had its headlights on. He lost control of the car and side-swiped a tree with his rear wheel. Dierks, who had fallen asleep, was hurled against the window and lost consciousness. Drüke merely suffered some minor skin abrasions. Nothing happened to his Swiss friend Wälti, who sat next to him. Both tried in vain to wake Dierks. An ambulance took him to the nearest hospital. From there, Drüke called the duty station, and Captain Böckel came immediately.

By the time Captain Böckel arrived at the hospital, Dierks was dead. He died without ever regaining consciousness. Drüke was beside himself. Böckel arrived just in time to knock the pistol out of his hand, with which he aimed to take his own life.

Dierks's death was a shock to everyone. It had happened so unexpectedly, and everything seemed to be so senseless. When Vera was informed, she demanded immediately to be sent to England as a parachute agent. Drüke also wanted to get into the action. Both told me they did not want to wait any longer, but they wanted to be dropped together with the Swiss fellow.

It did not seem advisable to us to move them across the Channel by boat after various such undertakings had failed. Following lengthy negotiations, it was decided to send all three with Captain Böckel to Stavanger in Norway, where they would pose as employees of a military duty station.

They discussed all possibilities of crossing with the X Luftwaffe Corps, and they finally agreed they would not parachute but would instead be dropped from a flying boat on the Scottish coast near the Shetland Islands. From there, they were to go to Southern England on bicycles.

The bicycles had to be English. After an extensive search, they found three bicycles that had belonged to the former British consul in Stavanger. They could hold out for a long time with everything we would provide them. Besides, they had a secret transmitter. Their code could be deciphered only as a result of gross negligence or due to betrayal. They had received further training in Hamburg, and a few days after their arrival in Stavanger, everything was ready for them to take off.

Captain Böckel assumed full responsibility for the mission. He was quite anxious about Vera and Drüke. Since Dierks's death, a noticeable change had come over them. Both had become completely apathetic, and their mood was such that Böckel had to redouble his attention. He was afraid they might take their lives even before taking off or that Drüke would betray the mission as a result of complete indifference. He tried to talk to him, but Drüke disregarded all warnings.

"Nobody will get me alive," he said simply.

With Vera it was not much different. Böckel's advice seemed neither here nor there with her. Early on the morning of the sixth day, the two flying boats took off in the direction of Scotland. Approaching land, the flying boat with the two men and Vera onboard landed about 150 meters out from land, where the coast in the haze looked like a beach. Immediately after the flying boat came to a halt, a large rubber raft was launched. Vera and the two men stepped in and began rowing toward their uncertain future.

Shortly after their landing, they could hear the explosions from heavy bombing in the distance. The other flying boat had continued further inland, above a little factory, to deceive any possible antiaircraft artillery and to divert attention from the landing aircraft. Before anyone could recover from the shock of this sudden and seemingly unprovoked barrage, the two flying boats were on their way back to Norway, and the three "strangers" were secured on Scottish soil.

The radios in Wohldorf were set on receive, and again we waited. We knew we could hardly expect any news for two weeks. During that time, our bicycle riders could have already reached the outskirts of London. They had a long and dangerous road ahead, and they had instructions never to travel together and, at all costs, to avoid empty roads as well as buses or train stations. They should, as quickly as possible, try to reach more populated towns and cities where they could easily blend into the crowd. The Swiss Wälti was to make his way to the west coast. Vera had the address of the duchess in London. Drüke's territory was London and Southern England. It was left to him whether and how he wanted to stay in contact with Vera.

After one week, as anticipated, we had not yet heard anything, and no one was concerned. However, when after two weeks there was no activity, we became anxious. After four weeks, we explored various avenues to discover the fate of the three. The informants in England, whom we queried cautiously, knew nothing. Our analysis station for foreign newspapers was directed to look out especially for any reports on arrests.

After a while, we received an entry from a Swiss newspaper about the arrest of a Swiss citizen in Scotland who reportedly worked for the German military intelligence service. That could be none other than Wälti, but we did not know what had happened. And what might have happened to Drüke and Vera?

Again, a couple of weeks later, another report appeared. A German agent, Belgian or German, had been arrested by the British Security Service.

Böckel had repeatedly warned us. "He was too indifferent and too careless," he said. "He threw my advice to the wind."

Maybe we could still do something for him.

Now the legal department of the Abwehr went into action. Since Wälti was a Swiss citizen, contact was established with the appropriate agencies there. Here is what turned up. After the landing, Wälti, on the way to Edinburgh, contrary to his instructions, had inquired at a small railroad station about the departure time of the next train. However, because it was common knowledge that this particular line had been closed for quite some time, he immediately aroused suspicion. During questioning, the police discovered he did not live in the area and that he had an obvious foreign accent, which would not have been as evident in a big city. He was arrested, and, as we learned later, he was tried in court. He confessed and was sentenced to death by hanging.

Drüke had arrived in Birmingham by way of a long detour. There he was arrested just as he was trying to get on a train going to London. True to his promise that nobody would ever catch him alive, he pulled out his pistol, shot at one of the men who wanted to arrest him, and then tried to shoot himself. But fate did not seem to have it in store for him to take his own life. Just as Böckel had knocked the pistol out of his hand before, this time a British police officer did the same thing. Drüke was taken to prison.

We did not find out how they had been alerted to him. We presumed that perhaps the Swiss had betrayed him after his arrest. All we knew at the time was that both were still alive. Berlin offered an exchange, but the British Secret Intelligence Service was not interested. They wanted to retain both Wälti and Drüke. Either they seemed to be too valuable, or the Security Service needed them to provide evidence of its successes in the interest of the public mood.

Allegedly, a court trial took place; Drüke and Wälti were hanged at Wandsworth, Drüke on September 6, 1941, and Wälti on August 6, 1941. We heard nothing from Vera until the war was over.

The mission to Africa was now immediately before me. It was to begin in March 1941. On March 20, I reported to Canaris. He seemed to be more worried than before. From vague hints, I thought I gathered that it was not the political situation that worried him, but rather the activity of the Gestapo.

"Watch out for the SD *Sicherheitsdienst* and when you are in Africa, keep in mind that you are not working *for* Rommel, but rather *with* him. By the way," he added, more lost in thought, "I'm not very hopeful about this." With this rather somber hint, he let me go. He wished me luck and said he would visit me down there someday. But I never saw him again.

When I arrived in Munich, where the mission was to commence, Röder was already waiting with the men from my detachment. He had volunteered for service in the Luftwaffe and had quickly been promoted to lieutenant. On his request, I was glad to have him transferred to my outfit. Now our name was "Reconnaissance Detail Northeast Africa (Special Detachment Major Ritter)," and we were attached to the X Luftwaffe Corps, which in the meantime had been moved to Sicily.

We had no idea how long we would be gone. We were supposed to retrieve the Pasha out of Egypt under the very eyes of the British. In addition to very careful preparations, this called for a march through the desert, establishing a base, and making aircraft available. We also had to take on an additional task, namely, dropping two agents behind the British-Egyptian lines.

I was very much intrigued by Africa, but I regretted that I had to pass on to somebody else something I had built up—above all, personal contact with my informants—particularly since Böckel, who in the meantime had been promoted to major, was transferred to Berlin.

Munich was under a big blanket of snow when we were given permission to take off on March 23. I wrote to my wife from Taormina, Sicily: "The clouds lay over the Alps up to an altitude of 5,000 meters, and since our tin donkey, the good old Ju-52, cannot go higher than 4,500, and since there was danger of icing between 2,000 and 5,000 meters, we were stuck in Munich for two days. The Alps are beautiful, grandiose, magnificent, awe inspiring, or whatever else you want to say in their praise. With a free look out of the cockpit, they are overwhelming."

It was already summer on the other side of the Alps. In Forli in Northern Italy, we made our first stopover. We reached Naples at sunset. From my hotel room in the glow of the setting sun, the view across the gulf toward Mt. Vesuvius was indescribably beautiful.

I had arranged for our continuation flight to leave at nine o'clock the next morning, but we didn't take off until 11:15 a.m. That was my fault. My *Thousand Words in Italian* told me that the Italian "subito" means "immediately" in German. I didn't realize at the time that it actually means "near future."

The headquarters of X Luftwaffe Corps was located in Taormina. I settled myself in the Hotel Diodoro with a radio terminal as relay facility. I checked in with the commander, General Hans Geissler, who listened to my report with great interest, but obviously very little understanding. At any rate, he promised his support.

As I briefed him on our plan, the staff intelligence officer, Captain Kleienstüber, said, "That's the cat's meow." I could not have found a more understanding assistant. He made First Lieutenant Blaich available to my special detachment. Blaich had brought his own Bf 109 from his farm in South Africa.

So I wrote to my wife, "You can hardly imagine our emotions when, for the first time, we saw the coast of the 'Black Continent' emerging out of the shimmering haze, like some endlessly long, narrow white strip. . . . I will fly ahead alone to Derna, and I have decided to set up my headquarters there. In Tripoli, we are too far from the action. How I will achieve my mission is not yet known to me. I feel a little forlorn."

On April 27, Almásy and I were riding in our desert vehicle on the Via Balbo, heading in the direction of Tobruk. At the kilometer 14 marker, which every African combatant knows, we turned off, heading toward the coast to Rommel's tent camp. While we were there, we experienced an air raid on Tobruk. Rommel displayed interest in our mission but did not hesitate to express his doubts about our success. When I reported to him about our ring of transmitters around the Mediterranean that supplied daily weather reports for his Luftwaffe units, he was impressed and let us proceed. On our return, as we arrived at the Derna airfield, forty-five Ju 52 aircraft were just rolling in and unloading a full-strength engineer battalion.

Derna, which I had now finally picked as the headquarters of my detachment, was the largest and most fertile oasis in Northern Libya along the Mediterranean. On one of the side streets, I had found a little whitewashed settlement house that was ideal for our purposes. It had two large rooms: one was set up as the radio station, and the other was used as a dining and day room. Several smaller rooms were bedrooms and offices.

Before Rommel had started his first big triumphant march, the house had been inhabited by Australians who had, in their hasty escape, left it in a mess and deliberately deposited their excrement in every corner. I asked a nearby camp to send me some prisoners to clean the house. They sent us a couple of Hindus, but when Röder showed them their job, they refused because it was against their religious regulations to touch human waste. Initially, I was rather angry, but then we respected their feelings, gave them a couple of cigarettes, and instead fetched a couple of Australians.

In the meantime, I flew with First Lieutenant Blaich to Tripoli, where Almásy was waiting with the rest of the detachment, because it was there we had to procure everything necessary for our move to Derna: suitable vehicles, technical equipment, and so forth. We had to overcome unforeseeable and time-consuming obstacles because our requirements were difficult to meet and, above all, because we had to convince uncomprehending and stubborn administrative officials, mostly Italians, that a detachment such as ours required specific items, even though Rommel himself needed them urgently. But the "Armed Forces High Command" was the magic word that finally overcame the resistance.

After we had gathered everything, I flew back to Derna, while Almásy and the rest of the men in the laboriously assembled convoy followed along the Via Balbo, the narrow asphalt road that ran through the desert and connected the various oases to each other. On the way, they were taken by surprise by the dreaded Sirocco, or the Ghibli, as the Italians called it—the harsh, dry wind that comes out of the Arabian Desert and, with increasing speed, sweeps with hurricane force toward the Mediterranean, carrying masses of dust and sand that darken the sunlight. Anyone who is not prepared for it is buried or choked to death. Without the experienced desert expert, Almásy, the entire convoy would probably have been lost. But they managed—1,500 kilometers through the desert.

During a similar storm, while on a reconnaissance patrol, I almost died. I had reported my experiences to my friend Thoran in Berlin, and when he let Canaris read my letter, the admiral said, "These guys are daredevils. Tell Ritter that I send him special greetings and that I will try to visit him in Derna myself."

In the meantime, we had daily radio contact with Cairo. Our secret transmitter was housed in a church that was visited by members of the Hungarian Embassy. Even the priest was in on it and permitted radio messages to be sent during services. The meteorologist for General Fröhlich (Luftwaffe Leader Africa) waited impatiently for the daily weather reports.

Now we began our preparations for Mission Pasha. The Hungarian ambassador had established contact with the Pasha, and the latter basically agreed to our plan. Initially, he insisted that he be picked up by submarine, but finally he concluded that the undertaking would be too difficult and agreed to our plan with the aircraft.

The invasion of Crete began on May 20, 1941, and by June 1 the island of Crete was occupied by German airborne troops. That made it considerably easier for Rommel. For me, it meant that the required aircraft would now be available for our mission. With First Lieutenant Blaich, I flew in the small Bf 109, with an auxiliary tank, across the Mediterranean to Athens, where, after reporting to General Geissler, I discussed all details with the chief of staff.

After some difficulties, they gave us two He 111s with their crews. When the two aircraft arrived in Derna, Almásy and I briefed the pilots and observers. The

Pasha had received and approved all the details of this elaborate and carefully developed plan that applied to him. As the meeting point, Almásy had proposed the "Red Djebel"—a major elevation not far southwest of Cairo along the road that linked Cairo with the southern oases in the desert. There, the Pasha was to lay out a landing cross marker consisting of large white bed sheets. One of the aircraft was to land and fetch the Pasha, while the other plane would circle above for protection.

Our first attempt was scheduled for June 5. On the evening of June 4, we received a radio message from Cairo that the mission had to be postponed because the Pasha had had a little auto accident. As a matter of fact, the accident was staged because the duty officer who collaborated with the Pasha had been relieved unexpectedly and would not be available for duty during the next two days.

The two He 111s took off punctually at 1500 hours on June 7, 1941, and disappeared behind the dangerous mountain on the other side of Benina [Libya]. Berlin forbade me from flying along. The aircraft were to be ready on the dot at 1800 hours. By 1930 hours, they should have flown through the most dangerous leg over enemy-threatened territory. They should have resumed radio contact around 1935 hours.

By 1945 hours, they had not checked in yet. I never left the radio operator's side. I was responsible for the agents, and I was responsible for the aircraft, which I had managed to inveigle out of the X Luftwaffe Corps with the greatest difficulty.

At 2015 hours we still had no contact. This helpless waiting was sheer torture. Finally, at 2045 hours, the lead aircraft checked in. It was in the vicinity of Tobruk, heading back. I breathed a sigh of relief, but at the same time, it grabbed me again. Where was the second aircraft?

I ran to the landing site and looked for the landing lights. No landing lights were to be seen. I ran to the operations tent and demanded the landing lights be laid out, but there simply were no landing lights! I lost my patience. I knew that this was not a regular airfield, but everything had been discussed in advance with the Italian commander. He should have provided the illumination.

I was beside myself. Suddenly, I spoke fluent Italian. I did not know whether they would understand me or not. I would not fall for their "subito" or "pronto." I pressed them to hurry up, pitching in myself. They were not accustomed to that from a major. Somehow, they found a long cable, but there were no electrical bulbs. I literally tore them out of the lamps. Within half an hour, the landing lights were ready and in place. I ran back to the radio station. At last! The second aircraft had also checked in. It was about thirty minutes behind the first one. The time difference could mean they had landed, and that they had the Pasha on board, I hoped.

Then the engine noises of the first aircraft approached. The improvised landing lights were turned on. One He 111 circled at a low altitude over the field and prepared to land. I stood at the end of the runway as the aircraft touched down. It rolled along the landing lights and stopped directly in front of me.

The engines were turned off. I could hear the hatch being opened, and I shouted, "Almásy?"

"Yes, Major," he responded out of the darkness. I walked toward him.

"Now . . ."

Almásy stood in front of me, saluting with his hand to his cap, reporting back for duty.

And before he finished talking, I knew the Pasha had not come along. After takeoff, both aircraft had continued flying low across the desert to avoid enemy reconnaissance aircraft; then they had climbed to a couple of thousand meters, and shortly before the landing field, they had come down again to fly under the enemy radar. Everything had gone according to plan. They saw the Red Djebel and looked for the Pasha's landing cross, but there was no cross. They were greatly disappointed. Their tension grew. What should they do now? They calculated that they had enough fuel for another half hour in the air. They continued for quite a way along the highway heading toward Cairo on which the Pasha was bound to come. The highway was empty, like the entire desert. They kept up their hopes. When their time was up, they reluctantly turned around and, greatly disappointed, started to fly back.

The pilots were angry and convinced the Pasha had left them in the lurch, but Almásy knew his man. Something must have gone seriously wrong. Otherwise, the Pasha would have been at the rendezvous point.

He tried to console me. "There is no need to worry about it now," I said, and tried to act calm. "All we can do now is wait for the next messages from Cairo." I thanked the men for their commitment and took my leave.

The next morning at the specified time, we received the first message from Cairo: "Pasha arrested." Nothing further. We asked for clarification. After a short silence, "Cannot be provided at this time." The weather report followed thereafter.

On the occasion of a visit to Cairo after the war, the Pasha personally told me what had occurred. Everything had gone according to plan in Cairo. The Pasha, who originally was to arrive by car on June 5, suddenly had to change his plans. The moment he wanted to get into the car in front of his apartment, he received the news that the British commander had changed the operations plan on the airfield so the Pasha's friends would not be on duty again for two days. So, he decided to scrap the original plan and go to the Red Djebel by aircraft.

The duty officer at the airport in Heliopolis, who would be back on duty on June 7, was a friend, as was the officer supervising them. Special care had been taken to select the pilot, and the Pasha trusted him, although he did not know him personally.

When the pilot checked out with the British control officer, according to regulations, he became nervous, as did so many young Egyptian officers who had been trained by the British and who had been inoculated with inexplicable fear of British disciplinary measures. That had made him hesitant. Nevertheless, he managed a good takeoff. They had hardly lifted off when they noticed a British aircraft heading toward them. The pilot pushed the machine's nose back down, skimmed the crown of an olive tree, and the aircraft dipped down. At first, the Pasha assumed something was wrong with the engine and that they would have to make an emergency landing. But then he found that the pilot had simply lost his nerve. The pilot jumped out and ran away without worrying about the Pasha, while some guards came to the latter's aid. When the English found out who the aircraft passenger was, they ordered his arrest. But since the officer of the guard was his friend and since no Egyptian soldier would ever have dared lay a hand on the "hero of the country," the Pasha was able to hide. An Egyptian major, who looked so much like him that he was often confused with him, voluntarily took his place in prison—something the English discovered much later.

From Palestine, the Pasha succeeded in establishing contact with Berlin. Ultimately, our initiative still influenced our objective, but it was too late to influence our events favorably in Egypt.

23

Desert Devils

Now we had to focus on our next assignment: dropping two informants behind the Egyptian-British front. I had always kept the personnel strength of my detachment as low as possible. We were an almost international family, bonded for better or worse.

An Egyptian cook cared for our physical well-being. He did an outstanding job of preparing *piccante* meals using rations and some local ingredients, for which he bargained with Arabs in the bazaar with some lire we had managed to save among ourselves.

The Italian driver, whom I had "borrowed" in Tripoli for the transfer of my detachment to Derna, had in the meantime been "adopted" by us. He had refused to return to his Italian unit in Tripoli and preferred to stay with us without pay in return for good treatment and good food. In Tripoli, he had apparently been written off, but I didn't concern myself about that. So, we had a willing driver, cleaning man, and odd-jobs worker.

Along with his desert expertise, the Hungarian Almásy contributed much to our entertainment during our free time. The others, of course, were Germans, but all, except for two, had lived abroad for many years, as had I.

In addition, we were directly under the Wehrmacht High Command, and we were ordered to cooperate with all other duty stations. This meant that they could never use us for routine garrison duty, and consequently, everyone else viewed us with suspicious respect and guarded envy. Once I was asked to report to the Italian commanding general in Barce; we were located in his area of command jurisdiction. Allegedly he wanted to find out more about us, but in fact, he wanted to inform me he had heard that all of us ate the same rations and that we sat at the same table with simple Italian soldiers.

He argued that this would undermine the discipline of his soldiers, and he asked me to adopt their habits. In other words, the Italians still had three different types of rations. According to him, it was improper for officers and non-commissioned officers to sit at the same table with the enlisted men. I told him I disagreed, that our German system, if anything, strengthened discipline, and that we, therefore, had far less difficulty in inspiring our men.

Per orders from Berlin, the two agents, whom we were supposed to drop behind the lines, had already completed their practical training. I didn't appreciate that. The essential personal connection is best established by providing on-site training oneself, particularly in the case of such special missions.

The first, Klein, was a short, roundish man in his middle forties, a dark type with black hair and clever brown eyes. He had been a noncommissioned officer in World War I; he had gone to Egypt as a young man and returned to Germany shortly before this war broke out. He'd been employed in the armament industry and had volunteered for employment in Egypt. I was unable to establish any meaningful rapport with him.

With the second, Mühlenbruch, the situation was different. His outward appearance, with his slim shape and his blond hair, was the exact opposite of Klein. His blue eyes and his open manner immediately produced sympathy.

Theoretical training was left to me. Since both of the men were so different in terms of character, I took them one at a time. Klein was scheduled to go to Alexandria, where he had lived before the war. Mühlenbruch was supposed to go to Haifa via Egypt. Formerly, he had owned a little boat that he used to run shipments along the coast, but he was not known there as being German. Both men spoke Arabic; both were certain they could work successfully once they reached their destination. The difficulty for us was to sneak them into Egypt without being noticed.

Almásy proposed the south, where they would be less likely expected. To get there, we either had to join a caravan, or we had to cross the desert in an airplane and drop both men in Egypt, at, or as near as possible to, the border. The caravan would have been the safest way to go, but we did not have that much time. With an aircraft it would go faster, but the operation would also be more dangerous. However, I had Almásy for this problem.

All the options were carefully reviewed. It was impossible to drop them in the narrow upper Nile country that was under constant British air surveillance, but the caravan route from the oasis Tarafrah to Dairut [Egypt] looked good. About 100 kilometers from the Nile, a lonely hill was an outstanding terrain reference point in the otherwise flat desert. Immediately to the south, there was a wide field strip of a hard serir [a pebble-strewn desert] all the way to the Egyptian border where an aircraft could easily land and take off again.

The distance to the pebble-strewn landing location amounted to barely four and a half flying hours. That meant eight to nine hours round-trip. My detachment now included only the small liaison aircraft "Storch" and First Lieutenant Blaich's Bf 109. So, I just needed to procure the suitable aircraft. I talked to General Fröhlich, the Luftwaffe Commander, Africa, but this aircraft was out of the question. Consequently, I flew with Blaich across the Mediterranean again to the X Luftwaffe Corps. Our need of the planes was verified. Finally, they promised me two He 111s.

I was pleased, but then the Chief of Staff added, "As soon as we can spare them." At any rate, I knew I would get them, eventually. I flew to Kifissia to the KG [bomber wing] and asked for the same crew that had flown on the "Pasha mission."

The greatest difficulty was surmounting the last hundred kilometers from the landing site to the Egyptian border. Here again, Almásy took control. Using specially equipped cars, he had covered the same distance shortly before the war during one of his expeditions. We could not take a car along in the aircraft, but we could do the job with a motorcycle.

Now we had to find an appropriate motorcycle. It should not be too small, but it should be stable enough for two men, and its dimensions should be such that it could be stowed in an airplane. It had to be an Italian make, as is the custom in North Africa, and the tanks had to hold enough gasoline. Klein had to learn how to ride a motorcycle. Mühlenbruch was an experienced motorcyclist, but Klein had to be prepared to help out in an emergency. Everything had to be coordinated. We made measurements and calculations: distances, times, speeds, weights, gasoline consumption, rations, clothing, lire, Egyptian pounds, and so forth.

Fortunately, we did not have to wait too long for the airplanes. The crews were the same, with the exception of one pilot. I would have preferred the old one, but he had temporarily been transferred to another wing. I had to be content with who was available.

The armor plating was removed from both aircraft in order for us to take more fuel along. We were ready to take off. All we needed now was the proverbial good luck! At 1300 hours, we left Derna for the airfield. One aircraft commander, his observer, Almásy, the radio operator, Winter, and I were in the first car. The rest of the crew followed in the second car, with First Lieutenant Blaich and, finally, Klein and Mühlenbruch on their motorcycle. The higher the car struggled up the serpentine paths from the Derna oasis to the airfield, the more torturous became the heat. High up, the air was glowing hot and dry, mixed with mealy dust. Beyond the airfield, the air shimmered.

Everything was ready for takeoff at the airfield. I had issued my last instructions, when one of the mechanics reported that a tire on one of the landing gears was defective. That was the aircraft that was supposed to land. Its pilot was particularly experienced and courageous. Waiting for a spare tire to arrive would signify a time loss of one and a half days, and who knew whether and when I would get the aircraft again. Klein and Mühlenbruch had to get to Egypt. The front lines were waiting for information regarding enemy activities. I had to take a chance.

Because I was not able to swap the crews, I had to designate the other aircraft for the desert landing, and along with Klein and Mühlenbruch, we joined

Nikolaus Ritter with comrades, returning from mission in Ju 52. From the editor's private collection.

the less-experienced pilot. I crawled forward through a narrow shaft and sat in the fuselage between the pilot and the observer, Captain Leicht. I put on the earphones and the throat microphone for onboard voice communications. The engines roared; the door snapped shut. We were cleared for takeoff. At first, we flew very low. There were no clouds into which we could disappear, and there were no mountains. The eternal desert wind played with the fine sand and whipped it along in hundreds of little swirling whirlwinds. The Arabs call them *afrit* winds; afrits are little desert ghosts.

The sun was bright, and the white sand was blinding. But before us hung a dirty wall that rose out of the distant desert. Again, it was the dreaded Ghibli. We had to try to fly over it. The fine dust was bad for the engines. The inexperienced pilot cursed the hazy air. He refused to believe we were flying in a fine sand dust. Things were no better at an altitude of 3,000 meters. Visibility became clearer at about 4,000 meters.

We flew southeast, heading toward the high ridges near Djerabub, behind which lies the great oasis Siwa. Captain Leicht made some precise calculations. There were no outstanding reference points here. We flew in bright daylight, and yet we had to fly blind. All we saw was the endless desert. It was eerie but captivatingly beautiful with its ever-changing colorations. In this barren waste, we

Nikolaus Ritter in front of Junker 52. From the editor's private collection.

were eager to find a strip of hard serir where we could land. I kept thinking of the day a year ago when we were looking for *Johnny* on the endless waste of the sea.

We were supposed to be on location around 1730 hours. We had already cleared the first elevations. The sun was behind us. The shadows marked bizarre figures on the white sand and made the tiniest pebbles look like boulders. The instrument needles lay calmly on their scales. The engines roared. Captain Leicht was making measurements and calculations. He touched my arm and indicated to me to put my earphones on again. He pointed at a lonely cone that rose in front of us out of the flat plain. That was our destination. Just another hundred kilometers and we would have reached our goal.

The aircraft commander pushed the bird's nose downward. The sun was low already; we did not have much time to lose. There were no landing lights here. After a couple of minutes, Leicht found the right spot. We decided to land. Our nerves were on edge to the very last moment. A smoke bomb indicated the wind direction. I crawled to the rear and made a sign for Klein and Mühlenbruch to get ready. The aircraft commander prepared to land. I held on to the fuselage. There were no safety belts.

Suddenly, the pilot pulled the bird up again. I shot Leicht a quizzical look. "Mensch, what's your problem!" the aircraft commander snarled. The pilot flew in a curve and tried to land once again.

I saw he was nervous, or was he afraid? The strange feeling I had had when I first saw him was back again. I had suppressed it because I didn't want to be prejudiced, but now I knew I had been right. And it was too late. Those in the other aircraft above us were bound to wonder why we were not landing.

"Go, already! Why are you hesitating?" Leicht asked, with tension in his voice as he tried to suppress his anger.

"It can't be done!" the pilot brayed back. "There are too many boulders."

"Those are not boulders!" Leicht shouted now. "They're just little stones!"

Too late. The pilot stepped on the gas again. The sand raced along below us. We turned west!

According to the laws of aviation, the pilot alone is responsible for the safety of the aircraft, even if he is merely a sergeant and the observer happens to be a captain. He had made his decision not to land, and no power on earth could force him to change his mind.

"Son of a bitch!" Leicht snarled with restrained fury.

I said nothing. What could I say? The fellow was afraid. I should not have swapped the airplanes. The other aircraft above us would have landed. Leicht interrupted my thoughts. "Those two guys are going to have to jump, Major," he said.

I understood him only too well. He, too, did not want to make this flight in vain, but I was responsible for the lives of two humans. That would have been murder. On foot, they could never have covered the 100 kilometers through the desert. The Arabs figure on fifteen to twenty kilometers for one day's trip, with their gear adapted to the conditions. Leicht was ready to remonstrate, but he also knew neither of them could possibly have marched on foot. Resigned, he bent over his charts.

In the meantime, we had climbed up again to 1,000 meters. The desert was brown, black, dead, and cold. The sun had already dipped into the sand. We chased after it. The higher we flew, the brighter it became again. Suddenly we saw the fiery red ball once more emerge before us, but soon it disappeared again. The colors of the desert changed from red to brown and violet into a deep blue. But a tiny flash of light loitered at the end of the world. The blue in the sky became deeper, and the stars became brighter. The last shimmer of the old day had gone out. We were alone. We were limited to use the radio briefly every thirty minutes.

The second aircraft turned on its own course to the west. We had barely enough fuel to reach Derna. We still had three-quarters of an hour to go.

Suddenly, the radio operator sounded off, "No landing in Derna! Enemy air raid. Head for alternate airport in Benghazi!"

Automatically, our eyes went to the fuel gauge. We still would have to cover

300 kilometers to Benghazi. We couldn't make it. Suddenly, the tail gunner reported enemy bombers. The aircraft commander automatically pushed downward and went into a curve.

There was nothing to see. Left, on the instrument panel, a needle sprang up and down. The aircraft commander checked all levers. The uniform stroke of the engines had been interrupted. The left engine flap didn't function any more. The motor practically fell out.

We had to land quickly. Our last chance was Derna, despite all of the enemy aircraft.

Why shouldn't we have luck just this once on this unlucky flight! The radio operator was instructed to report our intention, but his receiver did not work any longer.

Leicht said, "We cannot do it, Major." I had suspected this all along. "We have to jump," Leicht said.

"How long can we hold out?" I asked.

"Thirty minutes."

"We can't jump out here, or else in three days we'll be parched, hanging on the rocks of a dry wadi. Let's try an emergency landing on the coast. It can't be that far away."

Leicht gave routine orders. The aircraft mechanic behind me was working on an instrument in the dark. Radio operator Winter kept trying to repair his radio. Monotonously, the engines sang their last song.

I was quite calm now. I didn't think about the fact my life would be over any minute. I had a melancholy thought of my wife. I felt genuine concern for her. Perhaps Dierks had been right when he warned me against marrying in view of the coming war.

Leicht had switched the searchlight on. He was looking for a strip of beach. There was nothing under us except water.

"Radio operator, signal SOS emergency landing at sea," Leicht said in a calm voice, and to the aircraft commander, he said, "Don't forget, before touching down on water, tail down!"

After a couple of seconds, the last command, "Systems off."

Communication with the world and among us was cut. We did not see the deep blue of the African midnight sky. We did not see the sparkling stars. We hardly heard the sharp hissing of the air. The engines were still!

Suddenly, an impact, hard as steel; that was the last my brain registered.

When I came around, I detected I was sitting in water up to my knees. It flowed in through an open hatch and slapped into my face. Vaguely, I saw Leicht in the water ahead of me; he was being tossed back and forth by the waves, and in the process, his head bounced against my chest. I heard his gurgling moaning. His mouth and nose were just barely above water. His dark hair floated back and forth, and his hands searched in vain to grasp hold of something. I tried to grab him with my right hand. It didn't happen. A stabbing pain went through my shoulder and arm. With my left hand, I pulled Leicht's head above water by his hair.

"Man! Pull up," I yelled. "What's the matter with you?"

"I don't know," he moaned. "My chest."

"We have to get out of here," I said.

Leicht raised his arms. It hurt, but he could use them. He pulled himself toward the frame of the exit hatch. I helped push with my left shoulder. He was outside. Now it was my turn.

Leicht could not help me. I climbed into the pilot's seat and with my left hand reached for the upper frame of the hatch. My right arm hung down motionless. I had unbearable pain. Don't collapse now, I thought. I had already accepted my death, but now I wanted to live. The water rose quickly. I searched for some support with my right foot, but my foot kept slipping off. If I let go, I'm finished, I thought. With my last bit of strength, I managed to push my right knee onto the frame. After a spastic turn, I sat on top.

Suddenly, I heard someone call out, "Where's the major?"

"Up front in the cockpit," Leicht replied.

Then someone screamed, "Get down from the cockpit, Major! It's breaking off! The suction will drag you down. We're clearing the rubber raft right now."

I was not afraid of water. I had always been a good swimmer, but I had no life jacket and only one good arm. I let myself slide off. The water was warm, and saltwater provided a good support. I floated on my back, and my arm floated next to me. I couldn't see anyone. It was too dark, and the waves were too high. But I could hear them.

"This damned oxygen cartridge does not work. We have to inflate the rubber boat with the foot bellows," someone railed.

After a while, Leicht called out, "We're coming, Major! Give us a yell so we can get your direction."

Finally, I saw a shadow slide over the waves, and then disappear again. It seemed an eternity until it was next to me again and until I was able with my left hand to grasp the tow rope.

Only four men were in the boat: Klein, Leicht, the mechanic, and the pilot. "Where are the others?" I asked.

"Winter is hanging on to the other side. Mühlenbruch is dead. Winter tried to pull him out, but he is trapped somehow and no longer shows any signs of life."

"Poor bastard," someone said.

It struck me hard, as it always does when you lose a comrade. "Is everybody else okay?"

"The radio operator and I, yes," said the pilot, who was about to rig up the little emergency sail.

"My left arm is cracked," Klein said, and stubbornly continued to paddle on.

"And what about you?" I asked Leicht, who was sitting particularly straight.

"Probably just a couple of broken ribs," he said, "but when I sit straight, I can use my arms very well."

They tried to pull me into the boat, but the moment the right arm came out of the water, the pain became so severe that I could hardly breathe. I was glad to be back in the water.

"Do you have any idea where we are, except somewhere in the Mediterranean?" I asked Leicht.

"We were in the vicinity of Derna when we crossed the coast. I don't know how much further we might have flown."

"Well," I said, "that's not much to start out with. Hopefully, they heard our SOS." "Which direction should we paddle, Major? I propose north," Leicht reckoned. "Impossible," I said. "We'll never make it. We cannot be that far away from the African coast."

"Does anyone have a compass?" Leicht asked. Nobody had one. Everyone but Klein and I had stripped everything off except for their undershorts. Only three had life jackets, the regulation issue for a standard crew. Our wristwatches had stopped shortly after midnight; that was the time we hit the water.

For me, it was clear our obvious chance lay in a southerly direction. It was impossible that we could have flown another half hour across the Mediterranean.

"So, we paddle south," I said firmly, and nobody objected.

But where was south? It wasn't merely dark; it was also cloudy. Occasionally, we could see a star. Once, I caught sight of the Big Dipper. That gave me the North Star, and now at least we knew where north was.

And I noticed with fixed pleasure that we had a north wind. Just a little bit of luck! And although the little sail flap was barely two square meters large, it did give the plump lifeboat some speed and made the paddling easier. The clouds disappeared gradually. I observed the North Star and saw to it we stubbornly stuck to our southern course.

Toward morning the wind picked up, and the swells became stronger. We must have been under way for four or five hours already. Gradually, I began to go limp. I had to try to switch places with the uninjured pilot, but that was not so easy. With Winter's help, pushing from the water, they finally heaved me into the boat. The pains in my right shoulder were excruciating until, with Klein's help, I managed to lay my injured arm on the edge of the lifeboat.

I do not know how long I had dozed when I was awakened by Leicht's joyful shout, "Land! You were right, Major."

"Let me see. Turn the boat around a little bit so that I can look past the sail," I said.

Indeed, there was something on the horizon that looked like land, but I did not trust this tranquil site. I knew the coast between Tripoli and Derna. What I saw was utterly alien to me. After a while, the "land" changed its contours.

I did not want to disappoint the others, and I simply said, "Fellows, hopefully these are not just fog banks, but that can also indicate the proximity of land."

The sun rose higher and warmed our exhausted, freezing bodies. Klein had stopped paddling. The pain in his arm was too much.

"What does our land look like now?" I asked.

"It's gone, Major," Leicht said.

The sun burned relentlessly down on our shoulders. Winter couldn't go on. We had to pull him out of the water. We crowded closer together. We had nothing to eat or drink. The shimmering saltwater was beckoning, and the thirst was doubly torturous.

Suddenly, Leicht called out again, "Land, land! This time it really is land." The others couldn't see anything. Perhaps they were too apathetic.

I looked over Winter's shoulder. I saw nothing. I closed my eyes and then opened them again to just slits. Winter turned back to me and shook his head.

"But, I did see land," Leicht insisted.

I pushed the sail aside, and now I thought I could see something. I rubbed my eyes and looked in another direction to check myself. Nothing. Now you're also out of it, I thought. But there it was again—very slightly. I strained to stare at the same spot, but then I could not hold back any longer.

"Land!" I called out. "Look ahead, half-left."

Winter perked up. "Land!" he yelled. "That really is land!"

Land! New hope. Rescue. Nobody asked how far away it was. Winter and the aircraft commander suddenly found the strength to start paddling again.

Now I, too, was quite sure. We had to be somewhere between Derna and Barce.

Suddenly, we heard something. The noise came from the west and was quite low. It could not be anything except a German aircraft. Just a couple of uncertain moments, a Ju 52, we shouted and waved. We forgot paddles and sail and waited for a signal. Nothing. The old Ju just continued on its course. It disappeared as quickly as it had come and did not see six men in a tiny boat. After a while, a second aircraft came. It was a flying boat. We could not shout anymore.

We just waved.

"Boys, they saw us. They're turning and coming down."

The flying boat began to land on the water about 100 meters away. We observed them putting out a rubber boat.

But what's going on? This is impossible! They pulled the rubber boat in again! We waved and shouted. We simply could not understand. The engines roared again. Slowly, the aircraft took off from the water, made a loop, and flew toward the coast.

And then Leicht said, "They are dropping an information capsule, but why so far away?"

"They dropped it on land," I said.

"The cowards, the swine!"

Let them curse, I thought. I would have liked to do the same. "Just let's keep calm," I said, and I tried to get myself under control. "They must have had a good reason. You saw that they had the rubber boat outside in spite of the high swell. Perhaps it was kaput."

"I don't believe that. They were simply too cowardly!" the aircraft commander said. "That's just speculation. Pull yourself together, man!" I snapped at him.

"That's right," the others agreed.

I was just as disappointed as they. "Okay, go," I said. "Pick up your paddles, and remember to steady your nerves as we head through the surf."

Klein and Winter gritted their teeth and pulled hard on the rudders. I held the sail as best I could. The pilot and the mechanic had to go into the water and keep the boat heading in a fixed direction. Then we came into the breakers. With titanic thunder, the waves raged. The spray blinded us. The suction dammed the water, and we were thrown back and forth like a ball. The sail ripped off and flew away. Only forty meters to go. We lost control of the boat. Now Winter also had to grab it from the outside. Leicht, Klein, and I were no longer able to hold on.

The boat reared up. I fell backward into the water. For the first time, I was really afraid. I tried to hold on with my legs. Leicht did a somersault. Klein grasped on to the broken mast stump. A wave crested above us and pulled us down. The boat was thrown back and forth, and then submerged again. Another wave shoved us forward. Suddenly, I felt a hard knock against my left knee. Ground! I had ground under me. With all my strength, I picked myself up. A new wave grabbed me and whirled me around, and before I knew what was happening, I was lying on wet sand.

The water ebbed back. Four arms grabbed me and pulled me completely onto dry land. The aircraft commander and Winter had no longer had the strength to hold on to the boat's line, but with their healthy limbs, they had been able to work their way forward until they had ground under their feet. Leicht and Klein had also been thrown ashore by the waves. I was the last one ashore, because my right foot had gotten tangled in the rope.

In the meantime, Winter had been successful in pulling the rubber raft ashore. He was thinking of the emergency rations, which I had stowed at the last minute: a small pouch of ship zwieback plus a half-liter bottle of cognac. While the mechanic supported my right arm, I stood up and took the bottle while everybody hung on it with eager looks. I had to be tough.

"Please open it," I said to Captain Leicht, and then turned to the others. "We are not yet rescued. We may, of course, assume that our comrades of the Naval Emergency Squadron will come to our aid, but that can take quite some time. Thirst is our worst enemy. Everything we have in the way of fluids is in this little bottle here. It will have to last us as long as possible, just so long as the salivary glands do not dry out. All you need is a couple of drops." I emphasized, "A couple of drops! We use that to moisten the mouth cavity, and the rest we spit back into the bottle. I know this isn't easy; not for me either. Winter, you are the youngest; start."

I did not let go of the bottle. Winter managed it. I knew it. He was some hell of a guy.

Then came Klein and then the mechanic. He had trouble, but pulled himself together. Then, the aircraft commander. I held the bottle firmly. He wanted to swallow, but Leicht watched him carefully and tore the bottle away from his mouth. Then he took a swig, spat it back in, and gave me the bottle. In spite of the thirst, I managed to use the liquid like the others, and it was still better than having to drink my urine.

We dragged ourselves about a hundred meters further, where a boulder offered some shade, and we sank into the sand, exhausted. Leicht found a reasonably comfortable position to avoid the stabbing pain in his ribs. I lifted the hand of my right arm and tried to kneel down.

Winter had to help. He grabbed my arm with both hands, and as I lay down, he laid it on my right hip. "We are certainly between Derna and Barce," I said. "That would mean that there would be vegetation just a few kilometers away from here and perhaps even a settlement. Between us and the open desert, we have the Via Balbo [civilian/military highway that runs along the entire east-west length of the Libyan Mediterranean coastline and is a section of the Cairo–Dakar Highway]. The question is whether we can get there on our own strength. Except for Winter and the aircraft commander, we are seriously handicapped. Moreover, they will certainly be looking for us. It's best we stay here temporarily. What time do you estimate it to be?" I asked Leicht.

"I estimate around 1400 hours."

"Me, too. We should now try to sleep a little bit. Aircraft commander, you take the first watch. Draw a line in the sand around the outline of the shade. Awaken Winter to relieve you after it has moved about half a meter."

When the protruding rock ceased to offer shade, we awoke.

"Why don't they come?" everybody asked. "They should have been able to send a second aircraft long ago."

I also became impatient. Should we wait until it turned dark? Sleep had given us a bit of strength and new courage.

"Should we perhaps try to move inland?" Klein suggested.

"That's also my opinion," Leicht agreed.

I would have also loved to move on, but I was thinking of the experience of others. "Experts say that you should stay in the desert where you crashed. That is the quickest way to be found."

"But we are not yet in the desert," the others argued.

Against my better judgment, I gave in this time. I allowed everyone to take a real sip out of the bottle, and I distributed the zwieback, but it was too dry and required too much saliva.

Someone raised my arm as I tried to stand up. They used the rest of the broken mast and rubber strips from the raft to make a little frame that I could support on my hip where we could then tie my arm. This way, the pain would not be quite as bad while walking.

With the sea at our back, we crept south, along the bottom of a dried wadi. The sun burned down on us just as relentlessly as at high noon.

The captain and the aircraft commander had taken their socks and sandals off before we jumped into the water. Soon, their feet were raw, and their naked shoulders were afire. I told Leicht to put my socks on. I still had my sandals. Then I asked him to remove my shirt, take my undershirt, and rip it into two parts so he and the pilot would have some protection for their shoulders.

My arm had dislocated and hung limply. The upper arm was smeared with dried blood because a bone splinter had penetrated through the skin.

The thirst tormented us. I recalled having read someplace that it is a good idea to put a pebble in your mouth. A little bit of salicylic acid is enough to stimulate the salivary glands. We found a few pebbles in the dry wadi, and we discovered, to our astonishment, that they not only provided a pleasant, cooling effect, but that they actually worked.

We did not talk much. The distances we dragged ourselves from rest to rest became shorter and shorter. Our feet refused to serve us. Suddenly, Winter stopped and, with a heavy tongue, stammered, "Huts."

We all saw them. With glassy eyes, we staggered on, but soon the huts disappeared again—a Fata Morgana or mirage. What remained was sand and a couple of broken rocks. The hot, shimmering air had distorted them. We collapsed together, and, as I thoughtlessly stared into the sand, I thought I saw tracks—one, two, three, and more. Tracks of a person and a hooved animal. I probed them with my hand; they were no illusion. The others did not want to believe it, but nevertheless, they crept up, and with trembling hands, they made sure that this was not another illusion. With our final bit of strength, we staggered and crawled along the tracks. We could not afford to lose them. After a while, we saw before us some low pine thicket, and we could distinctly hear the snorting of a horse or mule. Winter had tottered ahead impatiently. Then we heard him talking and a guttural voice replying. We crept on. The pines were somewhat bigger here. Suddenly, we saw Winter and, in front of him, an Arab with a black robe and a white turban, displaying a stony face, holding his mule by the reins. He obviously distrusted us. I pushed Klein forward.

"Go on, man" I urged eagerly. "Explain to him who we are. He has to help!"

Waveringly, and much too slowly for us, Klein offered him a ceremonial salaam. We became impatient. Finally, the Arab's face lit up. He moved his hands to his chest and then his forehead to greet us and said something. Klein told us, "He thought we were Englishmen. They are also Rommel's friends. They don't help Rommel's enemies."

"Don't create so many particulars," Leicht urged. "Ask him where we are, and where we can find water." We were near his tribe's camp. He would take us there, but first we had to prove to him we were Germans. I knew what it meant when an Arab talked about Rommel like a god. That was obligatory. I pointed at the German Eagle Badge on my shirt. The Arab bowed reverently and finally went into motion. With renewed hope, we hauled ourselves behind him. It seemed like an eternity until we reached a clearing, and then we were instantly surrounded by a crowd of men, women, and children.

After what seemed like endless preparations, they had some spruce needle tea ready for us. We could hardly restrain ourselves. We literally tore the filthy cups out of the women's hands. The disgusting, foul taste did not bother us in the least. It was just something to drink.

As I figured, the next oasis was Barce, about seventeen kilometers away. We could not manage that on foot. We wanted the Arabs to give us their mules. While we were still negotiating, bargaining, and threatening, I saw Winter jump up. "Aircraft," he shouted, and ripped the white shawls off the shoulders of two Arab women. He ran as best he could and, in the middle of the clearing, spread them out on the sand. We were saved!

Three Fi 156 Storks of the Emergency Desert Squadron had found us. Slowly, they began to glide in and stopped almost precisely on the fabric that had been laid out. "Thank God, Major," the young lieutenant said; I knew him from Derna. "Your SOS was correctly picked up, but we didn't have any cross bearing. The rubber raft was damaged when it was dropped into the water. We were ordered to pick you up along the coast, but when we did not find you there, we were afraid you might have drowned at the last moment. But then we searched, meter by meter, until we saw the landing cross here."

"Where are the others?" I asked.

"They barely managed to land in Benghazi with their last drop of fuel."

We received primary medical treatment at Barce. In Derna, my arm was repositioned and placed in a plaster cast. That relieved me from pain, but inwardly, I was depressed due to this failure.

I had to keep reminding myself of what I had been told by my tactical instructor at the Kriegsakademie: "Let it always be clear to you, no matter how good your plans are and how courageously you perform them, without Lady Luck by your side, you will have little success. Never forget to pay the Lady her proper due!" This time, Lady Luck had deserted me.

I was to be taken to the military hospital in Kifissia [Athens, Greece], but I insisted on remaining in Derna for a couple of days because I wanted to hand command over to Almásy. I told him, "I will request that they take me to the military hospital in Berlin. From there, I can support you. You now have to carry out our alternative plan and move the next two agents through the desert by car."

After toilsome weeks and under great hardship, Almásy succeeded. Both agents reached their destination and were able to establish contact with the Egyptian Revolutionary Committee. Their contact man was Anwar el-Sadat, today the president of Egypt [1970–1981].

Initially, they wanted to take off my right arm at the military hospital. I refused, and although it hangs down somewhat today, and is weaker and often painful, I can still use it.

I was discharged from the military hospital on July 2, 1941, and was ready for action again by the middle of August.

Much had changed in the Intelligence Department on Tirpitzufer. Major Brasser, with whom I had closely collaborated and who had always shown special understanding for our concerns, had been replaced by a young captain without any experience and little tact. I was relieved when I received another assignment. I was to be transferred to Rio de Janeiro as assistant to the Luftwaffe attaché in order to continue work against the United States from there. All preparations had been made. I had obtained the necessary instructions, had said good-bye to my wife, and had taken off on September 10 from Berlin. I had to wait in Rome for a military aircraft to Lisbon. From there, I was to continue to Rio on a commercial airliner. While in Rome, we had spent the evening celebrating with an old buddy, the aide to the local attaché, and I was late getting back to my hotel. I had just gone to bed when the telephone rang. An unknown voice from the Wehrmacht High Command said I was not to take off the next morning, but I was to return to Berlin immediately. I was speechless. I asked for the message to be repeated. Then, I called the embassy and received concurrence from them.

I returned to Berlin on the next aircraft and immediately reported to Colonel Piekenbrock. "Unfortunately, we had to call you back," he said. "Take a look at this." And he showed me an issue of the *New York Times,* dated September 10, 1941.

In big letters, I read the headline: "GERMAN SPY RING BROKEN German Espionage Ring Busted . . . Sebold testified . . . The Secret Intelligence Officer Nikolaus Ritter, alias *Dr. Rankin,* is cited as co-conspirator."

I stared at Piekenbrock and continued to read. A roster of seventeen German agents were arrested, including some of my own: Duquesne, Elsa Weustenfeld, Lily Stein, and *Paul. Tramp* had betrayed them all.

"That son of a bitch!" I said. "That traitor."

"But Ritter," Piekenbrock said calmly, "according to your own rules, *Tramp* was no traitor, not even a spy. He was a man who had worked for his new country."

24

End of War

After I had brought *Tramp,* by way of Genoa, to the United States, I had relinquished supervision. When his first reports were received in Wohldorf, my successor had already taken over Section I Air Hamburg. I was making preparations for Africa as well as getting ready for my last meeting in Lisbon with *Johnny.* Various departments of other intelligence stations had asked me to connect other agents with *Tramp,* but I had refused and had expressed these sentiments to Berlin.

I was already in Africa when it turned out that the technical chief in Wohldorf, without Trautmann's knowledge, had failed to put *Tramp*'s instructor on the receiver, something that would have been absolutely necessary, because only the latter really knew his pupil's "signature." In the meantime, contrary to instructions from Berlin, other agents had been tied to *Tramp,* and in June 1941, when the FBI struck in the United States, there were directly or indirectly seventeen agents and subagents who were tied to *Tramp.* [On June 1941, the FBI arrested thirty-three Nazi spies on charges of relaying secret information on US weaponry and shipping movements to Germany. (Duffy 2014)]

This case resulted in a severe clash between Canaris and Foreign Minister Joachim von Ribbentrop; Ribbentrop said, "If the United States now declares war, Canaris, it will be all your fault."

Canaris was asked for an explanation. On September 22, 1941, he gave the following briefing notes to the Chief of the Wehrmacht High Command; classified "Top Secret" under Number 3371/41, these were forwarded on September 23 to the State Secretary of the Foreign Office, Baron von Weizsäcker, and are reproduced here in excerpts:

> The determinations concerning the Sebold espionage case have resulted in the following findings:
>
> Sebold returned to Germany from the United States in February 1939 and was referred to the Hamburg field office via Gestapo Düsseldorf, Münster field office. He was sent to the United States in February 1940. Shortly after he started his work in the United States, the Foreign/Counterintelligence Bureau began to suspect that the mes-

sages—although often assessed by the Luftwaffe command staff very low priority but not judged unfavorably by Naval Operations—should be incorporated with caution.

The suspicion raised by the Foreign/Counterintelligence Bureau, which soon extended to the reliability of the person Sebold, was confirmed by the fact that the undercover agent asked for a code from another transmitter (Max) . . .

Despite urgings from several field offices, the Foreign/Counterintelligence Bureau rejected the plea to link other agents in the United States in with Sebold for the purposes of faster communication transmissions in order to protect these agents and their contacts.

From that point on, the orders that were given to Sebold by Intelligence contained deliberate deceptions to leave the enemy in the dark about the status of our explorations. This undertaking—as we can tell from the American press—was completely successful.

None of the officers who met Sebold in Germany gave their real name nor did they pose as members of the Gestapo.

Their assertion that the persons who had met Sebold indicated already in the autumn of 1939 that we are in possession of the Sperry-Bombsight . . . is not in keeping with the facts; on the contrary: to mislead the other side, it was radioed from here repeatedly that information about the bombsight and the address of the manufacturer's location continued to be of interest to us.

This deception also achieved its purpose completely, because the American military authorities did not order the bombsight to be released to England until autumn of 1940. This release was not authorized by American Intelligence until after a German aircraft was shot down in France, equipped with the American bombsight design.

Even then, *Tramp* had the American consul in Cologne provide him with some rules of conduct, and in February 1940, upon his arrival in the United States, he was immediately confronted by the FBI, who set him up with a transmitter and also supplied him with the appropriate bogus material. I was never able to find out how *Tramp* learned my real name, but it was probably from the owner of the boardinghouse where he was staying. Until then, he had known me simply as *Dr. Renken,* something he rendered during the trial as *"Rankin."*

All seventeen agents, except *Paul,* pleaded guilty and were sentenced to prison.

Paul later assured me that during the trial *Tramp* could not have supplied any further evidence except for some vague assertion that someone in Germany

Ritter (left), Commander of Flack Regiment 63, standing by downed enemy aircraft, 1944. From the editor's private collection.

told him they already had the Norden bombsight, which led everyone to conclude it was *Paul. Paul* actually never sent his drawings via *Tramp.*

This case produced a complete change in me. When Piekenbrock gave me the newspaper articles about the arrest, he also showed me a top-secret document, dated September 13. It was part of the voluminous correspondence between the attaché group and the Wehrmacht High Command concerning my case, and it read:

"Please do not register Ritter as assistant to the Air attaché if this has not been done yet. If registration has already been completed, please cancel it again immediately with the explanation that Major Ritter was seriously wounded."

It was feared there might be political complications in South America since my name had become known in the United States. That meant I could no longer work in the United States.

Piekenbrock offered me another section, but he understood my refusal and supported my request to return to active duty, something Canaris had refused earlier in the war.

I was too old for flying. The head of my personnel department in the Wehrmacht High Command made sure that after graduating from various training courses, I would again be assigned to active duty. I soon became a battalion

Hamburg, July 1943. Courtesy of the US Naval History and Heritage Command, Washington, DC. Photographer: Ardean R. Miller.

commander, and then, as battalion commander in the "Hermann Göring" Luftwaffe Panzer Division, I participated in the fighting in Sicily. In the autumn of 1942, I became a regimental commander; in September 1944, I was antiaircraft auxiliary combat commander of Hannover-Misburg, and on April 20, 1945, I

Hamburg, July 1943. Courtesy of the US Naval History and Heritage Command, Washington, DC.

ended the war as brigade commander with two antiaircraft regiments for antitank and antiaircraft defense in the Harz Mountains.

By that time, we had been surrounded by the Americans; we had blown up our ammunition and our last artillery pieces, and we had destroyed all papers. I had left it up to my soldiers either to go into captivity voluntarily or to try to break through the American ring with me. With a few men, I managed to get through the enemy lines at night without being noticed.

When we found there were no further German units we could join, we separated. I was able to make my way unrecognized between American and British troops, and finally, in stolen civilian farmer's clothing, I arrived in Hamburg on May 11, 1945, three days after the city's surrender.

I did not know whether my wife was still at home or had left Hamburg. Aware of the devastating bombing raids in July 1943, Operation Gomorrah, when over 40,000 persons were killed and one-third of the city's buildings and apartments were destroyed, I had a premonition that she had left Hamburg and had gone to Mecklenburg with our two-year-old daughter. It was not a pleasant thought for me when I learned that, in the meantime, the Russians had occupied that area.

Our house on the Rothenbaumchaussee was still standing. When I rang the bell, my mother-in-law opened the door. She was shocked when she saw me. At first, I thought this was because of my disheveled appearance, but then I realized she was afraid of the British, who had proclaimed by means of large posters everywhere that anyone who sheltered a German soldier would be shot.

The next day, I learned the staff of the antiaircraft division was still assembled in the central fire control headquarters, the large bunker on the Rothenbaumchaussee. They had been congregated there to secure their help with an orderly transfer. I knew the commander, General Wolz, from Africa and reported to him. We agreed that he needed a good interpreter and air defense expert for the British and that I should not assume that post as a prisoner of war but rather as a discharged colonel with the permission to live at home.

It was just the right moment. General Wolz told me that, in addition to the British, an American commission had also arrived; they wanted to study the Hamburg air defenses. That relieved me of my duty to report to the British or German authorities. Because all colonels were supposed to be brought to a special camp in Belgium, General Wolz put me on the list as lieutenant colonel, which didn't seem to concern anyone. The next day, I was presented to the commander of the American commission, General Smith of the Air Defense Investigation USSTAF (Rear) APO 413, and his chief of staff, Lieutenant Colonel V. Rapp, and I became their interpreter and military-technical adviser. They treated me like a comrade, and their first request of me was "Don't tell the 'Limeys' anything you tell us." They picked me up every morning with their car, and we drove to the old posts around Hamburg and Hanover.

But one day, as I returned from "duty," my mother-in-law told me a British officer had inquired about me. The next morning at nine o'clock the doorbell rang. At the door stood a British captain, his hands on his hips, a riding crop in one hand.

"Morning," he said, "Ritter?"

"Yes," I replied.

"Come with me for an interrogation."

"I'm sorry," I said. "I have an appointment with Colonel Rapp of the American Air Defense Commission. Couldn't you postpone your interrogation?"

"This is the British zone, and the Americans have nothing to say here," he replied curtly.

I realized now he was getting serious, and I asked, "Will it take a long time?"

"I don't know," he said. "Perhaps a couple of days."

"Then I will take some things with me."

"That is not necessary. We will take care of you!"

Then he asked me to accompany him to his car, and he drove me to his duty station, the official headquarters of the former Gauleiter, the Nazi Party district leader, of Hamburg.

He addressed me sternly and ordered me to sit down in the porter's room, closed the door behind me, and disappeared. Soon thereafter, the door was opened again and a tall, good-looking American officer from the Intelligence Service appeared and asked, "Are you Colonel Ritter?"

I was astonished at his politeness after the treatment by the British.

"Please come with me," he said. "I'd like to ask you a couple of questions, and bring your pipe along!" He asked me about some informants who had worked for me in the United States. I knew who among them had been arrested and was known to the Americans. I had never heard anything about some of the others! He smiled but did not pursue the question any further. Above all, he wanted to know something about Lily Stein. Because I knew I could no longer do her any harm, I told him how I met her and how I helped her leave Germany.

He paused, and I was convinced he would now ask me about my trip to the United States in the autumn of 1937. I had waited for that for quite some time. Actually, I was curious to see how much they knew about it, but he closed his file and just said, "That is all. Thank you!"

And then he took me back to the porter's room. When I picked up my coat and made ready to leave, he said, "Just one moment. The British want to talk to you. Good-bye."

The British Captain Bell first asked me to surrender my rings and golden keychain and put them in an envelope on which he wrote my name and some numbers and letters.

"What does that mean?" I asked.

"I have to take you to prison now," he said.

"To prison?" I asked, astonished. "I'm a soldier and not a criminal. If you have to arrest me, then take me to a prisoner of war camp but not a prison."

"Orders!" he barked. It was no use; I had to follow him.

Not a word was spoken during our ride. In the prison in Altona, he passed me on to the noncommissioned officer on duty, and when I requested an officer, he quickly cut me off. "For now, you will not see any officer," and then he disappeared.

A guard ordered me to follow him. He took me to the first floor, opened the door to a cell, and pushed me inside. Then he locked the iron door from the outside. I was stunned. I looked around the narrow cell: a bare wooden floor, an iron bedstead, a small narrow table and a stool, and in the corner a toilet seat.

Seeing the iron grills in front of the tall window, for a moment I conceived the idea to hang myself.

I could not imagine what all this might mean. What was behind all this? What caused such conservative people as the British to violate the Geneva Conventions? Something must have gone awry somewhere. I refused to think about anything else. I had done my duty as a soldier.

This treatment was absurd and incomprehensible. On tiptoes, I could look out of the high window across to another wing of our building. Through the bars of the window, I recognized the heads of two colleagues. One belonged to Böckel.

"Hey, Böckel!" I shouted. "How did you get here? What's going on here?"

"I believe that this is their peculiar way of intimidating us," he shouted back.

"How long have you been here?" I asked.

"Three days," he shouted in reply. "I heard from a guard that they'll soon take us to some other camp from here."

Behind me I heard the key in the door, and as I turned around, a guard put a plate of nondescript thin soup and a piece of dry bread on the table. Then the light was turned off from the outside, and after I forced myself not to think anymore, I fell asleep on the hard cot.

After three days, they took me downstairs. Among a group of men, I saw some acquaintances with whom I had worked in the Intelligence Station at the start of the war. They put us in a truck and took us to the former Neuengamme concentration camp near Hamburg. Most of us had never heard anything about it. One fellow told us he had stayed there once during the war, and it would be better than the prison from where we had come. But that was not true. Furniture and sanitary facilities had been removed, and ten of us were squeezed into a room for four. The food rations were barely enough to keep us alive. There was no diversion of any kind except for the endless roll calls every morning and every evening. In between, we were allowed to go out into the courtyard and into a pasture surrounded by barbed wire.

One day, we heard machine-gun fire. Some fellow prisoners, who happened to be lying in the pasture, were wounded, and one was shot and killed. A Belgian guard had fired blindly at the prisoners because he suddenly remembered that his brother had been killed during the war. It was his personal revenge!

After three weeks, another former Intelligence officer and I were taken out. We had to report to the gate. The others thought we would be discharged. Instead a truck turned up with only German Intelligence officers. All were chained to each other. They were taken to the open-air latrine, and when they returned, they chained us likewise and loaded us together with the others onto the truck.

I protested, but the officer again repeated, "Orders." We were taken to the notorious CSDIC camp in Bad Nenndorf and placed in solitary cells.

The "prison" was the old health resources house. The narrow bathrooms had been converted into cells; they simply took out the furnishings, put cement over the bathtubs, attached iron grills in front of the windows, and replaced the doors with iron doors. The new inventory consisted of a wooden bedstead into which, instead of a mattress, narrow little slats were placed at an interval of 20 centimeters, plus a stool, and a tiny table. We were allowed neither to read nor write. As far as our families were concerned, we were lost. Not even questions via the Red Cross were answered.

Once a day, we were chased outside. In a narrow courtyard, we were allowed to walk around in a circle for a while without talking. Then we were locked up again. At nine or ten o'clock in the evening, a guard threw two blankets into the cell. In the early morning, they took them out again. During the night, we were awakened by the duty officer, who flashed a light at us. Opportunity for appeal did not exist. No one listened. The food rations were on par with the treatment.

One morning, I heard a wiping sound on my door, and somebody asked in German through the keyhole, "Who's in there?"

"Ritter," I answered, excited. "Who are you?"

"Trautmann," he whispered, as he continued wiping the door. "I can't talk much. The guard is watching. This is an insane asylum here." He gave me the names of some other inmates whom I knew. "In a couple of days, they will fetch you for an interrogation. Tell them . . ."

"Hey, you bastard," a rough voice shouted. "Finish wiping that door."

The next day, my door was ripped open, and a wild-looking guard frisked me and took me to the basement. Below, I heard the murmuring of German voices, and as I was pushed into the dimly lit room, pale faces looked at me—men wearing grubby clothing with bright patches on the knees and elbows, who, astonished, called out my name. I recognized several former comrades from Intelligence, including Trautmann. They were cleaning vegetables.

"Have you been interrogated already?" someone asked.

"No," I replied. "Is this an interrogation center?"

"You're lucky," said Trautmann. "For certain, they brought you here by mistake. You're not allowed to be together with anyone before you've had your first interrogation. To begin with, you have to fill out a list with the names of everybody whom you knew in Intelligence. Take a good look around everybody here, and I'll give you some more names you can also write down without doing anyone any harm."

I had barely understood correctly what was involved when an excited noncommissioned officer, screaming ferociously, approached and indicated I had no business there, as if it were my fault. I was immediately taken back to my cell. At any rate, I had gotten somewhat wiser, although I could not understand why such treatment was necessary for an interrogation or why they took the prostheses away from the amputees and collected all the dentures, as I had heard in the basement. Perhaps they thought they could make us more talkative this way? But that was a big psychological mistake.

After a few days, it was my turn. When I was taken to the interrogation cell, I stood before a major sitting at a table with an open file in front of him.

I walked toward him, certain that I would be facing a somewhat better educated man with whom I could talk. Instead he yelled at me, "Stop where you are! You are at attention!"

I was dumbfounded as I involuntarily came to attention; when I took a closer look at him, I saw how the blood was pulsing through his neck vein, and I knew he had to force himself to act this way.

"And do not speak. I do the talking! You will tell us everything down to the last detail about what you did while you were working in Intelligence. If not, you stay here, and if you get as old as Methuselah, and if I should die before that, then my successor will take you on. The guard will give you paper and pencil, and you will write down the names of everybody with whom you came into contact during your Intelligence activities. This evening you will give the completed sheet of paper to the guard, and no funny business!"

"Very well," I said.

"Now get out!" he yelled, and pointed to the door, as if I were going to exit through the window.

That was the commencement of a long series of unpleasant interrogations. After about two months of solitary confinement, I was taken to a larger cell together with my old friend Böckel and Dr. Peter Kleist of the Ribbentrop Bureau. The interrogations would continue, but they were no longer as unpleasant as in the beginning. I was surprised no one seemed interested in my travels in the Balkans or my mission to Africa.

At one point, I was retrieved again after a long break because my interrogator thought he had discovered something I had kept secret from him (and that was really a hell of a lot). He insisted that in the autumn of 1939 I had had lunch with one of my informants in the Hotel du Vieux Doelen in The Hague at noon.

"Do you believe that I would have been so foolish as to take one of my best people to that kind of place where everybody knew it was a meeting point for international intelligence services?" I asked him.

"But, I know you were there," he said. "I can even tell you what you had to eat!"

"You are certainly mistaken," I said.

The next morning, he told me, "By the way, I was wrong about the meeting in The Hague. It was somebody else." That had most certainly been just a trick. "Do you smoke?" he asked then. I was surprised because we were forbidden to smoke. Apparently, he did not know that.

Politely, I said yes, and he gave me a box of Senior Service with whatever was left in it. I thanked him, and when he dismissed me, I said in passing, "We don't have any matches in the cell."

"Is that so?" He acted astonished. "Then tell the guard to give you some."

I put the cigarettes in my pocket so the guard would not see them. I showed them to my two cellmates, and they looked at me incredulously. What were we supposed to do with them now?

"Because the major said that we should ask the guard for a match, I'll give it a try right now," I said. I banged the door with my foot to call the guard.

"What do you want?" he barked.

"A match," I replied.

"Have you gone crazy?" he screamed at me.

"No," I said, "my interrogating officer gave me the cigarettes and told me I should get a match from the guard."

Without a word, he slammed the door in my face, and we waited for what was yet to come. It did not take long before the door was ripped open again, and I was summoned to report to the guard on duty. I was lucky. He was one of those who, in contrast to many other guards, could read and write and who belonged to the normal species of the human race. I told him my story. He laughed and actually gave me a box with four or five matches.

"You know, I'm not supposed to do that. Actually, you should give me the cigarettes. But, for God's sake, do not let any of the guards see you smoking!"

"Okay," I smiled, and triumphantly I passed the guard and returned to my cell. The two others had waited anxiously. With nervous fingers we lit a cigarette. It was the first one we had had in six months. We closed our eyes, inhaled deeply, slowly blew the smoke out again, and took another deep breath, and then the three of us, without saying a word, simply crapped out, dizzy from the unaccustomed nicotine.

We had barely pulled ourselves together and hidden the remaining cigarettes and matches behind a broken tile when the door was ripped open again and a grim-looking corporal—whom, on account of his bloodshot eyes, we called "Bloodeye"—shouted, "Give me those cigarettes now!" We gave him one cigarette stub and said that was all that was left. He slammed the door behind him, but we knew this would not be the end.

After about an hour, I was summoned to the front. A young lieutenant straightened himself before me and snarled, "You know that you are not allowed to smoke. You will be punished accordingly! Your interrogation officer was not entitled to give you cigarettes."

"Okay," I said.

The next morning, I was taken to an interrogation cell. Another officer was there waiting for me: "You received cigarettes from your interrogation officer. He did not know that you were not allowed to smoke. You should have told him that. The matter is hereby finished."

I hesitated a moment, but then I could no longer restrain myself, and said, "You always reproached us for knowing everything about the concentration camps, and you called us liars when we told you, quite truthfully, that we knew nothing. And here is a British officer, with us under the same roof, and he did not even know that we are not allowed to smoke."

"That's enough," the Englishman cut me off and dismissed me, but I knew he got my point.

In addition to our routine treatment in Nenndorf, there was, among others, a very peculiar trick played by the guards. When we came from outdoors, we had to strip naked and throw our clothes down the stairwell, then run after them and sort them out. We knew to whom we owed this incredibly humiliating treatment. Like the master, so is the servant! The commanding officer was Lieutenant Colonel Robin "Tin Eye" Stephens. He seemed to take the view that he could best belittle us if he starved us and humiliated us. He was backed by the senior British diplomat, Sir Robert Vansittart, the biggest German hater of all.

I had been taken before a tribunal of British Intelligence officers, which included my interrogator, Major John Gwyer and Lieutenant Colonel William Edward Hinchley-Cooke, also known as "Cookie," the same guy who had questioned Simon in England. Personally, I had seen Hinchley-Cooke only once before. They asked me about Vera and Drüke. I did not know what had happened to Vera and said as little as possible about her, but since I knew that Drüke was no longer alive, I told everything without hesitation. Hinchley-Cook asked me what Drüke looked like. While I tried to describe him, he showed me a couple of pictures of criminals, "Can you recognize him here?"

I looked at the pictures and said quite honestly, "No."

Hinchley-Cooke said angrily, "Of course, you can. You were long enough . . ."

But when I shook my head, my interrogation officer chimed in and said, "I believe, Colonel, it will not be so easy to recognize this man in these photos. They were taken after Drüke had been sitting in prison for quite some time."

Hinchley-Cooke calmed himself down and said, "Perhaps," and then he looked at me and said, "Drüke was a brave man, but we had to shoot him because he had aimed his pistol at one of our men as he was arrested."

The picture he showed me was certainly Drüke, but he looked so completely different from the man whom I remembered. For me, Drüke was a tall, strong, healthy man, always perfectly shaved and clothed. The man in the photo was emaciated with a narrow, shrunken face, but that's how all of us looked now, gaunt and shrunken—Trautmann, Böckel, Kleist, and I.

Christmas 1945 came and went. It was the saddest Christmas of my life.

Kleist, Böckel, and I forced ourselves to practice our daily language studies in an effort somehow to preserve our spirit and morale. Kleist spoke fluent Russian, Böckel was fluent in French, and I in English. We spent our time, good and bad, instructing each other and would finally alternate languages and try to converse in that language for one entire day.

Then one day there came a significant change. About thirty of us were assembled on a lower floor. All had previously been more or less essential personnel. In addition to us, there was the former senior General Staff officer at OKH, some captains of industry, an ambassador, and others. A British colonel told us the interrogations were over. All of us would be placed together on the same corridor, where during the day, we were allowed to communicate with each other. The corridor was closed off from the outside. At night, we were locked in adjoining cells.

I was appointed floor leader. By mutual agreement, I managed to get a permit to work in order to prevent any gradually developing prison psychosis. A good-natured guard had told me a group of eight men could carry out the cleaning work daily in the Officers' Mess. With the right attitude, we believed we could engineer something for ourselves there. I asked the sergeant who had to make the arrangements to go ahead and assign the work and the schedule.

There was not much serious work. The rooms of the officers were kept in order by British stewardesses. We had to clean the dining room, the bar, and the kitchen, and we had to wash dishes. And, basically, that was exactly what we were trying to achieve. Half-filled plates with untouched meals were brought down by the stewardesses, and we had orders to dump them in the garbage cans. Instead we smuggled them into the vegetable room where some of us were always sitting, cleaning vegetables. There, we hid the leftovers and distributed them whenever we had a little break.

The guard, who was supposed to watch us, was mostly in the kitchen flirting with the female cooks. We were particularly courteous to them—politer than the English guards, and that worked out well. Among them were two French women who had volunteered during the war and who were happy that, in contrast to the British guards, we treated them courteously and spoke French with them the moment we were no longer being watched. It was not long before they started bringing us bowls of untouched food, and not infrequently, they would bake a cake for us that they hid under their aprons and smuggled into the vegetable cellar while others distracted the guard.

One day, I was again told to report upstairs, where I was put into a cell with my old friend Röder. Röder had gotten to Nenndorf just recently. My interrogating officer had asked me whether I might not want to talk to him sometime and tell him he should not be so stubborn.

Initially I refused, but when he assured me I could help Röder, who reportedly was bordering on a nervous breakdown, I finally agreed.

When Röder saw me, he was close to tears. "I'm going to hang myself," he said. "What did I do anyway?"

"Control yourself, man," I said. "You can have my shoelaces. As you see, we have been allowed to use them again for some time."

"Why are you so sarcastic?" he asked me, and sank on a stool.

"Now, pull yourself together." I tried to persuade him gently. "Naturally, you did not commit any crime, and the brothers here know that, too. Don't let yourself be influenced by all of this theater. It's no secret that you worked for us."

"Be quiet," he interrupted me. "Don't talk so loud. They have a microphone here, and they're listening."

"Probably," I said, "but what can they find out? You didn't do anything other than what the British merchants have been doing forever and ever."

He gradually calmed down, and when I asked him whether he still wanted to have my shoelaces, he said, "Don't be so nasty." We shook hands, and I banged against the door to summon the guard to let me out.

The winter passed. We froze. The walls in our cells were covered with ice. As spring came, I asked that they also let us work in the large garden of the Officers' Mess. One day, Trautmann and I managed to evade the guard, and with our wheelbarrows, we passed close to the German gardener who had been strictly forbidden to speak with us. Every time we whispered a question, we received an answer on the way back. He also had been a reserve officer and did what he could to help us. Through him, we were able for the first time to inform our families that we were still alive. They had not heard from us for more than a year.

This gave us new hope, but an uncertain future still lay ahead of us.

On August 18, 1946, I was again told to report to my interrogation officer. With an obliging smile, he said, "I can inform you that you will be discharged from here tomorrow."

"Thank God," I uttered involuntarily.

But he continued, "But you will not go home right away. That requires some time-consuming formalities, but it will happen in another camp." And after a short pause, he added, "Forget what you experienced here."

"I hardly believe that this will be possible," I replied. He looked at me for a moment, went away, and left me alone with my thoughts and the guard who was waiting for me at the door.

About twenty of us were once again loaded on a lorry and taken to another camp near Hemer in Westphalia. It was almost like the freedom of long ago, without the roaring guards and the narrow cells, where we had been cut off from the rest of the world by a tall barbed wire fence and every move had been restricted. The food was worse because we didn't get any of the extra rations from the Officers' Mess or from our French "girlfriends."

But now, we could write to our families and receive packages "to a limited extent." The first news came on an open postcard: Notification: "Message to be written by internee (*No more than 25 words*)." We were able to write such cards once a week. It was difficult to compose them and certainly even more difficult to comprehend them.

What we were most worried about was the uncertainty concerning the fate of our wives and children. I had heard nothing from my wife for more than a year and a half. I did not know where she was, nor did I know whether she and our little daughter were still alive.

When I had returned to Hamburg for the first time, my mother-in-law had told me that by the end of the war my wife and daughter had been in the Russian zone, and that she had heard from a refugee that they were relatively well off, considering the conditions. When I was arrested, my mother-in-law had promised to try everything to notify my wife.

Since my wife had not heard anything from me for such a long time, she had, in the meantime, gone to a fortune teller. The woman had told her that I was alive, but sick, and that it would take a very long time before we would see each other again. She said, "Don't trouble yourself. He is alive, and he is in a fertile region not far from Hamburg. You will soon get news about him."

My wife did not believe her because there was no mail connection among the zones. Then three weeks later, a young girl arrived and brought her a letter from my mother-in-law, which stated that I had been at home but had been arrested. The first camp had literally been "in a fertile region not far from Hamburg"—Neuengamme in the Vierlanden.

After that, my wife heard nothing further from me for an entire year. In the meantime, she succeeded, under great danger and many hardships, to slip into the British zone and return to Hamburg. But even there, she did not hear any news about me until, one day, a fellow prisoner came; he had been discharged from Nenndorf and contacted our wives. And finally, in August 1946, she received my first card, but it took almost another year before we saw each other again.

We were moved to another camp in Eselheide. Formerly, this had been one of the largest military training areas. There began a new series of interrogations, this time regarding our political affiliation. One day, I was asked, "Were you ever a member of the National Socialist Party?"

"No," I replied, "you know that we are interned here for military reasons."

"That does not matter," the interrogator snapped at me. "Why were you not a party member?"

His crude manner annoyed me. "First of all, because I was abroad until 1935, and second, because being on active duty, I was not allowed to belong to any party," I said.

"What does that mean? You would have been a member otherwise?" he asked sarcastically.

"Yes," I yelled. I was already irritated and defiantly stared him in the face while inwardly I was pleased I had struck a nerve.

"Get the hell out of here!" he shouted. He never questioned me again.

Apparently, he did not know we were allowed to become party members later, after the attempt on Hitler's life in 1944. By this scheme, the party tried to gain more influence in the Wehrmacht and issued an invitation to all soldiers to join the party. Some responded to the call, but even though they might have been tempted initially to become party members, at that point there was no further reason to join.

Christmas 1946 led into Easter, and we were still waiting. On May 3, 1947, I was told by the Irish doctor, for whom I often interpreted, that I and some other fellows would soon be discharged. I told Böckel, whose name the doctor had mentioned, about it. That night, neither of us slept very much.

The next day, I washed my few belongings, including my suit; it was the same in which I had been arrested and which I had worn uninterruptedly, except in Nenndorf. I folded my trousers nicely along the seam, put them under the mattress and slept on them because I wanted to arrive home with a pressed crease in my trousers.

And then, it came true. On the morning of May 22, 1947, five of us were summoned to the camp directorate. We carried our bundles under our arms—with a homemade spoon, an old tin can with a self-fashioned handle, and a little, self-fabricated pipe.

The gates closed behind us, and there we stood—aliens in an alien world. Our wives had been notified by a comrade in camp management, who had also organized a car for us to take us to the nearest railroad station. We bought our train tickets with our discharge money. Nobody paid any attention to us. We boarded the train and sat down among all the other people. The closer we came to Hamburg, the more anxious we became. Would our wives be at the station? For the first time, we were to see them again after two and a half years of separation.

And then, there she was. We fell into each other's arms. We could not speak. Our little one was there. She looked at me with questioning eyes. Her mother had shown her pictures of me and had read my letters to her. I picked her up, and she let me kiss her and also seemed to be happy.

I looked at my wife. She looked well. She wore one of the dresses that I particularly liked, and she had preserved it carefully. She wore a big hat because she knew I liked it, even though she did not like it. Suddenly she saw Böckel, and said, "My God." He had always been one of the best-looking men in our group, and now I also noticed how gaunt and old he looked. The others were crying when they saw him.

I said to my wife, "Come," and we went home.

And there I sat again, just like after World War I, but worse. The country was split into four zones and occupied by enemy powers. Once again, a way of life lost; once again, not a penny. And the worst of all was no job. On top of that, I was twice as old as after the first war. My wife was working for a notary and earned 300 marks a month. One loaf of bread, if you could get it, cost 80 marks. Our bank accounts had been confiscated. We somehow managed by selling my wife's jewelry and some other valuables, as well as a large carpet.

Finally, I found a job as a self-employed associate of various import and export firms. Life gradually became bearable again.

25

Reflections

Since then, many years have gone by. During my extensive travels at home and abroad, in conversations with friends, acquaintances, and colleagues, I have been able to learn a few additional, interesting details about the main actors mentioned in this book.

I visited the Pasha in Cairo in 1952. He was closely allied with Nasser and, at that time, was supposed to become ambassador to Russia. He told me Count Almásy had survived the war and had been working again in Egypt and that, while on vacation in Hungary, he died of acute appendicitis.

In the United States, my informants had been sentenced to prison terms after the "espionage ring" had been discovered. Duquesne had failed in his attempt to escape and had died in prison. Elsa and Lily had finally been discharged from prison, and as far as I know, they still live in the United States today.

Paul, Herman Lang, had served nine tough years of his prison sentence and had been released prematurely on good behavior. He had returned to Germany and initially found it difficult to get settled. With the help of other acquaintances and some connections, I was able to help him get recognized as a returnee. Over the years, he managed to get a good position in industry, and today he lives in his own home in southern Germany.

My old sea dog, Walter Simon, had also survived his prison years in Ireland and had returned to Hamburg. He had been discharged at the end of the war and earned his living doing odd jobs. We had been able to secure a little pension for him. Now and then, he visited us, and together, we relived the years of his activity for the Abwehr and for me during its various episodes, sometimes with bitterness, but sometimes also with a cheerful smile. In the summer of 1959, he became very weak and died in November 1961 in a hospital near us. Captain Wichmann, two distant relatives, and I were the only ones who attended his final journey.

On the advice of his English girlfriend, *Hansen* had turned himself in to the British authority; his circumstances in England had become increasingly difficult and we were no longer able to help him. He had been under arrest for a relatively short time, and the British Security Service had maintained contact with us using his name long after my departure, in the firm belief we would take his information at face value. His girlfriend waited for him, and after his discharge they married. Today he is well off and lives with wife and children in England.

Nilberg had also managed to survive his imprisonment in England, but he never completely recovered from the effects of his jump. Seriously ill, he lives in Sweden and has completely lost his memory. His fellow prisoner, a former Intelligence officer who had sat with him in a cell and to whom he told his story as it is described here, visited him on several occasions and helped him in any way he could.

My cloverleaf of the three ladies, as I learned in the end, seemed to have deceived me. *Lady May,* the Duchess of Château-Thierry (Maude Manxx), and Vera von Shalburg, whom the British Security Service had labeled the "Erikson Group," purportedly had been tagged onto us from the very beginning. When Vera had been disguised in England as a communist, on orders from Dierks, she had been interrogated by the British, but then released. Because she had completely fallen for Dierks, she remained, as long as he lived, faithful and totally committed to him and to us. Only after she had been dropped in England and had established contact with the duchess, who had been working for MI5, was she said to have betrayed Drüke. Böckel and I categorically rejected that version. Vera survived the war and is still living in England with her husband, a British officer.

In this context, it must be pointed out that, among other things, it was and is the task of every intelligence service to approach enemy agents and harness them for their own purpose. This is entirely reasonable, and then the dispatching organization may be tricked. Very often, however, this maneuver is exposed, and the deception continues the other way around.

In 1941, for example, German Intelligence successfully turned all British agents who were dropped in Holland and Belgium by aircraft or boat and then maintained communication with the British dispatching agencies. This was so effective that the British supplied these agents for more than two and a half years with the entire equipment of arms, ammunition, and explosives, as well as substantial financial resources, without realizing their entire intelligence and sabotage organization was in German hands and was working against them.

Our little *Johnny* had played his restless and fascinating game to the very end. Throughout the years, he now and then sold his contact with the British Security Service and occasionally supplied it with information while he was loyally working for us.

While writing this book, I managed to get my hands on an extraordinary document concerning *Johnny.* It is an excerpt from an official British report on the work of double agents of the British Security Service (MI5) and the British Secret Intelligence Service (MI6) during the war.

One document maintains that *Johnny* was a double agent. At first, I was rather baffled when I read that, but then I realized this report served to enhance the value and the honesty of this little man for me. It says in the report that *Johnny*—or *Snow,* as the British called him—worked for the first time for Germany in 1936 after he allegedly had met some members of the Abwehr in Cologne. But indeed, we had first come into contact with *Johnny* in March 1937 after he had offered his services to the German Embassy in Brussels. His reply went to the cover address of Miss *Busch*'s grandmother. Any prior business trips in Germany were purely of a private nature. He never met German Intelligence officers in Cologne.

All informants were registered in Central Headquarters in Berlin, and if any duty station registered an agent who was already working for some other duty station, it was immediately informed thereof. In that way, it was impossible for an agent to work simultaneously for two different duty stations without each knowing about the other.

The British assertion that *Johnny* was working for the Security Service was correct, but what the British did *not* know was that this happened with my full consent and with my total support. If the British claim we did not use him as a double agent, then that is not in keeping with the facts. *Johnny* often asked me for bogus material so he could consolidate his position with the British. In Germany, he was always under our control so he could never have established any other connection.

As the British themselves, quite correctly, acknowledge, he brought us a great deal of valuable information. They also state we received written information about the Navy from *Johnny.* We actually did get information about the Navy from him but never in writing. Everything he delivered until the outbreak of the war he just handed over personally during our many meetings.

The British have limited knowledge of the details concerning *Johnny*'s work with the secret transmitter. Among other things, the British claim *Johnny* was given written instructions from us concerning the use of the transmitter. That is comical. He had been trained exclusively by us in Hamburg. It is also asserted that the first establishment of contact with the transmitter was difficult, and that his first radio message supposedly went like this, "Must immediately meet you in Holland. Bring code for weather report. Indicate city and hotel." We never received such a message. *Johnny* knew his code for the weather reports by heart. As regards the allegations that *Johnny* wanted to set up four secret transmitters for the dissemination of propaganda in England, neither Lieutenant Colonel Trautmann nor I, under whose command the secret transmission station in Wohldorf functioned, knew anything about such a plan.

Moreover, the document contained some other assertions that are simply not true. I never met *Johnny* with an associate in Rotterdam or Cologne, nor did he get any money from Mrs. Kraft in England. He always received money exclusively from me or my representative.

The British version of our failed meeting at sea is likewise false. It reportedly took place during the day and not at night, and it was not foggy, either. There was no aircraft cruising over the cutter in order to warn it by means of light signals. The captain simply had gotten cold feet. The assertion that the account of events came from *Biscuit* (alias for Sam McCarthy), as the second agent was called by the British, confirmed my opinion that the latter likewise deceived the British. Why should he invent such a story? When I talked about this with *Johnny* and *Brown*, *Brown* mentioned nothing at all about the cutter affair. He merely confirmed *Johnny's* story that the British Security Service offered me $200,000 in gold if they would bring me to England with them.

Besides, nobody told *Brown* anything, as the British maintained, about a South African who was waiting in Belgium to be dropped in England by parachute to help *Johnny*. At that time, we had no such man.

Brown remained in Hamburg about three weeks and was escorted back by a Reserve Lieutenant George Sessler, from whom he escaped in Madrid. The fact that he did not go to Lisbon or return directly to England confirms my suspicion that he was a communist. Of course, he did return to England again but not until three months later. And as Lieutenant Colonel Trautmann assured me, he did not get any secret transmitter from us, although the English maintained that he had brought one back.

My judgment concerning the two men remains firm. I believe *Brown* betrayed both the British and us, whereas *Johnny* only betrayed the British. If, as the British claim, he was their man, why did he not betray my friends Helmut Thimm, or *Hansen*, or *Don Carlos*, or *Rudolf*, or many others?

No, I am firmly convinced that he was always honest with me. It was quite obvious he had to show the British something so he could move around freely. I do not doubt for one moment that his hatred of everything English was genuine, and I know he would have come to Germany permanently with Lily and his child if I had permitted it. But when I met him the last time in Lisbon, it was certain he had become ineffectual for us, and I felt compelled to cut off all connection with him.

Today there is no further doubt that *Johnny* was a master spy. The information he brought was of the utmost value for Germany. Unfortunately, I have had no further personal contact with *Johnny*, but I learned from my reliable source that he is alive and healthy and lives somewhere in Ireland under a false name with Lily and his children.

Admiral Canaris was hanged in April 1945 in Flossenburg concentration camp a few hours before the Allies came in. He, like many others, could not appear as a witness. It was his undoing that he provided cover for his associate and confidant Hans Oster. Oster was the chief of Department Z of Intelligence, and everybody knew he blindly hated everything and everybody that was National Socialist.

Neither Admiral Canaris nor Intelligence as a group belonged to any resistance movement. Naturally, there also were those in Intelligence who personally opposed Hitler, but engaging in politics was not the task of Intelligence. Some associates who were in Berlin during the last days told me a notebook with defeatist comments was found in Canaris's armored safe.

That the admiral did make such remarks, I'd like to believe. He had foreseen the downfall of his Fatherland. He was always a nationalist, but never a National Socialist, and the longer the war went on, the more his dislike of the party grew. When I saw the admiral the last time, as I reported to him prior to my departure for Africa, we briefly talked about the possible entry of the United States into the war. I told him I believed that the psychological intelligence service of the American OSS (Office of Strategic Services, predecessor to CIA) was at work even then in Germany. Canaris also knew that, but he said, "One can overthrow the government in peacetime if one is dissatisfied, but if one does it during a war, then one betrays his own people."

That was the first time I heard any remark along those lines from him, but it confirmed my opinion of him, which I always held. He was no friend of the system, but he did not want to become a traitor.

As I write this in 1970, of my group, only Böckel, Trautmann, Röder, and Helmut Thimm are still alive, plus a few others. After his retirement, *The Skipper* moved to the countryside, where he died a few years later. After the war, we all went our different ways, but occasionally we still meet and talk about days past, which are in a different world.

Nikolaus Ritter

Nikolaus Ritter, 1972, at home. From the editor's private collection.

Epilogue

The history of espionage is as old as history itself. The Bible tells us about Moses, who sent twelve spies into the Promised Land, and Delilah, who was an agent of the Philistines sent to weaken Samson, the great enemy of their people. Ancient Greece and Rome had their spies, and even the Church used them into the Middle Ages. When the Mongols were at the height of their power in the thirteenth and fourteenth centuries, they had a far-flung espionage network. At the time of the feudal rule of knights in the Middle Ages, with their ideals of honor and morality, espionage was considered dishonorable. But after the blooming of the Italian city-states around the fourteenth century, spying was again considered necessary to maintain competitive capacity and security. At that time, ambassadors, who engaged in quasi-official espionage, were often capable spies. Today it is the mission of military attachés—of course, without engaging in espionage—to gather information in their fields.

Espionage has been considered a part of military science since the eighteenth century. Frederick the Great reportedly said of his enemy, Marshal de Soubise: "The marshal is always followed by 100 cooks. I am always preceded by 100 spies."

Napoleon believed all spies to be traitors, but he considered it necessary to build an extensive and expansive secret service. An effective espionage system was established on the battleship *Bismarck,* and almost thirty-six thousand spies and agents were said to be working in France before and during the war of 1870–1871.

In the United States, George Washington was convinced of the necessity of espionage, and admitted having used quite a few "adroit tricks." He used "every conceivable form of deception" in war, including cyphers, secret codes, invisible ink, and doublespeak.

Today, no war, hot or cold, is conceivable without espionage. And no modern government can reasonably and successfully execute its policies without informants and spies. Neither can industry. It is a question of self-preservation, which consequently compels one to shield against the breach of information. Every country has its own intelligence service, an organization that is recognized by domestic and international customs. And yet, like everything nontransparent, it is consistently seen by nonmembers as mysterious because it cannot operate in the open.

In one's own country, members have the same rights and duties as any employee of the civil service, but they are viewed by the general population with a mixture of fear, curiosity, and restrained approval. But as soon as they leave the borders of their own country, they cease to be recognized, and they are subject not merely to the jurisdiction of the country in which they reside, but, furthermore, to special espionage laws. Also, the secret intelligence officer, or anyone the agent oversees, is also liable to prosecution because they enlisted a third party to commit a crime.

The general application of espionage in all civilized groups necessarily leads to the question of clarifying the legal status of spies as well as of official members of the intelligence services. As we have seen from the earliest days of emperors, kings, presidents, and generals, and even churches, espionage has been practiced in earnest and is considered indispensable.

Among the ancient Romans, "disclosure of secrets that are of benefit to the enemy" warranted harsh punishment. Also punishable were those "who sent enemies of the Roman people a messenger or letter that gives signs, deliberately aids the enemies of the Roman people, or provides wrongful advice to the state council."

According to ancient Germanic law, "treason is a breach of trust against the commonwealth." The Friesians "took the traitor northwards to the beach and drowned him." The Alemannic people's law punished treason with "death and burning"; the Longobards confiscated property and possessions. Here, the trail of treason also includes "the unauthorized dispatch of messengers and negotiators as well as the conveyance of state secrets to foreign powers." Until the turn of the eighteenth century, there was only talk of treason. Not until the General Prussian Land Law of 1774 was the word "scout" found for the first time in writing and referred to as "foreign scouts (spies)" to be treated according to the rules of martial law. The word "spy" is found for the first time in 1813 in the Penal Code of the Bavarian Empire. However, no differentiation is made between a traitor of the native country and a foreign spy.

At the Brussels conference of 1884, espionage was recognized as an admissible instrument of war as long as it was confined to the theater of operation. It was not until 1907 in The Hague Rules of Land Warfare that specific definitions and agreements for the treatment of agents and spies were formulated, but again, without any differentiation between one who betrays his own country and one who labors for his own country against another. In previous conferences, these points were seriously debated, but finally a consensus was reached that in the interest of self-defense and deterrence, no distinction should be made. Justification for punishment was, therefore, acknowledged, and it was determined that under known circumstances, agents could be sentenced to death. Apart from that, however, every country has its own espionage laws.

The first espionage law in the United States was adopted by Congress in 1917, shortly after the country's entry into World War I. Generally, agents and spies are subject to common laws and to specific regulations regarding treason and espionage (in the Federal Republic of Germany, paragraphs 80–85 of the StGB [German Penal Code]). In this context, it seems warranted to insert a brief reference to the concepts "treason" and "high treason." Treason is directed against the external security of the state, whereas high treason is a violent assault on the constitution, state, or head of state that threatens the existence of the state. In every country, this is considered the most heinous crime that can be committed. High treason also includes "accidental" dissemination of subversive literature. To put it briefly, treason is the act of betraying one's country, especially by attempting to kill the sovereign or overthrow the government.

As history shows, perpetrators of high treason often become heroes. The general public will judge them on the basis of feelings, by sympathy or antipathy, seldom according to reason.

Most espionage laws had express provisions for the punishment of those who practice espionage "with disguise, under a false name, or concealment of professional status." Neutral states can extradite an agent or incarcerate him for the duration of a war. All of these provisions are valid in peace as well as in war. In peacetime, they are just as severe, if not even harsher, regardless of whether this involves military or industrial espionage.

According to international law, no spy may be punished without a court ruling; but over time, an unwritten common law has taken shape by which *foreign* agents and spies are not punished as severely as traitors. They are extradited or mutually exchanged.

True informants are those who place themselves at the state's disposal out of idealism or out of a patriotic sense of duty. Among all volunteers, they have drawn the heaviest lot because they are almost always lone wolves—often in a losing battle. Soldiers at the front, who are publicly acknowledged everywhere, derive their courage, boldness, and toughness not merely from their own morality or enthusiasm, but also from the support found in military discipline, a sense of duty, and, equally as important, in the camaraderie they share with fellow soldiers.

Undercover informants, who voluntarily go behind enemy lines, who daily risk their lives, yet are not allowed to defend themselves with weapon in hand, can only draw courage from within themselves, without the community of comrades or the certainty of a vested right, but purely on a moral right.

But we also need the others: the professional spy, the adventurer, the wheeler-dealer, and the opportunist, who from a moral viewpoint deserve the vilest interpretation of the term "spy" if they betray their native country. All of them can be of inestimable value.

A secret service, however, cannot achieve success if it does not remain secret. In other words, it cannot deliver the essential clandestine information and documents unless it remains a secret, even to the parliamentarians who are often reluctant to grant the funding necessary for its survival.

As long as our world is not a utopian society, free from nations, race prejudices, and ideologies, there will be a need for and there must be espionage, and we will just have to contend with it. And, even as spies provide a service to the general community, espionage will always remain the awkward, opaque hybrid—endorsed, yet illegal; admired, yet reviled.

Nikolaus Ritter

Acknowledgments

Dear Reader, despite the six years of frustration to bring this project to a close, the benefit is always the touch of those individuals who made the difference between an ordinary document and a professional publication. One of my research questions took me to the editor of World War II Magazine on HistoryNet, Karen Jensen. Karen's sincere interest and kindness resulted in her contacting Major General David T. Zabecki, a military historian, author, and editor who served in the US Army in Vietnam and US Army Europe in Germany. General Zabecki recognized the possible value to history of my project and opened the door to the University Press of Kentucky, with whom he had published previously. I'm most indebted to both Ms. Jensen and General Zabecki, who have offered their continued support. My deepest gratitude goes to General Zabecki, who took his personal time to edit and critique my manuscript in detail. My appreciation also goes to Major Gerald Geiger, posthumously. Major Geiger, a WWII veteran and Air Force officer, provided invaluable German to English translation service with keen comprehension and focus on military vocabulary and operations. Likewise, I'm grateful to the Australian author, Carolinda Witt, who has become my good friend over the nearly ten years that we have exchanged critical information on parallel projects. Her book *Double Agent Celery* is about her grandfather, Walter Dicketts, an MI5 agent, whom my father briefly considered for spying against Britain. A recent enlightenment to this project is Falk Hoffmann, an employee of the German Embassy in Washington, DC, who has become my "go-to" friend regarding pertinent information and who labored on my behalf to extract my father's awards from his voluminous military pay book. I'm equally indebted to Nigel West, British intelligence expert, author, and European editor of *The World Intelligence Review* for his willingness to readily share his in-depth knowledge of MI5 and MI6 matters.

Of no small importance has been the ready access to my two children, Ray and Haviland. Their computer and word processing skills have given me boundless comfort during my frustrations and high-anxiety moments. I should also say how much I appreciate their spouses, Karen and Ronn, for surrendering family time. Next, everyone should be so lucky to have a live-in thesaurus. With little cogitation my husband, Raymond, has never failed to deliver the perfect word to make my writing more articulate. I sincerely thank him. And while we're on the topic of family. Although she has been deceased for many years, I continue to be grateful to my mother, whose ceaseless sacrifices and deep devotion shielded my brother and me during the tumultuous war years and beyond.

Of course, what would any production be without the people behind the scene. The heartbeat of all publications is the editorial staff. They turn chaos into order and papers into products. I thank each member of the University Press of Kentucky for their expertise, professionalism, and approachability, and specifically, copy editor Janet Yoe, whose sociability eradicates all fear of any red mark. Also, I'm indebted to Melissa Hammer, acquisitions editor, and Sarah Olson, project editor, for guiding this project painlessly to the grand finale.

With much appreciation,
Katharine Wallace

Appendix

Nikolaus Ritter Military Awards, 1917–1945

Iron Cross Second Class (EK II) in World War I

Verwundetenabzeichen (Wound Badge) in black, for 2 wounds received in WW I

Silesian Eagle 2nd Class and 1st Class. This badge was established by the High Command of the VI Army Corps of the Border Protection East. It was awarded between 1918 and 1921. A member had to serve for a period of three months for the Second Class Eagle, and serve for a period of six months for the First Class Eagle.

Medaille mit Spange zur Erinnerung an den 01.10.1938 Besetzung des Sudentenlandes (Metal with clasp in remembrance of service in Sudetenland). Awarded on October 2, 1939 for active members of the Wehrmacht who were in service at this time and involved in the occupation of the Czech Republic or who were active fighters for the annexation of the Sudetenland.
The medal includes a special clasp which was an additional award for outstanding achievements in establishing the Protectorate of Bohemia and Moravia.

Clasp for the Iron Cross second class (EK II 1939). Ritter was already awarded the Iron Cross Second Class, therefore he received this newly created clasp on February 6, 1940 for his achievements in World War II. This clasp has four prongs at the rear and was attached to the ribbon of the Iron Cross Second Class.

Verwundetenabzeichen in Silber (Wound badge in silver for his third wound in 1941 in Derna), September 24, 1940

EK I, Iron Cross First Class for bravery and tactical success as a commander, September 1944

Eisernes Ehrenschild des L.G.K. XI (Iron Honor shield of the Luftgaukommando XI), September 1944. Luftgau was an air district. The commander was responsible for training, administrative activities, air defense, recruitment, etc.

Flakkampfabzeichen der Luftwaffe (Anti Aircraft Badge) was awarded for time and achievements as an Air Defense Commander and the successful organization of the Air Defense at Luftgau XI.

Deutsches Kreuz in Gold (German Cross in Gold), March 6, 1945. An award presented for multiple occasions of bravery or outstanding tactical leadership at the front. One has to have earned the Iron Cross first Class before this medal can be awarded.

Cross of Honor, awarded in 1935 and 1937 for participating in World War I and earning the Hungarian War Medal.

All awards have been approved and are part of Ritter's Soldbuch (military pay book) from World War I and World War II.

An exception is the German Cross in Gold because his command was encircled by Allied Powers in Harz in 1945, which ended the war and Nikolaus Ritter's military career.

Source: Freie und Hansestadt Hamburg
Behörde für Kultur und Medien—Amt Staatsarchiv
Kattunbleiche 19, 22041 Hamburg

Glossary

Abwehr—Literally, "defense." The German intelligence organization in World War II.

ad acta—This occurs most frequently in the German phrase "*etwas ad acta legen,*" which means to file away or shelve a topic (https://en.wiktionary. org/wiki/ad_acta).

afrit—(variant of afreet) "A powerful evil jinni, demon, or monstrous giant in Arabic mythology" (https://www.merriam-webster.com/dictionary/afreet).

Bad Nenndorf—Former spa in Germany that was converted into an interrogation center by the British.

Barbarossa—In the context of this book, used as slang for a red-bearded person. Barbarossa was a red-bearded Turkish admiral of the sixteenth century.

Bf 109—Messerschmitt Bf 109, "a German World War II fighter aircraft that was the backbone of the Luftwaffe's fighter force" (https://en.wikipedia. org/wiki/Messerschmitt_Bf_109).

Black Reichswehr—"The illegal paramilitary formations promoted by the German Reichswehr army during the time of the Weimar Republic; it was raised despite restrictions imposed by the Versailles Treaty. The secret organization was dissolved in 1923" (http://en.wikipedia.org/wiki/Black _Reichswehr).

Blitzkrieg—"lightning war" to bring about quick victory.

Boer—"(Dutch: 'husbandman' or 'farmer') A South African of Dutch, German, or Huguenot descent, especially one of the early settlers of the Transvaal and the Orange Free State. Today, descendants of the Boers are commonly referred to as Afrikaners" (https://www.britannica.com/topic/ Boer-people).

CD—On a license plate, this is the abbreviation for French *corps diplomatique,* or diplomatic corps.

Chain Home—British radar network along the Dover Coast, an early warning system built before and during the Second World War. "It was one of the very first practical radar systems, and played a vital role in the defense of Britain against Nazi Germany's *Luftwaffe*" (https://cromwell-intl.com/ travel/uk/swingate-chain-home/).

counterintelligence—*See* intelligence.

CSDIC—Combined Services Detailed Interrogation Center, operated by the British.

Deuxieme Bureau—French Military Intelligence organization.

djebel—A mountain or hill in Africa or the Middle East (https://www.merri-am-webster.com/dictionary/djebel).

Do 18—Dornier Do 18 flying boat (seaplane) (https://en.wikipedia.org/wiki/Dornier _Do_18).

Fi 156—Fieseler Fi 156 Storch (Stork), a small German liaison airplane (https://en.wikipedia.org/wiki/Fieseler_Fi_156).

fifth column—"Group of people who undermine a larger group from within, usually in favor of an enemy group or nation. The activities of a fifth column can be overt or clandestine" (https://en.wikipedia.org/wiki/Fifth _column).

fist—The characteristic modulation of a radio transmitter (jproc.ca/rrp/rfp_ tina.html).

Flemings—Large Belgium ethnic population that speaks mostly Dutch.

ghibli—"A hot, dry southerly wind of North Africa" (https://en.oxforddictio naries.com/definition/Ghibli).

Friesians—People from Frisia, an area in the northwestern Netherlands bordering on the North Sea.

Gestapo—Abbreviation of *Geheime Staatspolizei* (Secret State Police), the Gestapo was the official secret police organization of Nazi Germany and German-occupied Europe (https://en.wikipedia.org/wiki/Gestapo).

He 111—Heinkel 111, a popular World War II German bomber disguised as a cargo plane (https://en.wikipedia.org/wiki/Heinkel_He_111).

Heer—German Army (https://en.wikipedia.org/wiki/Heer_(army)).

Hofbrauhaus—A restaurant that serves typical German Bavarian foods.

Intelligence—"Intelligence operations involve the collection, analysis, and interpretation of information about an enemy for the purpose of predicting his capabilities, vulnerabilities, and intentions" (Zabecki 1999, 1216).

Ju 52—Junkers Ju 52/3m, a German transport aircraft used for military personnel and cargo; they were sometimes used as bombers (https://en.wikipedia .org/wiki/Junkers_Ju_52).

Ju 90—Junkers Ju 90, a forty-seat, four-engine Lufthansa passenger aircraft that was used for military transport by the Luftwaffe (https://en.wikipedia.org/wiki/Junkers_Ju_90).

Jungfernstieg—One of the main streets in Hamburg, along the inner Alster (lake), with many shops and cafes.

KG 200—"Kampfgeschwader 200 (in English 'Battle Wing 200' or 'Air Battle Group 200') was a German Luftwaffe special operations unit during World War II. The unit carried out especially difficult bombing and transport operations, long-distance reconnaissance flights, tested new aircraft designs and operated captured aircraft" (https://en.wikipedia.org/wiki/Kampfgeschwader_200).

Kriegsakademie—War academy.

Lena—Operation Lena—planning for Sea Lion.

Luftwaffe—German for "air force"; also, the Nazi air force.

MI5—*See* Security Service.

MI6—*See* SIS.

Nagel—Nagel Restaurant and Brasserie in Hamburg.

Nazi—Short for National Socialist German Workers' Party. A far-right political party.

NCO—non-commissioned officer.

nebelbanke—Fog bank.

Norden bombsight—A footstool-size mechanical device to assist bomber pilots focus bombs on their intended targets with minimum population casualties (https://en.wikipedia.org/wiki/Norden_bombsight).

OKH—*Oberkommando des Heeres,* Supreme High Command of the (German) army of Nazi Germany.

OKW—*Oberkommando der Wehrmacht,* High Command of the Wehrmacht of Nazi Germany during World War II.

OSS—Office of Strategic Services, "a wartime intelligence agency of the United States during World War II, and a predecessor of the modern Central Intelligence Agency (CIA)" (https://en.wikipedia.org/wiki/Office_of _Strategic_Services).

RAF—(British) Royal Air Force.

Red Djebel—*See* djebel.

Reeperbahn—A street in Hamburg; a nightlife and entertainment district.

Reichswehr—German military organization, 1919–1935.

SD—See *Sicherheitsdienst.*

Sea Lion—Operation Sea Lion—The code name for the planned and later aborted invasion of Great Britain by Germany.

Secret Intelligence Service—(British) *See* SIS; MI6.

Security Service—(British) *See* MI5.

serir—"A flat area of desert strewn with rounded pebbles and boulders" (https://en.oxforddictionaries.com/definition/serir).

Sicherheitsdienst—The security service for the Nazi Party; a rival organization of the Abwehr (Zabecki, 1999, 1190). The SD, which cooperated with the

Gestapo, was a very frightening Nazi intelligence organization that served as an intimidating watchdog of every citizen in the Third Reich. Members were liable to prosecution at the Nuremberg trials.

SIS—(British) Secret Intelligence Service (MI6).

SS— "*Schutzstaffel,* literally, protection echelon. A unit of Nazis created as bodyguard to Hitler and later expanded to take charge of intelligence, central security, policing action, and the mass extermination of those they considered inferior or undesirable." They also cooperated with the SD and guarded the concentration camps (https://www.merriam-webster.com/dictionary/ss).

StGB—Strafgesetzbuch, the German Penal Code (https://en.wikipedia.org/wiki/Strafgesetzbuch).

Unter den Linden—Literally, under the linden trees. Main street of downtown Berlin.

USSTAF—"US Strategic Air Forces was a formation of the United States Army Air Forces. It became the overall command and control authority of the United States Army Air Forces in Europe during World War II" (https://en.wikipedia.org/wiki/United_States_Strategic_Air_Forces_in_Europe).

"V" or *Vertrauensleute*—Literally, trusted people. People in whom you can confide.

Wadi—A valley in the desert that is dry, except during the rainy season.

Walloon—French-speaking ethnic group in southern Belgium.

Wehrmacht—"The unified armed forces of Nazi Germany from 1935 to 1946. It consisted of the Heer (army), the Kriegsmarine (navy), and the Luftwaffe (air force)" (https://en.wikipedia.org/wiki/Wehrmacht).

Zillertal—Bierhaus and restaurant in Hamburg on the Reeperbahn.

Selected Bibliography

Below is a partial list of citations I consulted for my research, mostly to identify and cross reference aliases that my father used in his work. Several aliases were simply created on the spot to protect those individuals still living at the time the book was printed. They were never code names. For the past 47 years, since this book was published, identifying intelligence agent aliases is still a work in progress. Much has been published revealing new information—not all accurate. Every new intelligence publication is the "latest and greatest, with new and accurate information" only to be superseded by forthcoming revelations. Also, as we know, the winner has the last word. Therefore, the published literature is coming primarily from the WW II Allied countries and not from the Axis nations.

My observation has been that there is a clear "defensive undertone" in much of the intelligence literature. In other words, it seems that if one nation learns that their agent has been turned or if information has been compromised, this nation will give the impression that they already knew about the double-cross. In fact, my father implied that he knew that several of the agents dropped in England turned and sent back bogus information. Who really knows? Agents are trained to cover up, and they do—within their own organization or to the world. Intelligence communities rarely admit they were deceived.

Adams, Jefferson. *Historical Dictionary of German Intelligence and Counterintelligence.* Lanham, MD: Scarecrow Press, September 2009.

Barnett, Lincoln. "Mr. Piper of Cab-Haven." *Life,* October 29, 1945, 67, https://newspaperarchive.com/bradford-era-apr-23-1937-p-1/.

Duffy, Peter. *Double Agent.* New York: Scribner, 2014.

Farago, Ladislas. *The Game of the Foxes.* New York: Bantam Books, 1971.

Kelly, Saul. *The Hunt for Zerzura: The Lost Oasis and the Desert War.* London: John Murry Publishers, 2002.

Peis, Günter. *The Mirror of Deception.* London: Weidenfeld and Nicolson, 1976.

Ritter, K. F. (a.k.a. Katharine R. Wallace). *Aurora: An Alabama School Teacher in Germany Struggles to Keep her Children during WWII after She Discovers Her Husband is a German Spy.* Xlibris Corporation, 2006.

Ronnie, Art. *Counterfeit Hero, Fritz Duquesne, Adventurer and Spy.* Annapolis: Naval Institute Press, 1995.

The National Archives of the UK (TNA)—Security Service. *History of the Security Intelligence Department of the Defence Security Office, Gibraltar 1939–1945.* KV 4/259.

West, Nigel. *MI5: British Security Service Operations, 1909–45.* London: Triad/Panther Books, 1984.

West, Nigel and Madoc Roberts. *The Double Life of a World War II Spy.* London: Biteback Publishing, 2011.

Whiting, Charles. *Canaris.* New York: Ballentine Books, 1973.

Wighton, Charles and Günter Peis. *Hitler's Spies and Saboteurs.* New York: Award Books, 1958.

Witt, Carolinda. *Double Agent Celery, MI5's Crooked Hero.* South Yorkshire: Pen & Sword Military, 2017.

Zabecki, David, ed. *World War II in Europe: An Encyclopedia.* New York: Garland Publishing, Inc., 1999.

Index

Page numbers in *italics* refer to photographs or their captions.